Confederate Research Sources

A Guide to Archive Collections

Confederate Research Sources

A Guide to Archive Collections

By James C. Neagles

Ancestry Publishing

P.O. Box 476
Salt Lake City, UT 84110

15.45

Library of Congress Catalog Card Number 85-052453
ISBN Number 0-916489-11-6   (Hardbound)
ISBN Number 0-916489-16-7   (Paperback)

First Printing 1986
10 9 8 7 6 5 4 3 2 1

Printed in the United States of America

Contents

Introduction

This book was written for the ancestor hunter who may be descended from a soldier or sailor who fought in a military unit of the Confederate forces during the American Civil War. It will also be helpful to those who may be descended from a civilian who left some record of having contributed to or was otherwise involved with the Confederacy. By using this book as a guide, the researcher can efficiently track down information about his Confederate ancestor whether in a state archive, the National Archives in Washington, D.C., or in a state or other genealogical library. Use of this book should save considerable travel and search time because it points out what Confederate records there are and their exact location.

There is a section for each of the eleven Confederate states as well as for the territories and border states that provided military units to the Confederate armies or navies. To provide historical background, there is a summary of the role each state played in the war. In addition to the descriptions of the records in the state archives and libraries, there is a comprehensive description of the Confederate records housed in the National Archives. There is also a lengthy list of publications which contain names of persons involved with the Confederacy, especially those in the military forces.

The official records of the Union soldiers were preserved by the United States War Department, and they are generally more easily found than are the records of the Confederate soldiers whose records were only "compiled" by the War Department forty years after the war. The National Archives has extensive holdings of the files of Union soldiers, including their medical records. They have the pension files for the survivors or their widows or other heirs who might have qualified for federal assistance after the war. It has compiled service records and other related papers for Confederate soldiers, but no pension files. Any pensions awarded to Confederate soldiers were the result of legislation enacted by the individual states. Therefore, when researchers have completed their search at the National Archives, they are routinely referred to the state archives for pension material. However, seldom, if ever, are they given any information about the holdings of those archives. This book attempts to provide that information.

The author traveled to each of the Confederate and border states to determine exactly what Confederate records are to be found in those state archives and libraries. Those records are described and their exact locations are given. This information will considerably decrease the time the researcher needs to become oriented after arriving at any of the facilities, and should guarantee that a valuable genealogical source is not overlooked merely because the staff does not make specific reference to it. It is hoped that the archives and library staffs will appreciate this book as an effort to simplify their task of assisting the researcher looking for Confederate records.

"Some of you laugh to scorn the idea of bloodshed as a result of Secession, and jocularly propose to drink all the blood that will ever flow as the result of it. But let me tell you what is coming on the heels of Secession: the time will come when your fathers and husbands, your sons and brothers, will be herded together like sheep and cattle at the point of the bayonet, and your mothers and wives, and sisters and daughters will ask, where are they?

"You may after the sacrifice of countless millions of treasure, and hundreds of thousands of precious lives, as a bare possibility, win Southern independence, if God be not against you. But I doubt it. I tell you that while I believe with you in the doctrine of state rights, the North is determined to preserve this Union. They are not a fiery, impulsive people as you are, for they live in cooler climates. But when they begin to move in a given direction where great interests are involved such as the present issues before the country, they will move with the steady momentum and perseverance of a mighty avalanche. And what I fear is they will overwhelm the South with ignoble defeat."

--Sam Houston

ABOUT THE AUTHOR

James C. Neagles was born in Missouri and graduated from the University of Missouri. He did graduate work at Washington University, St. Louis, majoring in social work and corrections. He worked as a juvenile parole officer in Missouri and once was the superintendent of Boys Town of Missouri. He completed a thirty-year career in corrections in 1979, retiring from his position as Staff Director and Chief Hearing Examiner with the United States Parole Commission in Washington, D.C.

He has pursued genealogy as an avocation since 1970, compiling his own family histories, as a classroom instructor, and as a professional genealogical researcher in the Washington, D.C. area.

Mr. Neagles is the author of another Ancestry publication, *Summer Soldiers: A Survey & Index of Revolutionary War Courts-Martial.* He is also the co-author, with Lila Neagles, of *Locating Your Immigrant Ancestor, A Guide to the Naturalization Records,* and *Locating Your Revolutionary War Ancestor.* Mr. Neagles resides in Waldorf, Maryland.

CHAPTER 1

The Confederacy

SECESSION AND THE ARMY

Events Leading to Secession

For many years and even decades before the election of Abraham Lincoln as President of the United States, there was talk of secession from the Union. Historically, the Democratic Party and a friendly Supreme Court had enabled the South to protect its own regional interests with but minor and infrequent opposition or curtailment. As politics changed, however, sharp differences arose within the Democratic Party, split largely along geographical lines, with the South considered to be decidedly more conservative than the North, at odds on the tariff question, and fiercely protective of its right to protect the institution of slavery as a property matter. The drastic step of actually separating from the Union was shunned, though, in favor of attempts to reach compromises. Public and private debates on the means of reaching desired goals of the South resulted in two dominant camps. One urged separation and the other urged accomodation. When the question of secession came to a head in 1860 and 1861, both camps were represented by significant numbers of persons both in high and low places. Events were to occur, however, to swing the sentiments of the people away from the "Unionists" and toward the radical "fire-eaters." Those mind-changing events, in tandem, were the following, summarized below:

1. John Brown's raid on Harper's Ferry, followed by rumors and panic over stories of real or fancied slave insurrections;

2. The election of Republican Abraham Lincoln with the subsequent loss of political power of the badly split Democratic Party;

3. Lincoln's statement that the federal government would "hold, occupy, and possess" federal posts located in the South, and his refusal to surrender Fort Sumter;

4. Lincoln's call for a military force of seventy-five thousand men to form a Union army to retake or possess federal property in the South.

John Brown's Raid

Wealthy Southern slaveowners had insisted on the right to take the institution of slavery into the new territories of the country. The poor farmer could care less, but when tales of Negro violence upon whites were proclaimed and exaggerated, all white persons, rich and poor, came together in a combined urgency to keep the Negro in subjugation. Any talk in the North of abolition of slavery was seen as a direct threat to every white person in the South. Certain groups in Texas fanned the flames of fear and cried out against potential "Africanization." Newspapers headlined plots by radical slaves to overthrow their masters. When John Brown and his zealots rushed into Harper's Ferry to free slaves and to seize the stores of rifles and ammunition there, the Southerner was convinced that this was only a fore-runner of other such violence by northern agitators. The doctrine of "White Supremacy" had become a perceived necessity, if only for self protection, let alone for racial pride. The mutual distrust between the two geographical regions of the country soon heightened to proportions of hysteria.

Lincoln's Election

Stephen Douglas was considered the stronger choice for nomination as the Democratic Party candidate for president in 1860, but the party split and the "states' rights" Democrats of the South held their own convention and nominated John C. Breckenridge instead. A group bent on compromise was the resurrected Whig Party. It nominated Joshua F. Bell to run for the office. When the November election took place, Breckenridge was the overwhelming choice of the South; Bell received only a minority of the votes. Lincoln campaigned against Douglas in the North, and was elected with only 39.9 percent of the nation's popular vote, almost none of it coming from the

South. A "Black Republican" had been elected, and the South assumed disaster would follow under a regime controlled by the radical secretary of state, William H. Seward, and his puppet, Lincoln, the country buffoon.

Federal Posts in the South

Between the time Lincoln was elected in early November and his inauguration in March 1861, the deep South states, positive that they must leave the Union, began taking over federal posts within their own boundaries--purely as a defensive measure against the federal troops stationed there. In practically all instances, state troops marched in as the small cadres of federal troops evacuated without offering resistance. By the end of March, there were only four forts in the South still under federal control. Three of them were in Florida, and the other was Fort Sumter in the harbor guarding Charleston, South Carolina. One of the three Florida posts, Fort Pickens, guarding the Pensacola Bay, was retained under federal control by mutual agreement that the state would not attempt to take it in return for a pledge that it would not be reinforced with federal troops.

Fort Sumter was held by Major Robert Anderson. He had abandoned nearby Fort Moultrie on Sullivan's Island and the fort on the tiny island of Castle Pinckney, also in Charleston Harbor. Anderson had chosen to concentrate his troops on Fort Sumter because it was a stronger bastion. As soon as Lincoln was inaugurated, Anderson sent a recommendation that the fort, impossible to defend without massive reinforcements, be evacuated. Contrary to Seward's recommendation that Sumter be evacuated, Lincoln made up his own mind and sent a ship carrying provisions to aid the garrison. At the same time, he sent a message to South Carolina that troops would not be transferred to the fort unless it was fired upon. During the ensuing days, much discussion and many messages were exchanged by Anderson and the Confederate General Pierre Beauregard, who was in command at Charleston. Final agreement was never reached. On 11 April 1861, Anderson said that he would be forced to surrender at noon of 15 April, unless he received differing instructions or was attacked in the meantime. Not finding this statement satisfactory, Beauregard, without consulting with higher authorities, ordered the fort taken. Following an advance warning of one hour, a shot was fired on the fort from nearby James Island at 4:30 a.m. on 12 April. After thirty hours of shelling, with the federal troops sitting out the bombardment in underground tunnels and rooms, Anderson surrendered the fort with full military honors. None of his men had been killed during the siege.

Fort Pickens, as well as Fort Taylor at Key West, and Fort Jefferson in the Dry Tortugas, continued under federal control and remained so throughout the war.

Three days after the fall of Sumter, Lincoln issued a call for seventy-five thousand volunteers to serve for ninety days for the purpose of retaking the federal property occupied by the southern states. This call, in effect, forced the governors of the states to make decisions whether to furnish the quota called for or to refuse. The answer in the deep South states was obvious, but the decision placed heavy pressures on the states bordering the southern and northern halves of the country. The issue in those states was not only whether to join in the secession movement, but also whether to become a partner to "coercion" of their sister states.

Formal Secession

As early as October 1860, there had been much discussion and debate between the Southern governors as to how secession from the Union should be accomplished in the event Lincoln should win the presidential election. It was determined that one of the states should take the lead and the others would follow. Agreement was reached that South Carolina was the logical state to start the movement; the honor was not too reluctantly accepted. It was understood that as soon as South Carolina withdrew, the states of Mississippi, Alabama, and Florida would immediately follow. On the other hand, Louisiana, North Carolina, and Georgia said they would not secede merely because of Lincoln's election but would wait for some provocative act. As an example of the differing opinions between some states, the majority of the voters in Louisiana and Georgia voted for the Unionist Douglas rather than the "states' righter" Breckenridge. Conferences were held to attempt to reach compromises, but none of them sparked any large scale enthusiasm. The tide of secession grew. After the election, South Carolina called for a convention on 17 December in Columbia, its capital, but on that date, a smallpox scare convinced the delegates to move to Charleston. On 20 December, they unanimously voted to secede.

Despite more attempts at compromise, and despite delaying tactics by those who favored cooperating with the other southern states in some type of joint action, as opposed to "secession now," the states began to follow the lead of South Carolina. Secession votes were taken in the following states on the 1861 dates as shown below:

Mississippi	9 January
Florida	10 January
Alabama	11 January
Georgia	19 January
Louisiana	26 January
Texas	1 February

Of the above states, only Texas arranged for a later popular vote on the issue. That vote was 46,129 for secession and 14,697 against,[1] indicating, at least, that even in the face of overwhelming emotion in favor of separation, there were many who stood their ground against hasty action. This pattern was evident in all the states which seceded, and details are given in the individual summaries for each state to be found in later chapters.

The more reluctant border states which seceded later took their official actions on the dates shown:

Virginia	17 April (popular vote on 23 May)
Tennessee	6 May (popular vote on 8 June)
Arkansas	6 May
North Carolina	20 May

The border states of Kentucky and Missouri were not considered Confederate states despite the fact that the southern sympathizers in those states organized their own provisional governments and professed to speak for the state. The Confederate States of America accepted this distinction, proclaimed that they were part of the Confederacy, and added a star for each of them in their new flag.

The border states of Maryland and the later-to-be-created West Virginia, although contributing troops to the Confederacy, did not take official action to secede. The Territory of Arizona, with the support of its leaders and under military control of the Confederate troops, was briefly on the side of the Confederacy, but was shortly taken over by Union troops and placed under military control. At that time, Arizona was a part of the larger Territory of New

Mexico, where the Confederacy also claimed control for a short time before declaring that the Arizona Territory was to be considered a separate territory.

Creation of the Confederate States of America

A convention was called by the six states in the deep South which had so far seceded, to meet in Montgomery, Alabama, on 4 February 1861. The convention stayed in session for five weeks, during which time it drafted a new constitution to serve the new government. The constitution was closely based on the United States Constitution, but provided for a single six year term for the presidency. While outlawing slave importation from Africa, it guaranteed the right of slave ownership. On 9 February, the delegates unamimously elected Jefferson Davis the provisional president, to serve pending a national election at a later date. Davis was a West Point graduate who had preferred a military command in the Confederate army. A flag for the Confederacy (the stars and bars) was adopted. It was redesigned during the closing days of the war to resemble the Confederate flag more familiar to us today; the St. Andrews Cross on a field of red, with thirteen white stars. The city of Montgomery was not an ideal place for the capital. When Virginia entered the Confederacy, the Confederate Congress, on 10 May 1861, overrode Davis and agreed to move the capital to Richmond, as of 29 May. Davis, elected by popular vote in November 1861, was installed as president on 22 February 1862.

The usual procedure for adding new states to the Confederacy involved preliminary action by the states. Generally that took the form of some type of resolution by the state legislature to call a convention to decide the question of secession. In each case, any move to stay in the Union was put down by the elected secessionist delegates. It was known in advance which candidates were in favor of (a) immediate secession, (b) cooperation with other states, or (c) remaining in the Union. After a state legally seceded from the Union, it automatically became an independent, sovereign entity. It drew up a new constitution and set up new government organization. The next step was to petition for acceptance as a member of the Confederate States of America, thereby relinquishing its independent status. Finally, the Confederate States officially accepted it as a new state, and it was so proclaimed. In only one seceding state did this procedure produce an unusual effect. The northwestern counties of Virginia, disagreeing with the other counties east of the mountain, formed a "Reformed Government" and purported to represent the state in lieu of the state officials who had resigned from the United States Congress. This began a two year process which ended in those counties being admitted to the federal government as a new state.

Raising an Army

Whenever a state legislature called for a convention for the purpose of seceding, it also authorized the group to take whatever steps it felt necessary to create some form of military organization that would be used in the event the decision was to secede and the federal government then took steps to prevent such action. Also, the legislature normally took action to authorize the governor to increase the state militia, the home guards and the state guards, and to create new volunteer fighting units to be used if needed in defense of the state.

Meanwhile, the Confederate government was busy creating its own national fighting force by using troops recruited directly for the Confederacy and by accepting units recruited in the states and transferred to it. During the first year there were more volunteers than there were funds and supplies to support them, so thousands were lost to action because they could not be accepted until after long delays. Eventually, the mills and factories began turning out war material, and any volunteer was gladly put into service at once, usually with little or no training. Units raised in the states were to serve for only twelve months, while those raised or accepted by the Confederacy were required to serve either for three years or until the end of the war. Privates were paid $11 per month until 1864 when the pay was raised to $18-- but the depreciated value of the Confederate dollar made the pay worth much less than it had been.

In April 1862, as the twelve month terms were about to expire, the Confederate government enacted this country's first conscription law. The primary purpose was to convince the soldiers to reenlist rather than bear the stigma of having been drafted. The states continued to raise their own units, and the governors were constantly at odds with the Confederate government as to whether and how many of those units should be transferred to the Confederacy. There was bitterness also as to the extent that the Confederacy would use troops to defend the state. Governors and state legislatures also enacted conscription laws to fill out their volunteer units when necessary, and they enhanced the size of their militia and home guard units, usually insisting that they be used only within the borders of their own states.

The Confederacy passed conscription laws on the following dates, with the age limits as shown:

16 April 1862	eighteen to thirty-five years
27 September 1862	eighteen to forty-five years
February 1864	seventeen to fifty years

These laws provided that the very young and the very old would serve only in their own states.

The conscription laws, both Confederate and state, exempted many persons according to the occupation they followed or positions they held. These included government employees, most teachers, ministers, druggists, and those with skilled trade experience. They also exempted owners or overseers who were responsible for twenty or more slaves. This exemption was justified as a measure to control the rebellious slaves who might do physical damage to the property or harm the families left on the plantations. Near the close of the war, as the Union soldiers came and began to free Negroes, the ratio was reduced to fifteen Negroes to each owner or overseer. This was an unpopular exemption among the poor farmers who could not profit from it. In addition to exemptions, the hiring of a substitute was also possible, and they could be obtained for a fee of up to $1,000. Late in 1863 and early in 1864, this provision was eliminated because of its unpopularity, as well as the generally inferior abilities of the substitutes. Estimates show that the numbers of persons actually exempted or who provided substitutes amounted to only a few hundred in each state. Also, as time went on, the numbers of occupations meriting exemption were cut in half.

The Union armies actively recruited Negroes as they became available and organized entire units of Negroes. During the last days of the war, the Confederacy--in desperation--also authorized the use of Negro troops, but the end came before any of them saw service. Regardless, the records show that some Negroes did actually serve in Confederate units. Perhaps these were "servants" taken along by officers or free Negroes.

Confederate soldiers usually suffered from insufficient clothing, arms, and horses. Assistance from European countries was negligible because of the Union blockade and the reluctance of the European countries to throw in their lot with the Confederacy. Medical care was primitive, and it has been estimated that two to three soldiers died of disease for every one killed in battle. The use of chloroform and ether was infrequent. Any limb which developed gangrene was unceremoniously chopped off. Private organizations, such as the Georgia Hospital and Relief Association and the South Carolina Hospital Aid Association, collected and distributed medical supplies to the military hospitals and set up wayside houses along rail lines to provide free meals and lodging to passing troops. Occasionally, a register of soldiers using such houses has survived for posterity.

There are no reliable figures for the total numbers of fighting men who fought for the Confederacy, either as members of state units or of the Confederate army. Several historians have attempted to re-create such statistics, but their estimates are widely variable due to the lack of surviving Confederate records. It appears, though, that there were from six hundred thousand to more than one million Confederate soldiers and sailors. Approximately one-third of these were raised by conscription. These figures contrast sharply with the Union figures which indicate that there were three to four times as many Union fighting men as Confederate fighting men.

A Confederate army was composed of divisions, broken down into corps, then brigades, and finally into regiments (or battalions). Typical of the types and nomenclature of the various military units seeing service in the Confederate armies were the following:

Volunteer units: Heavy artillery (garrison, seacoast, seige) Light artillery (horse, mounted) Cavalry (dragoons, mounted rifle, partisan rangers, guerillas) Infantry (heavy, light, riflemen)
Legions (concentrations of artillery, cavalry, infantry)
Medical organizations
Local defense organizations (used in emergency situations or for special duty)
State Rangers (companies detached from a regiment)
Home Guards (served only with a state for defense purposes)
State Guards (protected state property or ceremonial)
Reserves and Militia (used for local defense or emergency)

Most military units were identified with the state where they were created. There were other units organized directly or otherwise formed or consolidated by the Confederate government itself. Many of those units were amalgamations of smaller units raised in more than one state. Others were the Corps of Engineers, the Nitre and Mining Bureau, the Signal Corps, the musical bands, and other such specialized corps not identified with a state. The National Archives has compiled service records of purely Confederate units as listed below. These records may be found in Microcopy 258, consisting of 123 rolls. See chapter four for a complete description of this series.

First Confederate Cavalry
First Confederate Regular Cavalry
First Battalion, Trans-Mississippi Confederate Cavalry (First Battalion,
      Arkansas and Louisiana Cavalry)
Third Confederate Cavalry
Sixth Battalion, Confederate Cavalry
Seventh Confederate Cavalry (Claiborne's Regiment, Partisan Rangers;
      Seventh Regiment, Confederate Partisan Rangers)
Seventh Battalion, Confederate Cavalry (Prentice's Battalion, Confederate
      Cavalry)
Eighth (Dearing's) Confederate Cavalry
Eighth (Wade's) Confederate Cavalry (Second Regiment, Mississippi and
      Alabama Cavalry)
Tenth Confederate Cavalry
Fourteenth Confederate Cavalry
Fifteenth Confederate Cavalry (First Regiment, Alabama and Florida
      Cavalry)
Twentieth Confederate Cavalry (Lay's Regiment, Confederate Cavalry)
Baxter's Battalion, Confederate Cavalry
Bell's Battalion, C.S.A.
Blake's Scouts, C.S.A.
Burrough's Battalion, Partisan Rangers (Princess Anne Partisan Rangers)
Clarkson's Battalion, Confederate Cavalry, Independent Rangers
Fort's Scouts, C.S.A.
Lyon's Escort, Forrest's Cavalry, C.S.A.
Martin's Escort, C.S.A.
Mead's Confederate Cavalry (Mead's Regiment of Partisan Rangers)
Murchison's Battalion, Cavalry
Powers' Regiment, Confederate Cavalry

Captain Baum's Company, Confederate Cavalry (Warren Dragoons)

Wheeler's Scouts, C.S.A. (Hawkins' Scouts, C.S.A.; Carter's Scouts, C.S.A.;
First Tennessee Mounted Scouts)

Wood's Regiment, Confederate Cavalry

First Regular Battery, Confederate Light Artillery (Semmes' Battery;
Barnes' Battery)

Braxton's Battalion, Confederate Artillery (Battalion C, Second Corps, Army
of Northern Virginia

Courtney's Battalion, Confederate Artillery

Cunningham's Battalion, Confederate Artillery

Cutshaw's Battalion, Confederate Artillery

Captain Davis' Company, Confederate Light Artillery

De Gournay's Battalion, Heavy Artillery (Twelfth Battalion, Louisiana
Heavy Artillery)

Captain Dent's Battery, Light Artillery, C.S.A.

Haskell's Battalion, Confederate Artillery

Huger's Battalion, Confederate Artillery

Lewis' Battalion, Confederate Artillery

Captain Lillard's Company, Independent Scouts and Rangers (Nelson
Rangers and Scouts)

Captain Madison's Company, Mounted Spies and Guides (Phillips' Mounted
Spies and Guides)

Captain Marshall's Company, Confederate Artillery (Brown Horse Artillery)

Martin's Battalion, Confederate Reserve Artillery

McIntosh's Battalion, Confederate Artillery (Battalion C, Reserve Corps
Artillery, Army of Northern Virginia)

McLaughlin's Battalion, Confederate Artillery

Montague's Battalion, Confederate Heavy Artillery (Fourth Battalion, Confederate Heavy Artillery)

Nelson's Battalion, Confederate Artillery (Thirty-First Battalion, Virginia
Light Artillery; Third Battalion Reserves, Light Artillery)

Lt. W. B. Ochiltree's Detachment of Recruits (Detachment of Regulars)

Maj. R. C. M. Page's Battalion, Confederate Artillery (Carter's Battalion of
Artillery; Braxton's Battalion of Artillery)

Palmer's Battalion, Confederate Artillery (Robertson's Battalion of Artillery)

Poague's Battalion, Artillery

Richardson's Battalion, Confederate Light Artillery (Battalion A, First Corps
Artillery, Army of Northern Virginia)

Major F. W. Smith's Battalion, Confederate Heavy Artillery
Stark's Battalion, Confederate Light Artillery (Battalion B, First Corps Artillery, Army of Northern Virginia)
Captain White's Battery, Horse Artillery
First Confederate Infantry (First Confederate Regiment, Georgia Volunteers)
First Battalion, Confederate Infantry (Forney's Regiment, Confederate Infantry)
Second Confederate Infantry
Third Confederate Infantry
Fourth Confederate Infantry (First Regiment, Alabama, Tennessee, and Mississippi Infantry)
Eighth Battalion, Confederate Infantry (Second Foreign Battalion, Infantry; Second Foreign Legion, Infantry)
Ninth Confederate Infantry (Fifth Confederate Infantry; Fifth Confederate Regiment, Tennessee Infantry)
Bailey's Consolidated Regiment of Infantry
Bradford's Corps, Scouts and Guards (Bradford's Battalion)
Brooks' Battalion, Confederate Regular Infantry
Brush Battalion, C.S.A.
Lieutenant Cunningham's Ordnance Detachment (Captain Cuyler's Ordnance Detachment)
Captain Davis' Company of Guides, C.S.A.
Exchanged Battalion, C.S.A. (Trans-Mississippi Battalion; Western Battalion)
Forrest's Scouts, C.S.A.
Gillum's Regiment (Henry Gillum's Regiment; Gillum's Regiment, Mounted Infantry; Gillum's Regiment, Mounted Riflemen)
Lieutenant Haskell's Co., Infantry
Jackson's Company, C.S.A.
Captain McDaniels' Company, Secret Service
Stirman's Regiment, Sharp Shooters
Tucker's Regiment, Confederate Infantry
Lieutenant Young's (Fifth) Company, Retributors
First Cherokee Mounted Rifles (First Arkansas Cherokee Mounted Rifles)
First Cherokee Mounted Volunteers (Waite's Regiment, Cherokee Mounted Volunteers; Second Regiment, Cherokee Mounted Rifles, Arkansas; First Regiment, Cherokee Mounted Rifles or Riflemen)

First Squadron, Cherokee Mounted Volunteers (Holt's Squadron, Cherokee
    Mounted Volunteers)
First Chickasaw Infantry (Hunter's Regiment, Indian Volunteers)
First Choctaw Mounted Rifles
First Choctaw and Chickasaw Mounted Rifles
First Creek Mounted Volunteers (First Regiment, Creek Mounted Rifles or
    Riflemen, Creek Regiment, Mounted Indian Volunteers; Second Regi-
    ment, Arkansas Creeks)
First Osage Battalion, C.S.A.
First Seminole Mounted Volunteers
Second Cherokee Mounted Volunteers (Second Regiment, Cherokee
    Mounted Rifles or Riflemen)
Second Creek Mounted Volunteers
Cherokee Regiment (Special Service)
Deneale's Regiment, Choctaw Warriors (Deneale's Confederate Volunteers)
Shecoe's Chickasaw Battalion, Mounted Volunteers
Washington's Squadron of Indians, C.S.A. (Reserve Squadron of Cavalry)
Captain Wilkins' Company, Choctaw Infantry
Miscellaneous Indian Reports
First Confederate Engineer Troops
Second Confederate Engineer Troops
Third Confederate Engineer Troops
Fourth Confederate Engineer Troops
Engineers
Nitre and Mining Bureau, War Department, C.S.A.
Sappers and Miners
Signal Corps
Bands, C.S.A.
Lieutenant Click's Company, Ordnance Scouts and Guards, C.S.A.
Infantry School of Practice
Invalid Corps
Officers Surnamed Morgan, C.S.A.
President's Guard, C.S.A.
Miscellaneous Records

CAMPAIGNS AND BATTLES

The Union war plan was to (a) control the Mississippi River, using both army and naval troops, thus splitting the Confederacy in half, (b) blockade the Atlantic and Gulf Coast ports to cut off the Confederacy from any European allies it might acquire and to prevent international commerce, (c) protect Washington, D. C., while attempting to conquer the Confederate capital at Richmond, (d) apply heavy pressure in the Tennessee area to tie down troops so they could not be used on other fronts, and (e) reduce the size of the enemy's fighting forces by inflicting as many casualties as possible in battle. The overall objective of both sides was not to gain or possess territory, but rather to destroy or control the rail junctions and ports, thus depriving the enemy of needed supplies and arms.

The Union named its various armies and battles, such as the "Army of the Potomac" and the "Battle of Bull Run" according to nearby rivers, streams, or places. In contrast, the Confederacy named its armies and battles, such as the "Army of Northern Virginia" and the Battle of Manassas" according to the geographical area or places. Both sides were led by ever-changing leadership, and reorganization was frequent. Neither side had an overall commander until 9 March 1864, when Grant was appointed supreme commander of the Union armies. Robert E. Lee received the title of General in Chief of the Confederate armies on 23 January 1865--only a few months before the war ended.

The war was fought in three major geographical areas. The heavier and more significant fighting took place in the East in the states along the Atlantic Coast. Another area, referred to as the western theatre, was west of the Alleghenies and east of the Mississippi, referred to as the Western theatre. The more scattered and lighter fighting took place in the states and territories west of the Mississippi, referred to as the Trans-Mississippi theatre. A brief summary of the major campaigns and battles in each of those theatres of action is presented here, purely for quick reference with no intention of duplicating the many descriptions and analyses of the battles fought in the Civil War. A word of caution is in order relative to the use of numbers used to show the severity of the fighting. The numbers of casualties, including wounded, captured, and missing must be only approximations. Because of the lack of accurate accounting available, the historians who have studied these battles and written extensively about them are often at odds with one another concerning numbers. Huge amounts of records of the Confederate armies and their participation in campaigns and battles have been lost to posterity. Figures are used here, however, to show comparisons between opposing armies and to illustrate the magnitude of the fighting forces used in a battle and the resultant casualties.

The most common tactical approach in battle was to make a massive charge by hundreds or thousands of men in a more or less straight line with more lines just behind. Similarly, the enemy would advance to meet them. All were equipped with muzzle loading rifles, usually the newer ones with bored barrels to increase the range and effectiveness. Thousands of men were killed or wounded within a few hours. Often both sides fell back because of inability to sustain further action. Artillery was used in support of the infantry and in seige operations where large shells needed to be shot over long distances. Cavalry was often used to protect the flanks of the infantry. More often, though, cavalry was the means of transportation for small groups such as rangers and guerilla bands which made fast raids in attempts to cut supply and communication lines.

War in the East

Using the volunteers Lincoln had called up to serve ninety day terms, the Union army under Gen. Irvin McDowell decided to march out of Washington, D.C., put the rail junction at Manassas, Virginia, out of commission, and then take the Confederate capital at Richmond. The green troops were met, however, at a stream named Bull Run, near Manassas, by a Confederate force led by Gen. Pierre G. T. Beauregard, the same man who had taken Fort Sumter. The date was 21 July 1861, and both armies were accompanied by hordes of civilians who went along to watch the glorious battle that would vanquish the enemy. McDowell repeatedly ordered his troops forward, but they were stymied by the heroic "stonewall" defense of Gen. Thomas J. Jackson. A Confederate counter-attack sent the federal soldiers fleeing back to Washington. This battle had no real significance except to make both sides realize that it would take a lot of bitter fighting before there would be a permanent victory. A massive program of gearing up for war began by increasing the stores of supplies and arms and pushing recruitment at full speed. Lincoln appointed a new general, George B. McClellan, and ordered him to recruit and train an army of one hundred thousand.

In 1862, with an army of one hundred thirty thousand, McClellan made a second stab at Richmond but was turned back just nine miles from the city. Meanwhile, General "Stonewall" Jackson's mission was to hold the Shenandoah Valley in the western part of Virginia in order to insure the continued agricultural production of that area and to keep it open for communication and north--south travel.

The Union forces, under various generals, attempted to take Richmond but always were turned back by Gen. Robert E. Lee, assisted by Generals Jackson and J.E.B. Stuart. Buoyed by his successes, Lee decided to march north and carry the fighting beyond the Virginia borders. He captured Hagerstown, Maryland, while Jackson captured Harper's Ferry on the Maryland border. Their advance ended at Sharpsburg, Maryland, when Lee fought McClellan in the bloodiest one-day battle of the war--on the banks of Antietam Creek. After suffering extraordinarily high losses, Lee managed to escape back to Virginia.

Battles were fought in the Fredericksburg, Virginia, area both late in 1862 and during 1863 for the purpose of repelling more attacks aimed at Richmond. In June, Lee decided once more to invade the North. He got as far as a small town in Pennsylvania named Gettysburg. There he attacked and fought a line of Union troops four miles long, commanded by Gen. George C. Meade. The combined forces of both sides numbered approximately one hundred sixty-three thousand. On the third day of fighting, 3 July, Confederate General George E. Picket ordered a frontal charge against the Union forces. He lost seven thousand of this fifteen thousand men in that charge, and the Battle of Gettysburg was finished. Failing to follow up, Meade let Lee get the remains of his army out and safely back into Virginia once more.

From a Southern point of view, the war took a decided turn for the worse in 1864. The armies were decimated by heavy losses in battle and the citizen population was crushed by poverty. Gen. Ulysses S. Grant, now in supreme command of the Union armies, decided to fight the Confederate armies on as many fronts as possible and to smash them with superior manpower, regardless of how many Union lives would be lost in the process. He launched three separate offensives in Virginia. One was directed toward the Shenandoah Valley; one was in the peninsula between the York and James rivers; and one was another push toward Richmond commanded by Grant himself. With 118,700 soldiers, Grant crossed the Rapidan River where he was met by Lee. There they fought what was to be called the "Battle of the

Wilderness," where losses were extremely high on both sides. They fought again at other Virginia locations including Spotsylvania and Cold Harbor, not far from Richmond. Grant then determined that a better technique to capture Richmond would be to move south and take Petersburg first. Eventually, he took both cities but only after long and horrible sieges designed to starve out the inhabitants. On 1 April 1865, Lee finally was forced to evacuate Richmond, and Grant moved in behind him. When advised by Lee that the city was to be evacuated, President Davis joined the others and left immediately. He was captured at Irwinville, Georgia, on 10 May, after refusing to capitulate. He was imprisoned at Fort Monroe for a time and later released.

Lee and what was left of his army made a run toward Danville, hoping to meet a supply train due there. Instead, they missed the connection, and the train went on to Richmond where it was greeted by Grant's troops. Lee turned here and there, hoping to join up with the remnants of the Army of the Tennessee, but Grant's troops faced him from every direction. Lee knew it was over and arranged to meet Grant in a farmhouse at Appomattox. A formal surrender was signed there on 12 April 1865, exactly four years from the date Sumter was fired upon. Grant agreed that the Confederate troops, including Lee, would be paroled upon taking an oath to obey the United States Constitution and to cease fighting. They would be permitted to take their horses and mules with them to go home and start the spring plowing. Lee went outside, mounted his horse, Traveller, and went with them.

Two weeks later, despite Jefferson Davis' objections, General Johnston also surrendered his army at Durham, North Carolina. His surrender was the culmination of a series of victories for the Union which had begun in Tennessee, moved through Georgia, and continued into the Carolinas. Gen. William T. Sherman, with 112,000 men, had taken Atlanta, the chief rail center of the South, then marched to Savannah, burning and laying waste a sixty-mile swath across the state. After a month's rest at Savannah, he headed toward Columbia, South Carolina, which his men burned before he arrived. From Columbia, they marched into North Carolina where they took Fayetteville and Goldsboro. During part of this campaign, Sherman was opposed by both Johnston and Gen. John B. Hood but was merely slowed down in his primary objectives of crushing the South and destroying their will to fight. When he accepted the surrender near Durham on 26 April, the war in the East was finished.

War in the West

In 1862, the mass of Union troops in the West under General Grant concentrated on Tennessee. They used gunboats to insure the fall of Fort Henry on the Tennessee River and then Fort Donelson on the Cumberland River. When Grant demanded unconditional surrender, thirteen thousand Confederate soldiers gave themselves up and were transported to Union prisons. Grant then turned his attention to Mississippi where he intended to capture Corinth, a rail center. Before he arrived there, on 6 April, a formidable force of Confederates met him at Shiloh Church, Tennessee, located near the Mississippi border. After two days of very heavy fighting by more than one hundred thousand troops, Grant was forced to pull his troops back a mile to the banks of the Tennessee River. The next morning, after being reinforced, he counterattacked and the Confederates were forced to fall back to Corinth.

During the summer of 1862, Col. John Hunt Morgan became famous by leading his "Kentucky Cavaliers" on cavalry raids against federal troops in his home state. Matching him was Gen. Nathan B. Forrest, who led his Tennessee raiders into Murfreesboro, Tennessee, and captured more than a thousand federal soldiers.

In August, Confederate General Braxton Bragg, commanding the Army of the Tennessee, marched into Kentucky, but after indecisive battles, he was forced to leave the state. Bragg was attacked by federal troops at Stone's River, near Murfreesboro, on the last day of 1862. There they fought for three days to a standstill during which both sides lost thousands of soldiers.

In November, Grant tried once more to win in Mississippi, but was pushed back to Memphis where he had previously been stationed. Meanwhile, Morgan's raiders were again riding through Kentucky taking federal prisoners and destroying whatever war material they could find.

In 1863, Grant launched a long-expected attack on Vicksburg, Mississippi. It required six months of fighting all around the city and a long siege to reduce the defenders inside the city to starvation and desperation. They surrendered on 4 July. This action permitted the federal armies unmolested use of the Mississippi River all the way to the Gulf of Mexico. It also split the Confederate armies west of the river from other Confederate armies, leaving them to fight alone on their own fronts.

In September 1863, the Union forces attacked General Bragg's army at Chickamauga Station, a few miles from Chattanooga, but before the fighting ended, Bragg overwhelmed his enemy and stood fast on the mountains over-looking Chattanooga. From there he conducted a siege of the city. In November, augmented by supplies and more troops, the Union army broke out and charged up the mountain side, causing the surprised Confederates to with-draw across the nearby Georgia line. This left both Chattanooga and the State of Tennessee under almost complete federal control.

1864 was the year of destruction by Union General Sherman. He was intent on breaking the South's morale by attacking at every possible point, killing and destroying as he went. With 112,000 trained soldiers, he left Chattanooga and started his march across Georgia. From that point on, his activities all took place in the East--with devastating results. The campaign in the West had been decisively won by the Union armies.

War in the Trans-Mississippi Area

During the early days of the war, there was a battle in the West, much like the first battle at Manassas in the East. It, too, had a sobering effect on both sides; making them realize that the other side would not easily be defeated. This western battle was fought at Wilson's Creek, near Springfield, Missouri, on 10 August 1861. Federal troops, under Gen. Nathaniel Lyon, attacked a Confederate force, but after an all-day battle and the loss of General Lyon, they were forced to turn back to Springfield and eventually back to Rolla, the terminus of the railroad. Following this battle, the Confederate troops were free to join with Arkansas units and fight on. They fought at other southern towns of Missouri, and eventually fought another major battle at Elk Horn Tavern (Pea Ridge), Arkansas, just south of the Missouri border. This battle took place in early March 1862. It ended in a victory for the Union army and left Missouri under federal domination except for the continuing and unceasing guerrilla activities.

The area west of the Mississippi was divided into three parts with head-quarter offices at Little Rock, Arkansas; Alexandria, Louisiana; and Houston, Texas. Eventually, in February 1863, Gen. Edmund Kirby Smith was placed in overall command of the area for the Confederate government, and he remained in command to the end.

As the war began in Texas, troops from that state made raids into the Arizona/New Mexico Territory and convinced many of the inhabitants there, mainly members of Indian tribes, to join the Confederate side. These expeditions were launched from the base at Fort Bliss at El Paso (then called Franklin), which the Confederates had taken over. From there, they claimed all the land as far as California but were never able to conquer it because of the distances and the difficulty caused by stretching supply lines. One major victory was a successful defense against Union troops in 1864 when Gen. Nathaniel P. Banks attempted to seize large quantities of cotton stored in Texas and then to seize Shreveport. His amphibious expedition up the Red River was forced back and was never again attempted.

After many losing battles in other parts of the South, the soldiers west of the Mississippi realized the war was about to end and began to desert in massive numbers (as Lee's men had during the last days of their battle). General Smith urged his men on, believing he could yet save the South even after Lee's and Johnston's surrenders in the East. Finally, with his troops straggling all over Texas, trying either to reach their homes or to escape into Mexico, Smith had to admit the cause was hopeless. Two of his generals, on his behalf, agreed to terms of surrender at New Orleans, on 26 May 1865. Smith headed toward Mexico. One group of soldiers heading to Mexico chanced to meet Smith, and one described him "mounted on a mule, wearing a calico shirt and a silk kerchief around his neck, with a revolver on his hip and a shotgun across the saddle."

War on the Water

The chances of finding a Confederate ancestor who served in the Confederate navy are slim. Although there was a navy of sorts, the vast majority of those who took to the sea were privateers, not a part of the organized navy. The Confederacy did have a few ships on the high seas and purchased some from England, but they were not a massive fleet. They also used gunboats to ply the rivers, hauling supplies back and forth on the streams and helping to defend the ports along their banks. At the first stroke of war, the Union took steps to bottle up the coastal ports, thus preventing Confederate ships from sailing in and out. Within a short time, the port at Port Royal, South Carolina, and other ports in Florida, fell to the federal naval and land troops. The cities of Wilmington, North Carolina, and Charleston, South Carolina, remained unconquered for most of the war years. Mobile and Galveston also remained unconquered until the very end. The ports of New Orleans and Vicksburg fell to amphibious attacks, and thus the Union controlled navigation on the Mississippi River.

Among the few bright spots for the Confederate navy was the duel between its ship, the *Virginia* (formerly the *Merrimack*), and the *Monitor*. These ships had been refitted with iron armor over the original wooden sides. The duel ended in a draw. The Confederate navy also pioneered a new invention called the submarine, although with disastrous results to several of its crew. It did, however, sink the USS *Housatonic*. The most prestigious efforts by the Confederate navy were the exploits of Ad. Raphael Semmes, who commanded two ships during the war. He roved over the open seas, taking countless prizes for the benefit of the Confederacy. His second ship, the *Alabama,* was sunk off the coast of France by the USS *Kearsarge*. In addition to Semmes' ships, the Confederacy also successfully sailed the *Florida,* the *Tallahassee,* and the *Shenandoah*.

Most of the naval action was engaged in by private boat owners and their crews. They used lightweight, speedy boats which could outrun the heavier and slower Union ships patrolling off the Atlantic and Gulf ports, blockading them from international commerce. The South, glutted with cotton, tobacco, and other agricultural products, knew that England needed those products and would pay dearly for them. Arrangements were made for the English to bring manufactured products, luxury items, and gold to the Caribbean Islands where they met the Southern boats laden with goods. Exchanges were made there. Fortunes were made on both sides from only one or two such escapades. Cotton purchased in the South for only a few cents per pound was sold to European purchasers at fabulous profits. The city of Wilmington, realizing the potential for profit, even operated its own blockade running ship, competing with the private entrepreneurs.

Illustrations

Page 23. Lee and His Generals

Left to right: Hood, Ewell, Bragg, Johnston (A.S.), Hampton, Smith Early, Hill (A.P.), Lee (Stephen), Anderson, Gordon, Holmes, Hardee, Johnston (Joseph), Buckner, Longstreet, Polk, Lee (Robert E.), Forrest, Beauregard, Jackson, Cooper, Stuart, Taylor, Pemberton, Hill (D.H.)

Page 24. Jefferson Davis

Page 25. Robert E. Lee

Photograph made especially for Queen Victoria, and thought to be only time Lee posed in full dress after surrender at Appomatox.

Page 26. Compiled Service Record Cards of Robert A. Taylor and J.F. Teague

Page 27. Pension Application of Confederate veteran Cary Warren

Page 28. Adjutant General's reply to query concerning service of James C. Taylor

Page 29. Pension Application (widow) of India Virginia Taylor, wife of James Coleman Taylor

Page 30. "Tenting on the Old Camp Ground," a popular Civil War ditty, from an 1883 songbook

(Confederate.)

42   Miss.

Robt. R. Taylor

3 Sgt.? Co. H., 42 Reg't Mississippi Vols.

Appears on

Company Muster Roll

of the organization named above,

for _Sept & Oct_, 1864.

Enlisted:
When _May 14_, 1862.
Where _Grenada, Miss._
By whom _Col. Miller_
Period _3 years_

Last paid:
By whom _Capt Cooper_
To what time _Apl. 30_, 1863.

Present or absent _Absent_
Remarks: _Prisoner of War_
Since July the 3 1863

Book mark: _____

Rict Buttey

(682)   Copyist.

(Confederate.)

42   Miss.

J. T. Teague

Privat?, Co. C., 42 Reg't Mississippi Vols.

Appears on

Company Muster Roll

of the organization named above,

for _July & Aug_, 1864.

Enlisted:
When _May 14_, 1862?
Where _Grenada Miss_
By whom _Col Miller_
Period _3 years or War_

Last paid:
By whom _Capt Cooper_
To what time _Feb 29_, 1864.

Present or absent _Absent_
Remarks: _Missing since_
Battle of The Wilderness
May 5 1864

Book mark: _____

G. E. Jones

(682)   Copyist.

O.K.D.

WAR DEPARTMENT
THE ADJUTANT GENERAL'S OFFICE
WASHINGTON June 30, 1930.

Respectfully returned to

State Comptroller,
    Pension Department,
    Richmond, Virginia.

The records show that Carey R. Warren, Capt. Thompson's Co., Va. Lt. Arty., (Capt. Carey F. Grimes' Co. (A) Maj. J. S. Saunders' Battn. Field Arty.,) (Portsmouth Light Arty.,) C.S.A., enlisted August 10, 1862, at Falling Creek.
Muster roll July & August 1862, dated Sept. 2, 1862, (latest on file,) shows him present, a Private.
Capture, parole or later record not found.
Not found as Cary R. Warren.

C. H. Bridges,
Major General,
The Adjutant General.
By *J.C.*

Form No. 074-A. G. O.

U. S. GOVERNMENT PRINTING OFFICE: 1930   3—6336

CITY } Portsmouth
COUNTY

COMMONWEALTH OF VIRGINIA
DEPARTMENT OF FINANCE
COMPTROLLER'S OFFICE

Richmond June 26, 1930

The Adjutant-General,
    War Department,
        Washington, D. C.
Sir:

I have the honor to request the official record of Cary R. Warren

Co. Grime's Battery Reg. Field Artillery
Colonel Maj. Saunders
Captain Cary F. Grimes

This information is to be used in connection with an application for a Confederate pension, which has been filed in this office.

Respectfully,
E. R. Combs,
Comptroller.

By
Pension Clerk.

Form No. 12
Received A. G. O. JUN 27 1930

PENSIONERS now on the Roll are NOT required to make new application, but must file annual certificate

THIS APPLICATION must be filed with the Clerk of the Corporation Court of Your City or Circuit Court of Your County

FORM No. 6

APPLICATION of a disable Soldier, Sailor or Marine of the late Confederacy under act approved March 26, 1928.

I, *Cary R. Warren* do hereby apply for a pension under the provisions of the act of the General Assembly of Virginia, relating to Confederate pensions.

I do solemnly swear that I am a citizen of the State of Virginia, and that I have been an actual resident of said State for two years next preceding the date of this application, and that I was a soldier (sailor or marine) of the Confederate States in the war between the States, and that I am now disabled, and that from the effects of such disability I am incapacitated from following my usual and ordinary occupation, or any other occupation for a livelihood; and that during the said war I was loyal and true to my duty, and never at any time deserted my command or voluntarily abandoned my post of duty, in the said service, and that by reason of such service and disability I am now entitled to receive a pension under the provisions of said act. And I do further swear that I do not hold a national, State, City or county office or any position which pays me a salary or fees exceeding Two Hundred ($200.00) dollars per annum; nor have I an income from any other employment or source whatever exceeding Four Hundred ($400.00) dollars per annum; nor do I receive from any source whatever money exceeding Four Hundred ($400.00) dollars per annum, nor do I own in my own right, nor does any one hold in trust for my benefit or use, estate or property either real, personal, or mixed, either in fee or for life, which yields a total income exceeding Four Hundred ($400.00) dollars per annum, or which yields an income, which, added to my income from all other sources, exceeding Four Hundred ($400.00) dollars per annum. I do further swear that I do not receive a pension from this or any other State, or from the United States nor do I receive necessary aid from any soldiers' home; board and clothing excepted; and that I am not an inmate of any soldiers' home. I do solemnly swear that the answers given to the questions which I am required to answer in this application are true to the best of my knowledge and belief.

Any assessment of property does not affect the right to pension, but the gross income from all sources must not exceed $400.00 per year.

1. What is your name? *Cary R. Warren*
2. What is your age? *83* years
3. Where were you born? *Norfolk County*
4. How long have you resided in Virginia? *83 years*
5. How long have you resided in the City or County of your present residence? *83 years* years.
6. In what branch of the service were you? *Field Artillery* Regiment. *Grimes Battery* Company.
7. Who were your immediate superior officers? Colonel *Major Saunders* Captain *Cary F. Grimes*
8. When did you enter the service? *Apr. 1861*, 186
9. Where did you enter the service? *Portsmouth, Virginia*
10. When and why did you leave the service? *Sept. 1862 — discharged by order of Gen. Lee being only 15 yrs. of age*
11. Where do you reside? If in a city, give street address. Postoffice *417 Fayette St.* County of *Portsmouth*, Virginia.
12. Have you ever applied for a pension in Virginia before? If so, why are you not drawing one at this time? *No*

13. What is your usual and ordinary occupation for earning a livelihood? *Helper.*
14. Are you following such occupation or any other occupation or employment at this time? If yes, state the nature and extent of same. *yes — at times*
15. What is your annual income? *600.00 on application ?*
NOTE.— By income is meant the total gross receipts derived from farms and all crops (whether sold or used), wages and other sources valued in dollars.
16. How much property do you own?
Real estate $ *none*
Personal Property $ *none*
17. What is the exact nature of your disability and the cause thereof?
18. Are you totally or partially incapacitated by such disability?
19. Give the names and addresses of two comrades who served in the same command with you during the war.
Name *Joseph Dukes & W. W. Picks*
Address *Portsmouth, Va*
Address *Portsmouth, Va.*
Name
20. Is there a camp of Confederate Veterans in your city or county? *yes*
21. Give here any other information you may possess relating to your service or disability which will support the justice of your claim. *After my discharge from the army I was employed at the Navy Yard, Charlotte, N.C.*

Cary R. Warren
Signature of Applicant.

A signature made by X mark is not valid unless attested by a witness.
WITNESS

I, *C. N. Markham*, notary public in and for the *City* of *Portsmouth*, in the State of Virginia, do certify that the applicant whose name is signed to the foregoing application personally appeared before me in my *City* aforesaid, having the aforesaid application read and carefully explained, as well as the statements and answers therein made, the said applicant made oath before me that the said statements and answers are true.

Given under my hand this *28th* day of *April*, 19*30*

C. N. Markham
Notary Public Signature of Officer.
My commission expires Sept 9-1930

29

WAR DEPARTMENT

THE ADJUTANT GENERAL'S OFFICE

WASHINGTON August 22, 1920.

IN REPLY
REFER TO O.R.D.

Respectfully returned to

Comptroller's Office,
Department of Finance,
Commonwealth of Virginia,
Richmond, Virginia.

The records show that James O. Taylor, not found as James Coleman Taylor, Private, Co. C, (Captain Andrew V. Scott), 2Z Regiment Virginia Infantry, Confederate States Army, enlisted May 15, 1861 at Winterham. Muster roll for November and December 1861 shows him absent, on parole taken prisoner July 13, 1861.
He was discharged at Richmond September 30, 1861.

Luty Mall
Major General,
The Adjutant General.
By O.R.O.

The Applicant must read, or have read to her, every word in this Application

PENSIONERS now on the ROLL are NOT required to make new application, but must file annual Certificate

THIS APPLICATION must be filed with the Clerk of the Corporation Court of Your City or Circuit Court of Your County

FORM No. 7

APPLICATION of a widow of a Soldier, Sailor, or Marine of the late late Confederacy under acts approved March 26, 1928 and March 10, 1928.

I, *India Virginia Taylor* do hereby apply for a pension under the provisions of the acts of the General Assembly of Virginia relating to Confederate pensions.

I do solemnly swear that I am a citizen of the State of Virginia and that I have been an actual resident of the said State for two years next preceding the date of this application, and that I am the widow of *James C. Taylor*, who was a soldier (sailor or marine) in the service of the Confederate States in the War Between the States, and that I was married to him before January 1, 1890 (See note below) and to the best of my knowledge and belief during the said war my husband was loyal and true to his duty, and never at any time deserted his command or voluntarily abandoned his post or duty in the said service, and that I was never divorced from my said husband, and that I never voluntarily abandoned him during his life, but remained his lawful wife up to the time of his death, and that I am a widow at the date of making this application, and that I am now entitled to receive a pension under the provisions of said act. I do further swear that I do not hold a national, State or county office, which pays a salary or less exceeding four hundred dollars ($400.00) per annum, nor have I income from any source whatever exceeding four hundred dollars ($400.00) per annum, nor do I own in my own right, nor is there held in trust for my own benefit, estate or property, either real, personal or mixed in lie or for life, which yields to said income exceeding four hundred dollars ($400.00) per annum, or which yields an income which, added to my income from all other sources, exceeds four hundred dollars ($400.00) per annum. I do further swear that I do not receive a pension from this or any other State, nor do I receive necessary aid from any source, board and clothing excepted. I do solemnly swear that the answers given to the questions which I am required to answer in this application are true to the best of my knowledge and belief.

Any assessment of property does not affect the right to pension, but the gross income from all sources must not exceed $400.00 per year. Certificates under B, C, E, not necessary if husband was pensioner.

NOTE.—Widows seventy-five years old or over can receive pension regardless of date of marriage. Widows under seventy-five years old are required to have been married prior to January 1st, 1890.

1. What is your name? *India Virginia Taylor*
2. What is your age? *76 years*
3. Where were you born? *Chesterfield Co. Va.*
4. How long have you resided in Virginia? *76 years*
5. How long have you resided in the City or County of your present residence? *17 years* years.
6. Where do you reside? If in a city, give street address. Postoffice *330 Broad St.* County of *Norfolk Portsmouth* Virginia.
7. With whom do you reside? *Charles Ernest Taylor (Son)*
8. What was your husband's full name? *James Coleman Taylor*
9. Which, where and by whom were you married? When? *November 4, 1883* Where? *M.E. Church So. Richmond Va.* By whom? *Rev. Lumpkin.*
10. When and where did your husband die? *Dec. 28, 1886. So. Richmond Va.*
11. What was the cause of his death? *Tuberculosis*
12. Have you married since the death of your husband? If yes, give full particulars. *No.*
13. In what branch of the army did your husband serve? *23d Virginia Infantry* Regiment. Company *E - Johnson Div - Jackson Corps* Company.

14. Who were his immediate superior officers? Colonel Captain *Andrew Scott*
15. Give the names and addresses of two comrades who served in the same command with your husband during the war. (Not necessary if your husband was a pensioner.) Name *Robert M. French* Address *Soldiers Home* Name *Richmond - Va* Address
16. What assistance do you receive, and what income have you from all sources? *None*

NOTE.—By income is meant the total gross receipts derived by you from all crops (whether sold or used), wages and other sources valued in dollars.

17. How much property do you own? Real estate, $ *None* Personal property, $ *None*
18. Was your husband on the pension roll of Virginia? If yes, in what county of his residence was his pension allowed?
19. Have you ever applied for a pension in Virginia before? If yes, why are you not drawing one at this time? *No.*
20. Is there a camp of Confederate Veterans in your city or county? *Yes. Stonewall Camp.*
21. Give here any other information you may possess relating to the service of your husband or the cause of his death which will support the justice of your claim. *Contracted pneumonia while in service*

A signature made by X mark is not valid unless attested by a witness.

WITNESS   *India Virginia Taylor*
                                                                                        Signature of Applicant
I, *A. H. Robinson* a *Notary Public* In and for the *City* of *Portsmouth*,

in the State of Virginia, do certify that the applicant whose name is signed to the foregoing application personally appeared before me in my *City* aforesaid, having the aforesaid application read to her and fully explained, as well as the statements and answers therein made, the said applicant made oath before me that the said statement and answers are true.
Given under our hand this *28th* day of *May* 1928

A. H. Robinson, Notary Public
                                                                                        Signature of Officer.

CHAPTER 2

Searching in the Confederate States

STATE ARCHIVES AND LIBRARIES

Before starting your search for your Confederate ancestor's records, decide how many and which state archives and libraries you need to contact or visit. Obviously, you should concentrate on the states where he lived during the years of the Civil War. Even though there is a chance he served in a military unit of some other state, you may still find related genealogical material back in his home state. If you uncover evidence that he did indeed serve in a unit of some other state, you must also contact that state. Many Southern sympathizers who lived in one of the border states of Kentucky, Missouri, Maryland, West Virginia, the Arizona Territory, or the Indian Territory crossed into Southern states to enlist. Also, anyone who lived close to his own state boundary might have crossed into a neighboring state to enlist with his friends or for some other reason of convenience or expediency. You should also contact any other state to which your ancestor moved after the war. He may have applied for a pension while in that state. Confederate pension laws almost uniformly authorized awards to its residents regardless of where they lived or enlisted during the war. In summary, you may be well advised to try to find evidence of your ancestor's existence in as many as three or more states, depending upon his mobility.

Before contacting or visiting any state archives or library, become thoroughly familiar with the information in this book; it lists and describes the material relative to the Confederate records which you may expect to find in each of the pertinent states. In this way you will be assured that a valuable source will not be overlooked, and you may ask specifically for a certain set of records despite the fact that a staff member may not voluntarily suggest it to you or may not even know of its existence. Be persistent and let no scrap of paper go unexamined if there is a possibility that it might bear your ancestor's name. If you visit the archives or library personally, or hire a professional reseacher in lieu of making a written request, be sure that all the promising sources are inspected.

Written Requests

All the state archives described in this book will respond to written requests for information about your Confederate ancestor. This service is free except for charges for any copies you may request. An exception is North Carolina which requires an advance payment of five dollars by a non-resident. Generally, staffs of the archives are small and budgetary limitations prevent them from making more than simple searches. If they cannot help you directly, they will often refer you to the National Archives or provide you with a list of local professional researchers whom you might engage. In every instance you are asked to make only one request at a time, for only one person, in only one set of records. In this way you have a good chance that the staff will respond favorably to your letter and will advise you that they do or do not have material about your ancestor. They will also advise you of the cost of making copies of any records they have found and will send them to you after they receive your payment. In most cases a brief telephone call asking for one specific piece of material will also be honored. Exceptions or modifications to this general procedure are spelled out in this book, and your attention is directed to the descriptive sections for each state.

Personal Visits

Except for simple searches which may be done by archives staffs in response to a letter or telephone call, a search will be more productive if you make a personal visit or hire a professional researcher to visit for you.

Each section of the chapters pertaining to a state lists the usual hours of operation, and the holiday closings. Because of changing policies, however, these listings are not reliable. Except for the obvious holiday closings, such as Christmas and New Year's Day, it may be wise to call ahead to be sure. While the search rooms and libraries generally are closed on state holidays, it is often impossible to know exactly just when those holidays occur in any particular state. Notice, too, that federal holidays are not always state holidays. Thus, Columbus Day or George Washington's Birthday, among others, may or may not result in the closing of a state facility. The federal Memorial Day, as well as the Confederate Memorial Day, is observed in many southern states, as are the birthdays of General Lee, General Jackson, and Jefferson Davis. Also, archives may be closed on the days just before or following a holiday. Frequently, decisions about closings are made by the state's executives just a few days before the holiday.

Upon entering an archives you will be required to register. In most cases a researcher's card or badge, identifying you while in the building, will be presented to you at no charge. As you register you probably will be given a written list of rules and regulations governing the use of the archives. You will be asked to sign it before you begin your search. A staff member will explain what resources are available to you and how to find them. That orientation varies from only a word or two to a full description. A pamphlet or sheet listing the holdings may be given. Regardless of the extent of the orientation, it is necessary that you become familiar with the listing of the records described in this book. Nowhere else will you find such a complete listing.

You will probably be directed to certain finding aids which will guide you to the material needed. The aids for each state archives are described in detail in each state section. Facilities in the archives vary quite widely, but generally they are spacious and conducive to pleasant research. Many archives search rooms are located adjacent to the state library, and some are integral parts of it. Microfilm readers are always available, but in some instances you may be asked to register for a specific reader and to relinquish it temporarily during times of heavy public usage. In other instances you may choose any reader available and use it at will. In one state, Arkansas, the staff insists that they personally place the roll of microfilm on the reader and remove it when you are finished with it; you never touch the roll. In nearly all archives, the rolls are refiled by the staff after you have placed them at a spot designated for that purpose.

Take along a supply of pencils, since most archives ban the use of ink or ball point pens, especially where publications or original papers are handled. All are careful that you treat their holdings with care, since they are valuable and subject to damage through mishandling. Extreme care is necessary when handling original manuscripts, and these are sometimes not made available to you at all, especially if they have been microfilmed.

Security over the rooms and the researchers is very strict in some archives. Often you will be asked to leave your wraps, purses, briefcases, large envelopes, and bound notebooks in an outer room or in a locker provided to you. All material in your possession is subject to search as you leave the room. In North Carolina, for instance, closed circuit cameras continually scan the search room. In some archives most of the material you desire may be obtained personally, while in others you will be required to use the finding aids or indexes first and then request that the material be brought to you. The varying procedures are set forth in this chapter. Becoming familiar with the local rules and procedures before you visit will smooth your research attempts.

Types of Materials Available

In an archives of a Confederate or border state, you will usually find the following broad classifications of records which relate to your ancestor:

1. National Archives microfilm of the "compiled service records" and related Confederate records which have been purchased by the state archives;
2. Pension records for residents of that state;
3. Military service records including muster and pay rolls;
4. Miscellaneous state records of the war including Confederate home registers, manuscripts, and other documents.

It is suggested that you inspect the material in the order listed above. By first examining the service records on the microfilm purchased from the National Archives, you will determine the names of the military units in which your ancestor served, the dates of his enlistment and discharge, and other information to be found in those films. Using that identifying data, you may next determine whether he applied for a state pension and, if so, inspect those records next. Following that, you may look at any of the other state records which might contain a reference to your ancestor. These include muster and other rolls, militia lists, and other miscellaneous items. After following this procedure, you may well conclude that a visit to the National Archives in Washington, D.C., is not necessary since you have found everything you need in the state records.

Historical Background

A part of each section of the chapter dealing with a particular state con-sists of a short summary of the role that state played in the Civil War. The moves toward secession from the Union and contributions in military man-power to the Confederate armies are described. A summary of the campaigns and major battles fought within the state's borders and the final surrender of its troops are also included. These things are set forth here to provide you with a ready reference to the historical background of the state's participation in the war. You will want to refer to it as you uncover material that refers to your ancestor's place of residence, the military units in which he served, and the battles in which he may have participated. For more detailed background, you are urged to select from the publications listed in the bibliography or from any of the hundreds of books which provide more detail in the back-ground of the Confederacy and the thousands of battles, actions, raids, and skirmishes--too numerous even to mention in this book.

Lists of Military Units

Each section of the state chapters includes a list of associated military units at least insofar as the National Archives has compiled personnel service records. Check these lists for a reference to the name or number of a unit that might mention your ancestor. Next, the publications in chapter five might refer you to a unit history containing a roster or list of men who served in that unit.

Often you will find a reference to a name or a military unit which is not included in some list of units. The reason for such a discrepancy may be that the unit was called by its local name rather than by the official designation given it by the Confederate government. In those cases you can find a cross-reference in publications which list both official and local designations. Your attention is directed to *Personnel of the Civil War,* by William F. Amman, and *Confederate Military Land Units,* by William J. Tancig, both of which are very complete in this regard. As an example, there you will find listed the "Tipton Rifles," and its official designation, "Company I," Fourth (Neely's) Tennessee Infantry.

ALABAMA
DEPARTMENT OF ARCHIVES AND HISTORY
624 Washington Avenue, Montgomery 36130
(across from the Capitol)

HOURS: 8:00 a.m.--5:00 p.m., Monday--Friday
9:00 a.m.--5:00 p.m., Saturday
closed: state holidays

The combined archives and library is on the first floor of the building. Next door to the building is the house where the Confederate States of America, with Jefferson Davis at its head, was created. After you register at the archives, a sketch showing the location of their holdings will be given to you. That sketch shows the areas and shelf numbers where the records will be found. Begin your search at area number twenty, the "retrieval area." Fill out a slip, giving the name of your veteran ancestor and any other information you may know about him, especially the county of his residence during the war or in the years following. Drop the slip in a box provided. The staff will consult their master card index to see if your ancestor or his widow is mentioned in one of their military rosters, muster rolls, or pension files. Whatever they find will be placed on a shelf near the desk for you to take to your table for examination. Return it to the same shelf when you are finished.

National Archives Microfilm

To help you identify your veteran, locate and examine the microfilm records dealing with Confederate soldiers which this archives has purchased from the National Archives. There is only one series of such film in this archives; it is in a microfilm room adjacent to the search room. It has been relabeled "Alabama Confederate Soldiers," but the official title is *Index to Compiled Service Records of Confederate Soldiers Who Served in Organizations From the State of Alabama.* These may be found in Microcopy 374, consisting of forty-nine rolls. See chapter four for a complete description of this series.

Pensions

On 19 February 1867, Alabama enacted legislation providing for Confederate veteran pensions and created a state pension commission to oversee the program. The probate judge of each county was authorized to receive pension applications and pass them on to the commission through the office of the state auditor. A clerk in the auditor's office was assigned to act as the secretary to the commission. An amendment in 1886 provided for pensions to widows also.

The original law provided funds only for the furnishing of artificial limbs to soldiers or sailors who had lost their arms or legs in battle. Future revisions, up to 3 February 1891, expanded the opportunities for financial assistance and increased appropriations. All applicants were required to prove desertion-free military service with the Confederate forces, not to include the home guards, the state reserves, or a militia of some other state. Both veterans and their widows had to be in indigent circumstances. They could not own real or personal property valued at more than $2,000 and could not live in the state soldiers' home at Mountain Creek.

To be eligible for any pension, according to later revisions of the law, widows must have married the veteran prior to July 1914, and not be remarried. They had to be Alabama residents and own no property valued at more than $2,000. Any qualifying widow who married the veteran before the end of the war in April 1865 was entitled to a full pension, but the widow who did not marry until after that month was entitled to only a one-third pension.

A typical application is replete with military and genealogical information including affidavits from others who could attest to the veteran's service. Sufficient personal data was required to prove the applicant's qualifications under the law. A widow's application was similar to that of the veteran with the addition of data concerning her marriage and her husband's death. There is no index of the Alabama pension applications, and they have not been microfilmed. Each pension file, arranged by county of residence, consists of a separate folder. Those folders will be brought to you for examination by the retrieval area staff.

Census of Pensioners

A census of pensioners in Alabama was taken in 1907 and again in 1921. During 1907, the state tax assessors personally canvassed all persons in the state who were then receiving pensions for Confederate service. Each interview was logged into a ledger type book. In addition to the pensioner's name, there was a brief synopsis of his military service, his place and date of birth, and his place of residence. During 1921, a questionnaire form was mailed to each Confederate pensioner with a request that it be completed and returned to the state. The form had several questions concerning the pensioner's military service, his occupation, and the names, addresses, and occupations of his living children. Each of the returned questionnaires, most of which were filled out with care, are filed in a folder and arranged in alphabetical order by name of the pensioner. Each name is included in the archives' master card index. You may examine both of these censuses by filling out a retrieval slip.

Military Service Records

The finding aids at location number twelve include a green, fiber-bound booklet entitled "Historical Reference File." It contains a list of titles relating to several military service records. These may be obtained by submitting a retrieval slip; write the title of the material and its "call number." A few examples of the kinds of material listed there which pertain to Confederate soldiers are described below:

Military Rosters

Each unit roster, clearly labeled by a cover sheet, is in a separate folder. These very large sheets contain names, ranks, ages, and enlistment dates. Requests should be made by the name of the military unit.

Lists of Alabama Commands (CSA)

These lists contain names of personnel and histories of various Confederate units from Alabama. Requests should be made by name of the military unit.

Roll of Honor

On 15 April 1915 (Confederate Memorial Day), the Ladies Memorial Association of the General Morgan Chapter, United Daughters of the Confederacy, presented to various Alabama veterans metal crosses with their names engraved on them. Information about the presentation of each medal is in a separate folder. One such folder inspected by the author still had a medal in it, apparently never having been presented. Requests to see these folders should be made by referring to the name of the veteran.

Miscellaneous State Records

The "Historical Reference File" also lists many other sources possibly of lesser value than those described above. They include folders containing miscellaneous material such as newspaper clippings, typed lists of names, letters, and similar material. In some libraries these kinds of folders are called "vertical files." The material in these folders is far from complete and varies in degree of usefulness. All of them bear the reference letter "W" which must be included on the retrieval slip. Some of the titles in this group are:

Biography--Confederates
Deaths in Hospitals
Oaths of Allegiance to the CSA (officers)
Casualties--Killed or Wounded
Substitutes or Exempts
Surgeons in Confederate Service

ALABAMA'S ROLE IN THE WAR

Despite stiff opposition by many Northern Alabamians who preferred to cooperate with the federal government to resolve their differences, the election of Lincoln convinced the majority of the state's citizens that the Republican Party was an "abolitionist party" intent on outlawing slavery wherever it existed. From the day of Lincoln's election, Alabama began to take precautionary steps including the seizing of federal forts and arsenals located within its borders, chiefly the port of Mobile and the Mount Vernon Arsenal. Those actions prevented the federal government from reinforcing them with its own troops.

A state convention was called to debate and decide the question of secession. The "cooperationists" argued for delay, patience, and the outcome of a popular vote on the question. A popular vote was never taken, but the delegates to the convention took an immediate vote instead. On 11 January 1861, the tally was sixty-one for secession and thirty-nine for staying in the Union.[2] By this action, Alabama became a sovereign state and soon joined South Carolina and its sister states in the Confederacy. Immediately after the vote, a huge Alabama flag was unfurled over the Capitol and the people were ecstatic.

It has been estimated that Alabama furnished seventy-five thousand men to the Confederate military; most served in battles outside of Alabama. For instance, there were thirteen regiments and three batteries of Alabama troops at Vicksburg, Mississippi, when it fell. Likewise, at Gettysburg there were sixteen regiments and several batteries and battalions. Alabamians also were present in large numbers with the Confederate army during its many battles in Virginia and the Carolinas. There was, however, no major invasion of Alabama by Union forces until near the end of the war.

On 23 August 1864, Admiral David G. Farragut approached and took Mobile. As he entered the bay, he disdained the presence of mines (then called torpedoes) which had been laid by the Confederates. It was there that he is said to have bellowed the immortal words, "Damn the torpedoes! Full speed ahead!"

After the disastrous battle at Shiloh, Tennessee, Northern Alabama was ripe for raids by Union troops. With most of the soldiers stationed elsewhere, the local defense was left mainly to home guard units assisting a few units of Confederate cavalry. One of the Union raids was led by Colonel Streight. Destroying the railroads which had supplied the Confederate units, he marched from Tuscumbia across the state to Rome, Georgia. Eventually, he was captured by Confederate Gen. Nathan B. Forrest at Lawrence, Alabama. Another raid was made by General Lowell H. Rousseau who marched from Decatur to mid-Alabama; he also destroyed railroads as he went. A third raid was a joint efort by Generals Croxton and Wilson who marched from northwest Alabama to Macon, Georgia.

After the losses at Vicksburg and Gettysburg, many soldiers, both Confederate and Union, deserted and straggled on foot into the mountains of northern Alabama, where they were often joined by hordes of draft dodgers and Union sympathizers. They tended to collect into roving bands which lived off the land and terrorized the local citizens who did not cooperate with them. The majority of the soldiers, though, continued to fight, and when Lee surrendered at Appomattox, Virginia, he had twenty regiments and three smaller units from Alabama with him. When Johnston also surrendered at Durham, North Carolina, he had ten Alabama regiments with him. The troops then stationed within Alabama soon surrendered at Selma and Citronelle.

Military Units

The National Archives has the compiled service records for the personnel who served in units from Alabama as listed below. They may be found in Microcopy 311, consisting of 508 rolls. See chapter four for a complete description of this series.

First through Fourth Cavalry
Fourth (Roddey's) Cavalry
Fourth (Russell's) Cavalry
Fourth (Love's) Battalion, Cavalry
Fifth through Eighth Cavalry
Eighth (Hatch's) Cavalry
Eighth (Livingston's) Cavalry
Ninth Cavalry
Ninth (Malone's) Cavalry
Tenth through Twelfth Cavalry
Fifteenth Cavalry
Twenty-fourth Cavalry
Captain Arrington's Company A, City Troop (Mobile)
Barbiere's Battalion, Cavalry
Captain Barlow's Company, Cavalry
Captain Bowie's Company, Cavalry
Captain Brooks' Company, Cavalry Reserves
Captain Callaway's Company, Cavalry
Captain Falkner's Company, Cavalry (Chambers Cavalry)
Captain Chisolm's Company
Forrest's Cavalry
Gachet's Company, Cavalry

Graves' Company, Cavalry
Hardie's Battalion, Cavalry Reserves
Holloway's Company, Cavalry
Captain Lenoir's Independent Company, Cavalry
Lewis' Battalion, Cavalry
Logan's Company, Mounted Reserves
Mobile City Troop
Moreland's Regiment, Cavalry
Captain Morris' Company, (Mounted Men)
Captain Moses' Squadron, Cavalry
Murphy's Battalion, Cavalry
Roddey's Escort, Cavalry
Stuart's Battalion, Cavalry
Young's Company, Cavalry (State Reserves)
First Battalion, Artillery
Second Battalion, Light Artillery
State Artillery
Bay Batteries
Twentieth Battalion, Light Artillery
Clanton's Battery, Light Artillery
Eufaula Light Artillery
Gid Nelson Light Artillery
Goldthwaite's Battery, Light Artillery
Hurt's Battery, Light Artillery
Jeff Davis Artillery
Kolb's Battery, Light Artillery
Lee's Battery, Light Artillery
Phelan's Company, Light Artillery
Captain Seawell's Battery (Mohawk Artillery)
Tarrant's Battery, Light Artillery
Captain Ward's Battery, Light Artillery
First Infantry
First Conscripts
First Mobile Volunteers
First Battalion, Cadets
First (Loomis') Battalion, Infantry
Second Volunteer Militia

Second Infantry
Third Volunteer Militia
Third Infantry
Third Alabama Reserves
Third Battalion Reserves
Fourth Infantry
Fourth Volunteer Militia
Fourth Reserves
Fifth Infantry
Fifth Battalion, Volunteers
Fifth Battalion (Blount's Volunteers)
Sixth Infantry
Sixth (McClellan's) Battalion, Infantry
Seventh through Thirteenth Infantry
Thirteenth Battalion, Partisan Rangers
Fourteenth Infantry
Fifteenth Infantry
Fifteenth (First) Battalion, Partisan Rangers
Sixteenth Infantry
Seventeenth Infantry
Seventeenth Battalion, Sharp Shooters
Eighteenth Infantry
Eighteenth Battalion, Volunteers
Nineteenth through Twenty-third Infantry
Twenty-third Battalion, Sharp Shooters
Twenty-fourth Infantry
Twenty-fifth Infantry
Twenty-sixth (O'Neal's) Infantry
Twenty-seventh through Thirty-second Infantry
Thirty-second and Fifty-eighth (Consolidated) Infantry
Thirty-third through Forty-eighth Infantry
Forty-eighth Militia
Forty-ninth Infantry
Fiftieth Infantry
Fifty-first Partisan Rangers
Fifty-third Partisan Rangers
Fifty-fourth Infantry

Fifty-fifth Volunteers
Fifty-sixth Partisan Rangers
Fifty-seventh through Sixty-third Infantry
Eighty-ninth Militia
Ninety-fourth Militia
Ninety-fifth Militia
Hilliard's Legion
Leighton's Rangers
Fire Battalion of Mobile
Montgomery Guards
Camp of Instruction, Talladega, Alabama
Calhoun County Reserves
Coosa County Reserves
Fayette County Reserves
Randolph County Reserves
Shelby County Reserves
Talladega County Reserves
Allen's Company
Captain Beiser's Company, Reserves
Captain Bligh's Company, Militia
Captain Campbell's Company, Militia
Captain Crawford's Company
Captain Darby's Company, Auburn Home Guards, Volunteers
Lieutenant Echols' Company, of Conscripts
Captain Fagg's Company, Lowndes Rangers, Volunteers
Captain Freeman's Company, Prison Guard
Captain Goldsmith's Independent Company, Volunteers
Captain Gorff's Company (Mobile Pulaski Rifles)
Captain Gueringer's Company, Militia
Captain Hardy's Company, (Eufaula Minutemen)
Captain Hert's Company
Captain Hunt's Company, Militia
Captain Lee, Jr.'s Company, Volunteers
Captain Lockett's Company, City Guards
Captain Meador's Company, Mounted Infantry
Captain Orr's Company, Morgan Defenders
Captain Palmer's Company, State Reserves

Captain Rabby's Coast Guard Company No. 1, Volunteers
Captain Rankin's Company, Reserves
Ready's Battalion, Reserves
Reed's Supporting Force, Second Congressional District
Captain Rives' Supporting Force, Ninth Congressional District
Lieutenant Stewart's Detachment, Local Defense
Captain Toomer's Company, Local Defense and Special Services
    (Chunchula Guards)
Captain West's Company, Militia
Captain Young's Company, Nitre and Mining Corps
Alabama Conscripts
Battalion of Conscripts and Reserves
Alabama Rebels
Alabama Recruits
Miscellaneous, Alabama

ARKANSAS
ARKANSAS HISTORY COMMISSION
One Capitol Mall, Little Rock 72201
(west of the Capitol)

HOURS: 8:00 a.m.--4:30 p.m., Monday--Saturday
closed: state holidays

This combined archives and library operated by the state History Commision is in a new, modern building. There is free parking in a lot down the hill along the railroad tracks.

When you register you will be furnished with a folder entitled "Historical and Genealogical Source Materials." Based on the titles in that pamphlet, you may submit a call slip for either the microfilmed or the published material. Staff at the counter of the reference desk will obtain the material and hand it to you. All microfilm and published material, with the exception of the books on the open shelves, are controlled exclusively by the staff. If you request a roll of microfilm, a reader will be assigned to you, and a staff member will place the roll on the machine for you. When you are finished, the staff member will remove it and place any other roll you may have requested on the machine. You are not allowed to load or unload the machine yourself.

National Archives Microfilm

This archives has purchased five series of microfilmed Confederate records from the National Archives, and they are available to you. You are not permitted to make copies from this film, however, despite the fact that the National Archives itself permits unlimited copying. See chapter four for a complete description of these series.

Consolidated Index to Compiled Service Records of Confederate Soldiers (all states). M253 (535 rolls).

Index to Compiled Service Records of Confederate Soldiers Who Served in Organizations From the State of Arkansas. M376 (926 rolls).

Compiled Service Records of Confederate Soldiers Who Served in Organizations From the State of Arkansas. M317 (256 rolls).

Confederate Service Records of Confederate Soldiers Who Served in Organizations Raised Directly by the Confederate Government. M258 (123 rolls).

Case Files of Applications From Former Confederates for Presidential Pardons (Amnesty Papers), 1865-1867. M1003 (Arkansas rolls only). The pamphlet provided you lists this series as "Ex-Confederate Amnesty Papers, Arkansas." Also available is an index to these types of papers filed from all the states.

Pensions

Arkansas enacted its first Confederate pension law on 1 April 1891. Any veteran who had served honorably in a Confederate unit and had become disabled because of war wounds or their later complications was eligible for a pension provided he had been an Arkansas resident for at least one year and was in an indigent condition. He could not own real estate valued at more than $400 and could not have an annual income of more than $150. In 1915 those amounts were raised to $500 and $250, respectively, and the value of his home was not included in the computation. The pension program was controlled by a state pension board, working through seventy-five local boards, one for each county. Applications had to be submitted to the local board by 1 July of the year. If approved, the applicant received one pension payment of $25 the following fall. Checks were sent from the state office to the local boards for distribution. In 1915 the amount of the pension was raised to a maximum of $100, subject to appropriation of sufficient funds by the legislature. Also during that year, widows born before 1878 and mothers of veterans also became eligible for a pension, but there were few applicants. Widows of qualifying veterans were entitled to continue to receive his pension as long as they did not remarry. In 1937 a widow might qualify for a pension in her own right even though her husband had not previously qualified for one. However, she must have married him before 1927. Two years later an amendment stated that she must have been born before 1870, thus had to be older than fifty-nine.

From time to time during the 1920s and the 1930s, the legislature authorized special pensions to certain persons who were not otherwise qualified under the existing pension laws. In those cases a pension file might not have been created by the pension board, and the archives may not be aware of it.

A typical pension file includes, in addition to the routine information concerning military history and personal status, a physician's statement and two statements from comrades-in-arms who could testify to his service. Widows' applications also added certain other biographical information.

Between 1891 and 1939, the period when the pension laws were administered by the State Department of Welfare, approximately fifty thousand persons received pensions. The files for that period have been microfilmed and are available for public inspection. After you identify your veteran from either the National Archives film listed above or from the WPA index listed below, the staff will bring you the microfilm roll which contains the pension file you requested. A copy of that file will be made for you upon payment of a $5 fee.

A collection of index cards entitled "Confederate Veterans and Widows Pensions Paid by the State of Arkansas" was created by the Work Projects Administration (WPA) in 1935 and 1936. The cards were microfilmed in 1968, and contain the name, application number, name of widow, military unit and service record, the date the application was approved, county of residence, and death date of the veteran or his widow. This index is available in the search room. At the time of this writing, it is being processed for publication by Frances T. Ingmire of St. Louis, Missouri.

Census of Pensioners

A census of veterans and widows then on the state pension rolls was attempted in 1911 and 1912, but only forty-four of the state's seventy-five counties participated, probably because the local tax assessors were paid only ten cents for each questionnaire they processed. Although there were thousands of pensioners in the state at that time, only 1,750 questionnaires were turned in. The material asked for included the last place of residence, date of birth of the veteran as well as his parents, his occupation, education, political party membership, and other material of a genealogical nature. These questionnaires have been alphabetized by name, and a file folder found at the reference desk contains the list of names. These questionnaires have also been published in three volumes by Bobbie J. McLane and Capitola Glazner who compiled the material in 1980.

Related Pension Records

Supplemental indexes available at the reference desk, found in red binders, should also be checked with regard to names of pensioners. They are titled as follows:

1. *Confederate Pensions.* Names are arranged by county and alphabetically thereunder. The microfilm roll number is given for each name;
2. *Confederate Deceased Pensioners.* Names are in alphabetical order, and the county of residence and identifying numbers are given;
3. *Miscellaneous Confederate Pension Records.* This index contains several names of persons not indexed in other sources and who had not been absolutely identified when other lists were prepared.

Military Service Records

An index titled "Arkansas Confederate Service Records" was begun in 1911 by the Arkansas History Commission. Data on the cards was obtained from various official sources and included the name, rank, military unit, names of commanding officers, and any enlistment data uncovered. When the National Archives published a similar index and made it available to the states, this local index was terminated. The cards were microfilmed, however, and the resulting thirty rolls are available for inspection.

Miscellaneous State Records

A resident of the state Confederate home was ineligible for a state pension. The home opened 12 November 1907 and closed approximately 26 August 1957. All the applications for admission received during that period have been alphabetized, whether or not the applicant was actually admitted as a resident. An index of the names of these applicants, showing their counties of residence, is available in a red binder found at the reference desk.

ARKANSAS' ROLE IN THE WAR

Despite the fact that a majority of the citizens of Arkansas were opposed to secession, its leadership pulled out of the Union on 6 May 1861. The result was a total debacle for the state, from beginning to end, on both military and civilian fronts. Nothing seemed to go right, and everyone suffered until the last shot of the war was fired--and for a decade or more later as well. The citizens were, for the most part, poor, uneducated farmers with small plots of ground to sustain them. The cotton culture was just beginning to flourish in the state and there were relatively few plantations with slaves. The state was strongly Democratic in politics, and the election of the Republican Lincoln solidified the feelings of opposition toward him and his philosophies. There remained, however, large parts of the population, mainly in the northwestern part of the state, who believed they should not leave the Union. The state's legislature agreed to permit a popular vote on the question as well as whether a convention should be called to make the final decision. The popular vote count was 23,626 for staying in the Union and 17,927 for secession, but the convention call was agreed to.[3] When the delegates to the convention met, they voted on 6 May 1861, to take the state out of the Union.

By the end of 1862, there were 21,500 Arkansas men under arms, either in units commanded by the state's General N. B. Pearce or with the Confederate General Ben McCulloch. Gearing up for war was poorly handled by the state's military board because of recruiting and supply problems. When it came time to transfer the state units to the Confederacy, there was much confusion and hostility between the respective leaders.

As soon as Arkansas opted to leave the Union, it took over the federal arsenal at Little Rock, forced the evacuation of federal troops from Fort Smith, and seized shipping facilities along the Arkansas and Mississippi rivers. Its neighbor, Missouri, was in the midst of intra-state fighting between those who wanted to secede and the federal troops who prevented them from doing so. When Missouri's Union General Nathaniel Lyon engaged Southern sympathizers from that state in the battle at Wilson's Creek, the Arkansas units, lead by General Pearce and General McCulloch, fought against him. After that battle, the Arkansas troops returned home and simply disbanded after attempts to integrate them into the Confederate army failed. Eventually, however, they were reorganized and placed under the command of Confederate General Earl Van Dorn. Their mission was to save Missouri for the Confederacy and to do what they could to turn around the war in the West.

On 7 March 1862, a major attack was launched by Van Dorn at the Elkhorn Tavern (Pea Ridge), just south of the Missouri border. Union General Samuel R. Curtis resisted Van Dorn's attempts to take Missouri for the South and, despite being outnumbered, battled for two days until Van Dorn had to retreat. Thousands of soldiers on both sides were killed in the battle. When the retreat was over, the Confederate army, feeling that the Arkansas and Missouri campaign was hopeless, pulled out of Arkansas and headed toward Mississippi, taking their arms and supplies with them. Exploiting the resultant vacuum, the Union troops then marched into the state and headed south. With this turn of events, Arkansas refused to send any of its men across the Mississippi River to fight in distant battles.

During the remainder of 1862 and into 1863, there was continued confusion over the leadership of the Confederate armies in the area, but General Theophilus Holmes was eventually placed in overall command of the Trans-Mississippi Department with headquarters at Little Rock. He remained in that city until the Union conquered Fort Smith on 1 September 1863 and Little Rock ten days later. From that time on, the Union troops plundered the poverty stricken farmers for whatever food they could find. Meanwhile, the Arkansas troops had to rely on food shipments from Texas to keep them alive.

During the remainder of the war, there were many small battles and skirmishes in Arkansas with only one brief moment of victory. This was when Union General Frederick Steele was ambushed by Arkansas troops near Pine Bluff and suffered the loss of two thousand men who were killed before they could escape.

In April 1865, when Lee and Johnston surrendered in the East, the Arkansas soldiers, owed pay for up to two years, turned from their camps and walked toward home.

Military Units

The National Archives has the compiled service records for the personnel who served in units from Arkansas as listed below. They may be found in Microcopy 317, consisting of 256 rolls. See chapter four for a complete description of this series.

First Cavalry
First (Crawford's Cavalry)
First (Dobbins') Cavalry
First (Monroe's) Cavalry
First Mounted Rifles
First (Stirman's) Battalion, Cavalry
First State Cavalry
Second Cavalry
Second Mounted Rifles
Third Cavalry
Sixth Battalion, Cavalry
Seventh Cavalry
Eighth Cavalry
Tenth (Witt's) Cavalry
Fifteenth (Buster's) Battalion, Cavalry
Forty-fifth Cavalry
Forty-sixth (Crabtree's) Cavalry
Forty-seventh (Crandall's) Cavalry
Forty-eighth Cavalry
Anderson's Unattached Battalion, Cavalry
Carlton's Cavalry
Davies' Battalion, Cavalry
Gipson's Battalion, Mounted Rifles
Gordon's Cavalry
Harrell's Battalion, Cavalry
McGehee's Cavalry
Nave's Battalion, Cavalry
Poe's Battalion, Cavalry
Witherspoon's Battalion, Cavalry
Wright's Cavalry

Abraham's Company, Mounted Volunteers
Baker's Company, Mounted Volunteers
Hooker's Company, Mounted Volunteers
Reeve's Company, Cavalry
First Field Battery (McNally's Battery)
Fifth Battery, Light Artillery
Clarkson's Battery, Light Artillery (Helena Artillery)
Etter's Battery, Light Artillery
Hart's Battery, Light Artillery
Key's Battery, Light Artillery
Marshall's Battery, Light Artillery
Owen's Battery, Light Artillery
Pine Bluff Artillery
River's Battery, Light Artillery
Thrall's Battery, Light Artillery
Wiggins' Battery, Light Artillery
Zimmerman's Battery, Light Artillery
First Volunteers
First Infantry
First (Consolidated) Infantry
First Battalion, Infantry
First (Colquitt's) Infantry
Second Volunteers
Second Infantry
Second (Consolidated) Infantry
Second Battalion, Infantry
Third Infantry
Third (Consolidated) Infantry
Third State Infantry
Fourth Infantry
Fourth State Infantry
Fourth Battalion, Infantry
Fifth Infantry
Fifth Militia
Fifth State Infantry
Sixth Infantry
Seventh Infantry

Seventh Militia
Eighth Infantry
Eighth Battalion, Infantry
Ninth Infantry
Tenth Infantry
Tenth Militia
Eleventh Infantry
Eleventh and Seventeenth (Griffith's) Consolidated Infantry
Twelfth Infantry
Twelfth Battalion, Sharp Shooters
Thirteenth Infantry
Thirteenth Militia
Fourteenth (McCarver's) Infantry
Fourteenth (Powers') Infantry
Fifteenth Infantry
Fifteenth (Johnson's) Infantry
Fifteenth (Josey's) Infantry
Fifteenth (Northwest) Infantry
Fifteenth Militia
Sixteenth Infantry
Seventeenth (Griffith's) Infantry
Seventeenth (Lemoyne's) Infantry
Eighteenth Infantry
Eighteenth (Marmaduke's) Infantry
Nineteenth Infantry
Nineteenth (Dawson's) Infantry
Nineteenth (Dockery's) Infantry
Twentieth through Twenty-sixth Infantry
Thirtieth through Thirty-eighth Infantry
Forty-fifth Militia
Fiftieth Militia
Fifty-first Militia
Fifty-eighth Militia
Sixty-second Militia
Adams' Infantry
Borland's Infantry
Cooke's Infantry

Crawford's Battalion, Infantry
Desha County Battalion, Militia
Hardy's Infantry
Williamson's Battalion, Infantry
Captain Ballard's Company, Infantry
Captain Clayton's Company, Infantry
Clear Lake Independent Guards, Infantry
Ernest's Company, Infantry
Kuykendall's Company, Infantry
Louis' Company, Militia
Sparks' Company, Infantry
Willet's Company, Infantry
Miscellaneous, Arkanas

FLORIDA
FLORIDA STATE ARCHIVES
500 South Bronough Street, Tallahassee 32301
(R. A. Gray Building)

HOURS: 8:00 a.m.--5:00 p.m., Monday--Friday
closed: state holidays, including New Year's Day, Memorial Day,
Independence Day, Labor Day, Veteran's Day, Thanksgiving Day
and the Friday following Christmas.

The archives is on the first floor of the building and the state library is on an upper floor. The archives is extremely well organized and designed to permit most searching without staff assistance. After you register, you will be shown the many simple-to-understand finding aids and indexes. The microfilmed records stored adjacent to the search room are also organized to permit a high degree of self help.

National Archives Microfilm

There are four series of microfilm which have been purchased from the National Archives. The index (listed first below) is stored in gray fiber boxes in the microfilm room. You may find your Florida Confederate ancestor in that index, by name and military unit, and then go to the search room where you will find the microfilmed records of his military service. Those are stored in gray steel file cabinets in a corner of the search room. See chapter four for a complete description of these four microfilm series.

Consolidated Index to Compiled Service Records of Confederate Soldiers. M253 (535 rolls).

Compiled Service Records of Confederate Soldiers Who Served in Organizations From the State of Florida. M251 (104 rolls).

Compiled Service Records of Confederate General and Staff Officers and Nonregimental Enlisted Men. M331 (275 rolls).

Florida personnel have been extracted from this series, and the resultant collection has been titled "Compiled Military Service of General and Staff Officers for the State of Florida." The names in this series are arranged in alphabetical order; thus no index is needed.

Records Relating to Confederate Naval and Marine Personnel. M260 (7 rolls).

Pensions

In 1885, Florida enacted pension legislation to benefit needy Confederate veterans. At that time a state pension board empowered to approve or disapprove all pension applications was created. Only those who had served in formal Confederate units were eligible according to that first legislation, but in 1887 those who had served in state militia units were also included. In 1889, widows of Confederate veterans also became eligible. Subsequent amendments to the basic law were frequent but minor, and were primarily concerned with changes in residence requirements and the annual amounts of funds authorized for payment of pensions.

Between 1885 and 1954, applications for 12,755 pensions were approved, and there is a file for each of these as well as a file for each application which was disapproved. The files contain much genealogical information, including personal data, military information, and battle wounds. Statements from comrades-in-arms are often included. In addition to the information required of a veteran, a widow's application has data about her marriage and the date and place of her husband's death. Each pension file has been numbered, microfilmed, and made available to the public.

Finding the pension files of your ancestor is a two-stage process. First, consult the computer printout containing the alphabetized listing of names of all the applicants. Each name has a file number. The next step is to consult the companion printout which lists the files according to the file number. This list is comprised of two sections, one for the approved applications and one for the disapproved applications. The applicant, his military unit, the name of his spouse, his county of residence, the number of pages in his file, and the year he submitted his application, are given. Similar data is listed for widows' applications. The microfilmed copy of the actual file may be examined after obtaining the proper roll form the gray, steel cabinets in a corner of the search room. These are filed by number.

If you write for this pension material, the staff will try to locate your ancestor in the computer printouts and will advise you on the number of pages in the file and the cost for copying them. A typical file has from four to twenty pages.

The state pension board kept all of its incoming correspondence; it has also been microfilmed. As it was handled, the content of each letter was summarized on the reverse side, the date noted, and the general content of the board's reply summarized. This correspondence is arranged chronologically in nine volumes. They cover the period from 7 July 1887 to 8 November 1905. Each volume is indexed according to the name of the letter writer. There are six additional boxes which contain loose folders covering the years from 1885 to the 1950s. These boxes are numbered as well as the folders they contain. Special notice is taken of box six, folder sixteen, which contains names of officers of Florida military units, widows granted pensions by special acts of Florida legislature, lists of soldiers killed at the Battle of Olustee, and a muster roll of the Thirty-third Alabama Regiment. In addition to its correspondence collection, the pension board issued biennial reports which contained rolls of persons who were then receiving pensions. Archives staff will obtain these for you upon request if you can specify the years your ancestor might have been on a pension roll.

Miscellaneous State Records

Supplementing the pension material, there is a collection of manuscript material which may turn up something of interest to you. Ask to see the three bound volumes which describe this material. You will find listed such things as diaries, letters, unit registers, and personal narratives. You may request that any of these be brought to you by giving a staff member the five digit location number at the upper right hand corner of the page where the material is described.

In addition to the published holdings of the state library, this archives has its own extensive collection of genealogical books, journals, and magazines. Staff will provide you with a notebook which lists those holdings.

FLORIDA'S ROLE IN THE WAR

By 1860, Florida had developed a thriving plantation, slave-owning economy. Almost one-third of the white people in the state owned at least one slave.[4] Many of the state's citizens, made up largely of farmers who had migrated from Georgia, the Carolinas, and Virginia, had found prosperity and feared that Lincoln's election was a serious and direct threat to their way of life. With the exception of a pro-Union faction centered mainly in Taylor and Lafayette Counties, most Floridians were eager to join with South Carolina in seceding from the Union. Within a few weeks after Lincoln's election, the state legislature was convened for the purpose of calling a convention specifically to secede and declare itself a sovereign nation. On 10 January 1861, the convention delegates voted sixty-two to seven to leave the Union. Four of the seven dissenting votes were cast by delegates from western Florida. A new state flag, containing three stars was unfurled over the state Capitol. The stars represented the three states, South Carolina, Mississippi, and Florida, that had voted so far to secede.

Four days before the above vote was taken, Florida troops had taken over the Appalachicola Arsenal. A few days after the vote, they took over Fort Barrances, Fort McRea, and the Pensacola Navy Yard. The federal troops stationed at Fort Pickens on the island of Santa Rosa which guarded the Pensacola harbor refused to surrender to the state troops and agreed instead to a truce. In return for a pledge that the Florida troops would not attack the base, the federals agreed that the fort would not be reinforced. After two months, federal ships arrived and stood offshore. Construing this action to be a reinforcement, Confederate General Braxton Bragg, on 9 October 1861, launched a nighttime raid on the fort. Heavy casualties were suffered by the New York unit known as Wilson'a Zuoaves, but there were equally heavy casualties in the defending force. With this action, fighting had come to Florida for the first time. Throughout the entire war, Fort Pickens remained under Union control as did Fort Taylor at Key West and Fort Jefferson in the Dry Tortugas.

Soon after it seceded, Florida organized two regiments financed by funds from private donations and filled by extensive use of volunteer soldiers. On 1 March 1861, the Confederate States army was offically organized, and it recruited five thousand men specifically for "duty at Pensacola." Of that number, five hundred came from Florida, with the remainder coming from Georgia, Alabama, Louisiana, and Mississippi. The First Florida Infantry, organized 5 April 1861 to serve a term of twelve months, headed immediately for Pensacola. After the mandatory term of twelve months, the soldiers headed home; only a minority of them reenlisted. At that point conscription by the Confederate government became a necessity.

As wartime conditions worsened, many Floridians who had been opposed to secession from the beginning and those who later jumped to the side of the obvious victor began to speak out in public and to organize themselves as loyalists. They hoped to turn around the political climate in the state and eventually to align it with the Union. One such group, organized in 1864 and known as the "Independent Union Rangers," was made up of so-called "Union men" mainly from Taylor and Lafayette Counties and of deserters from the Confederate army. When their primary goal was thwarted, these and similar groups disintegrated into guerrilla bands and outlaw gangs who terrorized the local citizenry with violence and bloodshed.

The strategy of the United States navy was to sail south along the Atlantic, take over the port cities, and blockade the Confederate coastline. It gained control over Port Royal, South Carolina, and then took over Fort Ferdinana, Georgia, and then Jacksonville and St. Augustine. Just prior to these last two engagements, Florida troops burned and destroyed as much equipment and stores as they could before withdrawing inland in the face of overwhelming superiority. Joining the fleeing soldiers were thousands of civilians who trailed along as refugees. Those who remained behind in the cities presented themselves to the conquerors as Union sympathizers and pledged their loyalty and cooperation. A month after the official surrender of Jacksonville on 11 May 1862, the Union troops abandoned the city only to retake it at will at least three times before the war ended. Pensacola, like Jacksonville, had been abandoned by the Florida troops in March 1862, after much burning and destroying of military stores and equipment to prevent them from falling into enemy hands.

In February 1862, the Confederate army had determined that instead of having soldiers from neighboring states coming in to defend Pensacola and other places in Florida, troops stationed in Florida should be sent to Tennessee where the Union army was massing large numbers of men and arms and appling heavy pressure. All the troops in Florida, except a few who were instructed to remain and hold out as long as possible, were ordered to vacate the state and become part of the Army of the Tennessee. Of the 6,500 troops stationed at Pensacola, 5,000 moved out; of the 4,000 troops in the eastern and central parts of the state, 3,000 moved out.[5] This left the coastal areas defenseless. Florida began to believe that the Confederacy had abandoned it to the enemy; indeed it had.

Since inland Florida was able to continue to grow crops and raise cattle and hogs, and despite a rail transportation system severly damaged by Union forays, large amounts of foodstuffs were shipped to Confederate units outside the state. Union forces made many raids into the state to try to curtail its agricultural output and to recruit or capture slaves for the Union army. Major raids were directed toward Palatka, Tampa, Gainesville, and St. Mark's. Some of this fighting consisted of shelling from gunboats which sailed up and down the rivers and creeks. At Olustee, near Lake City, in February 1864, Confederate units--5,200 strong--under the command of Gen. Joseph Finegan threw up a series of embankments and dug in to repel any further Union attacks. The clash resulted in the Union troops being pushed back to Jacksonville after suffering more than eighteen hundred casualties. The Confederates suffered only 934 casualties.

The last battle in Florida was the successful defense of Tallahassee in February 1865. The Union forces, made up largely of Negro troops, Confederate deserters, and some regular Union soldiers, were turned back in their attempt to gain control of the state capital. The Southern cause was hopeless by then, however, and Confederate Generals Lee and Johnston were in predicaments which would inevitably result in a surrender in the near future. When they did surrender, the Florida soldiers, unpaid and destitute, and wherever they were at the time, began to walk home. Six thousand of them congregated at Tallahassee. Two thousand others gathered at Tampa, Lake City, and other Florida cities to give themselves up and to become the subjects of the martial law imposed by the North.

During the course of the war, Florida had enlisted or drafted an estimated fifteen thousand men. This unofficial number may be high because many men served multiple terms. Whatever the number, approximately five thousand of them were killed in battle before it was all over.[6]

Military Units

The National Archives has the compiled service records for the personnel who served in units from Florida, as listed below. They may be found in Microcopy 251, consisting of 104 rolls. See chapter four for a complete description of this series.

First Cavalry
First Battalion, Special Cavalry
Second Cavalry
Third Battalion, Cavalry
Fifth Battalion, Cavalry
Captain Fernandez's Mounted Company
Captain Pickett's Cavalry Company
Captain Smith's Cavalry Company
Captain Abell's Light Artillery Company
Captain Dunham's Milton Light Artillery Company
Captain Dyke's Light Artillery Company
Kilcrease Light Artillery
Captain Perry's Light Artillery Company
First Infantry
First (Reserves) Infantry
Second Infantry
Second Battalion, Infantry
Third through Eleventh Infantry
Conscripts
Campbellton Boys
Captain Harrison's Company
Captain McBride's Company
Captain Parson's Company
Miscellaneous, Florida

GEORGIA
DEPARTMENT OF ARCHIVES AND HISTORY
330 Capitol Avenue, S.E., Atlanta 30334
(On I-20, near the stadium)

HOURS: 8:00 a.m.--4:00 p.m., Monday--Friday
        9:30 a.m.--3:30 p.m., Saturday
closed: state holidays, including Confederate Memorial Day and Jefferson
    Davis' Birthday, (3 June).

If you write to this archives seeking assistance in finding a record of a specific veteran, you will be notified on a standard form describing what material, if any, relative to that veteran has been located and the cost for a copy of it. When your payment is received, the material will be sent to you within three weeks.

If you make a personal visit, you may park at the rear of the building where there is a nominal charge. As you register in the front lobby, you will be informed that all the Confederate records have been microfilmed and may be found in the microfilm room adjacent to the library reading room on the first floor.

Before attempting to find a particular record, it will pay you to familiarize yourself with the indexes to the Confederate material. These are in a wooden card catalog in the microfilm room, specifically in the two upper left-hand drawers. The top drawer is labeled "Georgia Official Records." The second drawer is labeled "U.S. Records." This latter index pinpoints the exact drawer of the gray, steel cabinets which contain the film purchased from the National Archives.

National Archives Microfilm

In many of the series listed below, the names of the Georgia personnel have been extracted from the National Archives material. In those instances, only the Georgia troops will be found. It may be difficult to identify some of these films according to the correct National Archives titles. The Georgia archives has blocked out the titles on the roll boxes with white tape on which is written the drawer and roll number--nothing else. Likewise, the index cards are a bit confusing since the National Archives titles have been modified to some degree. To lessen any such confusion, the drawer and roll numbers are listed here opposite the National Archives titles. See chapter four for a complete description of this series.

Index to Compiled Service Records of Confederate Soldiers Who Served in Organizations Raised Directly by the Confederate Government and of Confederate General and Staff Officers and Nonregimental Enlisted Men. M818 (26 rolls). Located in drawer 258, rolls 58-108.

Compiled Service Records of Confederate Soldiers Who Served in Organizations Raised Directly by the Confederate Government. M258 (123 rolls). Located in drawer 258, rolls 1-47.

Compiled Service Records of Confederate General and Staff Officers and Nonregimental Enlisted Men. M331 (275 rolls). Located in drawer 279, rolls 1-33.

In addition to the series listed above, this archives also has other microfilm presumably purchased from the National Archives but not identified as such. The titles of those series as designated by the Georgia archives are the following:

Muster Rolls of the Georgia Confederate Units. Located in drawer 279, rolls 62-93.

Reference File Relating to Confederate Organizations from Georgia. Located in drawer 279, roll 104.

Reference File Relating to Confederate Medical Officers. Located in drawer 279, rolls 105-107.

Adjutant and Inspector General's Office (CSA), General Orders, 1861-1865. Located in drawer 279, roll 108.

Adjutant and Inspector General's Office--Special Orders, 1861- 1865. Located in drawer 279, rolls 109-110.

Pensions

In 1870, Georgia enacted legislation to provide artificial limbs for Confederate veterans disabled in action. Later, a needy veteran could qualify for a pension regardless of disability. Veterans' widows became eligible for pensions in 1891. Much later, after most of the Confederate veterans had already died or were quite old, amendments provided for pensions regardless of financial need.

A pension file recounts the applicant's military history, gives the state and county of residence, and provides information related to the applicant's economic status, especially the value of any property owned and the amount of current earnings. Related documents from physicians and community witnesses are often included. A widow's application includes the date or her marriage and a statement that she had not remarried. A marriage certificate may be found in these files.

Each pension file is indexed on a card which shows whether the applicant was a soldier, a widow, or was a witness to someone else's application. Also shown on the card are the county of residence, military unit, and name of a widow's spouse. These card have been alphabetized and microfilmed and may be found in drawer 261, rolls thirteen to fifteen. In addition to the purely alphabetical listing, the cards have also been arranged by county, and alphabetically thereunder. The pension files themselves have also been microfilmed and may be found in drawers 271-76, plus a few supplemental files in drawer 277.

Military Service Records

Mrs. Lillian Henderson, who headed the Georgia Division of Pensions and Records for many years, compiled a general index of that state's Confederate soldiers. In gathering the data, she used documents turned over to the federal government after the war--Georgia pension files, and many other sources, both official and non-official. Errors in her index are possible because she used of hearsay sources such as correspondence from relatives, newspaper clippings, and similar material. All her findings were put together in a six volume work, *Roster of the Confederate Soldiers of Georgia, 1861-1865*. This index was turned over to the state archives in 1960 and microfilmed, and is located in drawer 253.

On roll seventy-one of Mrs. Henderson's microfilmed cards is a grouping of a few miscellaneous categories. Examples are: "Men in units from Alabama, Arkansas, and Virginia regiments," and "Naval and Marine personnel." On rolls seventy-two and seventy-three are: "County volunteers and militia," "Widows (deceased)--date of death and county," and "Soldiers (deceased)." Unfortunately, this last category contains only those names beginning with the letters A through C; the rest are missing.

Supplementing Mrs. Henderson's work, there are other records of Georgia veterans on microfilm. Indexes to that material are in the drawer of the wooden cabinet cited earlier under the label "Georgia Official Records." Some of the more helpful of those records are described below:

Roster of Commissioned Officers in the Georgia Militia Under the Reorganization Act of 1864. These names are arranged by military district and thereunder by county. They are located in drawer 40, roll 18.

Militia Enrollment Lists, 1864. These entries are difficult to read but contain much information such as county, age in years and months, occupation, place of birth, cause of exemption (where applicable), whether the soldier possessed a gun and its condition, and, if in the cavalry, whether he owned a horse, saddle, or bridle. There is a typed index of the names in these records. They are located in drawer 245, rolls 4-10.

Miscellaneous State Records

Other lists which may mention your Confederate ancestor are the following:

1. *Adjutant and Inspector-General Letters Sent January 5, 1864-April 4, 1864.* These hard-to-read letters are indexed by name. They are located in drawer 277, roll 48.

2. *Register of Equipment Issued and Amount of Bond Posted by Company Officers Going into Confederate Service.* This is located in drawer 40, roll 18.

Other material such as personal narratives and diaries, may be found in drawer 56, roll 63; drawer 70, roll 6; drawer 71, roll 28, and drawer 180, roll 80. Also, archives staff members who specialize in Civil War records may be able to guide you to other miscellaneous lists and sources not yet microfilmed. It may pay you to seek out such persons and ask for advice.

GEORGIA'S ROLE IN THE WAR

Before the war, Georgia had risen to a pinnacle of prosperity among the southern states. It was a major center for industry of many kinds, operated several textile mills, grew cotton, corn, and other crops in tremendous quantities, and was second only to Virginia in the miles of railroad running between its borders. Because of those assets, Georgia became a valuable part of the Confederacy. At the same time, it became a prime target for Union raids bent on destroying the Souths ability to create a war machine. Georgia's governor, Joseph Brown, was an outspoken, charismatic person who led his legislature and the public in a forceful way. As soon as it became evident that Abraham Lincoln would be elected to the presidency, Brown came out strongly in favor of early secession from the Union. His legislature quickly appropriated one million dollars for him to build a military organization within the state to protect itself should the North prove to be a threat. At the same time, the legislature issued a call for a state convention to determine whether Georgia should secede after Lincoln's election. That convention met at the capital, Milledgeville, on 16 January 1861. Three days later, an overwhelming vote of 208 against eighty-nine took Georgia out of the Union. The eighty-nine "cooperationists" who voted to remain in the Union mainly represented the thinking of those citizens in the mountainous northeast portion of the state; a few represented those in the flat lands in the heart of King Cotton country.

On 23 January, between the time of Lincoln's election and his inauguration, Governor Brown seized the federal arsenal at Augusta. Early in March, Georgia formed its first military company and assigned it to the Confederacy along with large amounts of military supplies and equipment. It also turned over the forts and ships along its shores and within its borders. In April, the governor issued a call for recruits, and volunteers flocked in. Already organized local companies became part of the state military organization. These included some companies with heavy foreign membership such as the "German Volunteers" and the "Irish Jasper Guards" from Atlanta and Savannah. Three training camps, Camp McDonald, Camp Stephens, and Camp Davis, were set up. By early May, there were eighteen thousand Georgians in six regiments and two battalions. The civilian population went all out to forge the war materials needed by the South. Mills worked around the clock to manufacture both heavy and light artillery, guns, the well-known butternut uniforms, and blankets. War fever was at a high pitch, and the patriotic public supported the Governor in his inspiring efforts on behalf of the Southern cause. He was reelected and remained in office without serious opposition throughout the war years.

During the four years of war, Georgia's civilian population and its military forces suffered from several Union raids long before the most devastating raid of all--the march by Gen. William T. Sherman across the state to Savannah. The first of the early raids, which destroyed thirteen railroad bridges and committed much other destruction, was led by Capt. James J. Andrews with his Ohio regiments. Then, in April 1863, Col. Abel D. Streight and his troops marched in from Alabama and went as far as Rome, Georgia, where he was forced into a retreat. In April 1865, Gen. James H. Wilson also led a march from Alabama and went to Macon.

The major battle in Georgia was at Chickamauga Station, an outgrowth of the battles at Chattanooga, just over the Georgia-Tennessee line. The Army of the Tennessee fought at Chickamauga on 19 September 1863, along the banks of the Chicakamauga Creek on a six mile front. After two days of bloody fighting, the Confederate casualties totaled more than eighteen thousand, with Union casualties almost as great. The next day when it was over, the Confederates were in control of the area but were too exhausted and decimated to follow up on their victory. After this battle, there was little other heavy fighting in the state except in defense against the Union raids until Sherman marched in toward the close of the war.

With the tide against the South, rivalries and jealousies broke out between Governor Brown and Jefferson Davis and his army leaders. There were disputes over the requirement that enlistments be for three years or until the end of the war rather than for twelve months as required by the state. Georgia was also hostile about having its own units taken over by the Confederacy and broken up or reassigned to other units. Georgia also disagreed over regulations for conscription and exemptions. Some Georgia citizens, especially those in the northeast, bitter over exemptions of certain occupational classes, often fell in with the Union. In many cases they hid in the mountains or in the Okefenokee Swamp to escape military duty and were often joined there by deserters from both Confederate and Union armies. They foraged through the countryside striking terror in the farmers who dared to oppose them. Others organized themselves into political groups intent on returning the state to the Union. One such organization was the Peace Society which was active in western Georgia.

After General Grant defeated the Confederate army at Chattanooga, he left that area to meet Robert E. Lee head-on in Virginia. In leaving, he placed General Sherman, with ninety thousand men, in charge of an army poised to cross the South, to conquer any opposition, and to lay waste to the country as he went. Sherman entered Georgia on 4 May 1864 and proceeded on to take Atlanta. Defending against this march was Confederate General Joseph E. Johnston with 432,000 men. These two engaged each other at various points, but always Johnston chose to withdraw, hoping that Sherman would eventually over-extend his supply lines. Impatiently, Jefferson Davis replaced Johnston with Gen. John B. Hood who attacked Sherman but succeeded only in losing many of his men. In the two and one-half months of fighting, the Confederacy had ten thousand men killed, wounded, or captured. The Union had seventeen thousand killed, wounded, or captured.[7]

Governor Brown, realizing the desperate situation near Atlanta, sent his militia to help reinforce Hood and rebuked Jefferson Davis for not sending more of his own troops. At that point, Brown called up every man in Georgia able to bear arms, between the ages of sixteen to fifty-five, including those who had been previously exempted.

One supplemental objective of the Union's drive to Atlanta was to liberate the prisoners of war confined at Andersonville prison in Georgia. General George Stoneman moved around Atlanta for this purpose but eventually had to surrender his troops to the Confederate forces. The prisoners were transferred to Savannah and Charleston and later to Millen, Georgia. The twelve thousand who had died there in recent months were buried at the prison site.

Meanwhile, Sherman, supported by his patrols of "bummers," foraged for provisions and raided plantations and homes along the way, freeing slaves as they went. They burned and pillaged almost at will, often without any clear orders from higher echelons. The legislature at Milledgeville fled after destroying the military facilities there. Sherman took the city on 23 November. He then continued east through Sandersville, Tennile, Louisville, and Millen. The only resistance came from Gen. Joseph Wheeler whose men sometimes also plundered homes as they traveled across country. Sherman reached Savannah on 10 December, and Confederate General William J. Hardee evacuated the city nine days later, leaving it open for occupation shortly after by Sherman, who then gave his troops a month's rest.

By March 1865, the entire Georgia coast was under Union control. A few days after Lee surrendered in Virginia the next month, the Confederate troops at Macon surrendered to General Wilson. Wilson then ordered Governor Brown to surrender in favor of a military governor. Confederate soldiers were allowed to return home if they signed a pledge not to bear arms against the federal government.

The symbolic act capping the defeat of the Confederacy occurred on Georgia soil; Jefferson Davis was captured on 10 May 1865 at Irwinville, Georgia.

Military Units

The National Archives has the compiled service records for the personnel who served in units from Georgia as listed below. They may be found in Microcopy 266, consisting of 607 rolls. See chapter four for a complete description of this series.

First Cavalry
First Battalion, Cavalry
First Battalion, Reserve Cavalry
First Gordon Squadron, Cavalry (State Guards)
Second Georgia Cavalry
Second Georgia Cavalry (State Guards)
Second Battalion, Cavalry
Third Cavalry
Third Cavalry (State Guards)
Fourth (Clinch's) Cavalry
Fourth Cavalry (State Guards)
Fifth Cavalry
Sixth Cavalry
Sixth Battalion, Cavalry (State Guards)
Seventh Cavalry
Seventh Battalion, Cavalry (State Guards)
Eighth Cavalry
Eighth Battalion, Cavalry (State Guards)
Ninth Battalion, Cavalry (State Guards)
Tenth Cavalry
Tenth Cavalry (State Guards)
Tenth Battalion, Cavalry (State Guards)
Eleventh Cavalry
Twelfth Cavalry

Twelfth (Robinson's) Cavalry (State Guards)
Twelfth Battalion, Cavalry (State Guards)
Twelfth (Wright's) Cavalry (State Guards)
Thirteenth Cavalry
Fifteenth Battalion, Cavalry (State Guards)
Sixteenth Battalion, Cavalry (State Guards)
Nineteenth Battalion, Cavalry
Twentieth Battalion, Cavalry
Twenty-first Battalion, Cavalry
Twenty-second Battalion, Cavalry
Twenty-fourth Battalion, Cavalry
Twenty-ninth Cavalry
Sixty-second Cavalry
Captain Alexander's Company, Cavalry
Captain Allen's Company, Cavalry
Captain Arnold's Company, Cavalry
Captain Asher's Company, (Murray Cavalry)
Captain Boddie's Company, (Troup [County] Independent Cavalry)
Captain Bond's Company, Cavalry (State Guards)
Camden County Militia (Mounted)
Captain Corbin's Company, Cavalry
Dorough's Battalion, Cavalry
Captain Floyd's Company, Cavalry
Captain Gartrell's Company, Cavalry
Captain Hall's Company, Cavalry
Hardwick Mounted Rifles
Captain Hendry's Company, Cavalry (Atlantic and Gulf Guards)
Captain Humphrey's Company, Independent Cavalry (Reserves)
Captain Logan's Company, Cavalry (White County Old Men's Home
     Guards)
Captain Mayer's Company, (Appling Cavalry)
Captain Nelson's Independent Company, Cavalry
Captain Newbern's Company, Cavalry (Coffee Revengers)
Captain Pemberton's Company, Cavalry
Ragland's Company, Cavalry
Roswell Battalion, Cavalry
Captain Rumph's Company, (Wayne Cavalry Guards)

Captain Russell's Company, Cavalry

Lieutenant Waring's Company, Cavalry

Captain Young's Company, Cavalry (Alleghany Troopers)

Ninth Battalion, Artillery

Eleventh Battalion, Artillery (Sumter Artillery)

Twelfth Battalion, Light Artillery

Fourteenth (Montgomery's) Battalion, Light Artillery

Twenty-second Battalion, Heavy Artillery

Twenty-eighth Battalion, Siege Artillery

Captain Anderson's Battalion, Light Artillery

Captain Baker's Company, Artillery

Captain Barwell's Battery, Light Artillery

Captain Brooks' Company, (Terrell Light Artillery)

Captain Campbell's Independence Company, Siege Artillery

Captain Carlton's Company (Troup County Artillery)

Captain Clinch's Battery, Light Artillery

Captain Croft's Battery, Light Artillery (Columbus Artillery)

Captain Daniell's Battery, Light Artillery

Captain Ferrell's Battery, Light Artillery

Captain Fraser's Battery, Light Artillery

Captain Guerard's Battery, Light Artillery

Captain Hamilton's Company, Light Artillery

Captain Hanleiter's Company, Light Artillery (Jo Thompson Artillery)

Captain Havis' Battery, Light Artillery

Captain Howell's Company, Light Artillery

Captain Hudson's Company, Light Artillery (Arsenal Battery)

Captain King's Battery, Light Artillery

Captain Lumpkin's Company, Artillery

Captain Massenburg's Battery, Light Artillery (Jackson Artillery)

Captain Maxwell's Battalion, Regular Light Artillery

Captain Maxwell's Regular Light Battery, Artillery

Captain Milledge's Company, Light Artillery

Captain Moore's Battery, Artillery

Captain Pritchard's Company, Light Artillery (Washington Artillery)

Pruden's Battery, Artillery (State Troops)

Captain Ritter's Company, Light Artillery

Captain Scogin's Battery, Light Artillery (Griffin Light Artillery)

Siege Train (Major Buist) Artillery
Captain Slaten's Company, Artillery (Macon Light Artillery)
Captain Tiller's Company, (Echols Light Artillery)
Captain Van Den Corput's Company, Light Artillery
Captain Wheaton's Company, Artillery (Chatham Artillery)
First Infantry
First Regulars
First Light Duty Men
First (Consolidated) Infantry
First Local Troops, Infantry
First Infantry (State Guards)
First (Fannin's) Reserves
First (Olmstead's) Infantry
First (Ramsey's) Infantry
First (Symons') Reserves
First Confederate Battalion, Infantry
First Militia
First Battalion, Sharp Shooters
First Battalion, Infantry (State Guards)
First City Battalion, Infantry (Columbus)
First Troops and Defenses (Macon)
First State Line
Second Infantry
Second Militia
Second Reserves
Second Battalion, Infantry
Second Battalion, Sharp Shooters
Second Battalion, Infantry (State Guards)
Second Battalion Troops and Defenses (Macon)
Second State Line, Including Stapleton's and Storey's
Third Infantry
Third Reserves
Third Battalion, Infantry
Third Battalion, Sharp Shooters
Third Battalion (State Guards)
Fourth Infantry
Fourth Reserves

Fourth Battalion, Infantry (State Guards)
Fourth Battalion, Sharp Shooters
Fifth Infantry
Fifth Reserves
Fifth Infantry (State Guards)
Fifth Battalion, Infantry (State Guards)
Sixth Infantry
Sixth Infantry (State Guards)
Sixth Militia
Sixth Reserves
Sixth State Line
Seventh Infantry
Seventh Infantry (State Guards)
Eighth Infantry
Eighth Infantry (State Guards)
Eighth Battalion, Infantry
Ninth Infantry
Ninth Infantry (State Guards)
Ninth Battalion, Infantry
Tenth Infantry
Tenth Militia
Tenth Battalion, Infantry
Eleventh Infantry
Eleventh (State Troops)
Eleventh Battalion, Infantry (State Guards)
Twelfth Infantry
Twelfth Militia
Thirteenth Infantry
Thirteenth Battalion, Infantry (State Guards)
Fourteenth Infantry
Fourteenth Battalion, Infantry (State Guards)
Fifteenth Infantry
Sixteenth Infantry
Seventeenth Infantry
Seventeenth Battalion, Infantry (State Guards)
Eighteenth Infantry
Eighteenth Battalion, Infantry

Eighteenth Battalion, Infantry (State Guards)
Nineteenth Infantry
Nineteenth Battalion, Infantry (State Guards)
Twentieth through Twenty-third Infantry
Twenty-third Battalion, Infantry, Local Defense (Athens Battalion, Enfield Rifle Battalion)
Twenty-fourth Infantry
Twenty-fifth Infantry
Twenty-fifth Battalion, Infantry (Provost Guard)
Twenty-sixth Infantry
Twenty-sixth Battalion, Infantry
Twenty-seventh Infantry
Twenty-seventh Battalion, Infantry
Twenty-seventh Battalion, Infantry (Non-Conscripts)
Twenty-eighth through Thirty-second Infantry
Thirty-fourth Infantry
Thirty-fifth Infantry
Thirty-sixth (Broyles') Infantry
Thirty-sixth (Villepique's) Infantry
Thirty-seventh through Fortieth Infantry
Fortieth Battalion, Infantry
Forty-first through Fifty-seventh Infantry
Fifty-ninth through Sixty-first Infantry
Sixty-third through Sixty-sixth Infantry
Arsenal Battalion, Infantry (Columbus)
Augusta Battalion, Infantry
City Battalion, Infantry (Columbus)
Coast Guard Battalion, Militia
Cook's Battalion, Infantry (Reserves)
Rowland's Battalion, Conscripts
Youngblood's Battalion, Infantry
Cobb's Guards, Infantry
Cherokee Legion (State Guards)
Cobb's Legion
Floyd Legion (State Guards)
Phillip's Legion
Smith's Legion

Captain Alexander's Company, Infantry
Captain Anderson's Company, Infantry (Anderson Guards)
Athens Reserved Corps, Infantry
Captain Atwater's Company, Infantry
Captain Bard's Company, Infantry
Captain Barney's Company, Infantry (Richmond Factory Guards)
Captain Brook's Company, Infantry (Mitchell Home Guards)
Captain Caraker's Company, Infantry (Milledgeville Guards)
Captain Chapman's Company, Infantry (Defenders)
Captain Clemons' Company, Infantry
Captain Collier's Company, Infantry
Captain Collier's Company, Infantry (Collier Guards)
Conscripts, Georgia
Captain Dozier's Company, Infantry
Captain Ezzard's Company, Infantry
Captain Fuller's Company, Infantry
Captain Garrison's Company, Infantry (Ogeechee Minute Men)
Captain Green's Company, Infantry (State Armory Guards)
Captain Grubb's Company, Infantry
Captain Hamlet's Company, Infantry
Captain Hansell's Company, Infantry (State Guards)
Captain Harris' Independent Company, Infantry (Brunswick Rifles)
Captain Hendry's Company, Mounted Infantry (Pierce Mounted Volunteers)
Captain Holmes' Company, Infantry (Wright Local Guards)
Captain Howard's Company, Infantry (Non-Conscripts)
Captain Hull's Company, Infantry
Captain Jackson's Company, Infantry
Captain Jones' Company, Infantry (Jones Hussars)
Captain Kay's Company, Infantry (Franklin County) Guards
Captain Lane's Company, Infantry (Jasper and Butts County Guards)
Captain Matthew's Company, Infantry (East to West Point Guards)
Captain Medlin's Independent Company, Infantry (High Shoals Defenders)
Captain Milner's Company, Infantry (Madison County Home Guard)
Captain Moore's Company, Infantry (Baldwin Infantry)
Captain Moring's Company, Infantry (Emanuel Troops)
Captain Pool's Company, Infantry
Captain Porter's Company, (Georgia Railroad Guards)

Captain Preston's Company (Railroad Guards)
Ridgon Guards
Captain Roberts' Company, Exempts
Captain Russell's Company (Newton Factory Employees)
Captain Taylor's Company
Captain Thornton's Company (Muscogee Guards)
Lieutenant Weem's Detachment, Camp Guard (Augusta)
Captain White's Company
Captain Witt's Company (Express Infantry)
Captain Wyly's Company (Mell Scouts)
Whiteside's Naval Battalion, Infantry (Local Defense)
Miscellaneous, Georgia

LOUISIANA
STATE ARCHIVES AND RECORDS SERVICE
Essen Lane, near the intersection of I-10 and I-12
P.O. Box 94125, Baton Rouge 70814

HOURS: 8:00 a.m.-4:30 p.m., Monday-Friday
closed: state holidays

A large, modern building at the above location is being constructed as
the new state archives. Previously a wholly inadequate building located in an
industrial part of town at 1515 Choctaw Drive served as the archives. The
planned extensive use of computers in the new building promises to make
finding aids and indexes easily accessible to patrons and with less assistance
required from staff members. Frequent users of Louisiana records should
consider placing their names on the mailing list of the archives' quarterly
newsletter, *Legacy.* All accessions are listed in this helpful publication.

National Archives Microfilm

This archives has chosen not to purchase the index to the compiled
records of Confederate soldiers in Louisiana organizations. They prefer using
the state's publication, *Records of Louisiana Confederate Soldiers and Commands,* compiled by Andrew B. Booth. It does have the National Archives
microfilm of Louisiana soldiers but not the index. It has the following three

microfilm series purchased from the National Archives. See chapter four for a complete description of these series.

Compiled Service Records of Confederate Soldiers Who Served in Organizations From the State of Louisiana. M320 (414 rolls).

Compiled Service Records of Confederate Soldiers Who Served in Organizations Raised Directly by the Confederate Government. M258. Only those rolls of this series which pertain to Louisiana military personnel are available here. An index of the names in these rolls has been typed and may be found in a notebook which is available to you.

Compiled Service Records of Confederate General and Staff Officers and Non-regimental Enlisted Men. M331 (274 rolls).

The State Library is located in another part of Baton Rouge, at 760 Riverside North. It also has some Confederate records on microfilm purchased from the National Archives. This includes the index to the compiled service records not available at the archives. The holdings of the library are listed below.

Index to Compiled Service Records of Confederate Soldiers Who Served in Organizations From the State of Louisiana. M378 (31 rolls).

Compiled Service Records of Confederate Soldiers Who Served in Organizations From the State of Louisiana. M320 (414 rolls).

United States War Department. *Official Records of the Union and Confederate Navies, 1861-1865.* M260 (31 rolls). This is a microfilm copy of the publication by the same name. There are 31 volumes.

Pensions

In accordance with the 1898 constitution, Louisiana enacted legislation creating a five member Board of Pension Commissioners with authority to approve or disapprove applications for pensions filed by Confederate veterans or their widows. The board's discretion was limited to making awards not to exceed eight dollars per month provided the applicant was indigent. To show indigence, the applicant had to prove that he was unable to earn a livelihood by his own labor or skill, was not employed by the state or any other government, and have no other means of financial support. His military service had to be continuous until he was either discharged or paroled, and service in the militia or home guard did not qualify. A widow was eligible only if she qualified as being indigent, had been married some time prior to 1 June 1865, her husband had lost his life from a service-connected wound or disease, and provided further that she had not remarried.

Residence requirements stipulated that the veteran or his widow must have either resided in Louisiana at the time of enlistment in any regular Confederate unit or had served in a Louisiana military unit if he had not been a Louisiana resident at that time. Exceptions were allowed for those with no Louisiana connection at the time of the war if they had been Louisiana residents for fifteen years prior to filing the application. Otherwise, only a five year residency was required. To prevent unscrupulous attorneys from profiteering at the expense of indigent veterans or their widows, the legislation imposed a five dollar ceiling on any fee charged by an attorney who prepared and handled an application.

An amendment in 1900 permitted a widow to be eligible if she married the veteran before 1 January 1870, whether or not he had died during the war period. A 1904 amendment advanced the latest possible date of her marriage to 1 January 1875. A further amendment in 1920 spelled out the specific procedures involved in furnishing artificial limbs. If the veteran preferred, he could have the cost of the limb instead. Every four years thereafter, a replacement limb or the money equivalent was also furnished.

A new constitution adopted in 1921 provided that the monthly pension could be as high as thirty dollars per month and set the annual income ceiling at $1,000. State residency was reduced to five years for all applicants. A widow of a veteran might qualify if she had married him before 31 December 1900 and had not remarried. The amount of the award to either a veteran or widow was scaled according to the individual's need. The basic pension was set at $20 per month, but if the person's total assets were less than $2,000, he or she could receive $30 per month. In addition to pensions, the constitution provided for the maintenance of the state soldier's home, Camp Nicholls.

The pension applications contain much genealogical data, including military service, wounds, place and date of surrender, commanding officers, and statements from comrades-in-arms. A widow's application added data concerning her marriage, with the name of the minister, the date of her husband's death, his place of burial, and her means of support.

The pension files are fragile and not open for public inspection, but they have been microfilmed. They are indexed by name of the applicant and include those where the application was disapproved. A widow's application is indexed according to the name of her husband. You are permitted to make notes in unlimited quantity from these microfilm, but if you wish to have a file copied, the standard fee is $10 regardless of the number of pages in the file.

Supplemental pension material may be found in reports published by the Board of Pension Commissioners. This includes names of pensioners on the rolls at the time of issue. The reports for 1906, 1916, and 1922 are available. The names listed therein are arranged first by parish and then alphabetically by name.

A special 1911 census questionnaire was sent to all pensioners. The form asked for information concerning age, military unit, state from which enlisted, property owned, means of livelihood, physical infirmities, and the date of a widow's marriage. There is no index to this census, but the papers are arranged by parish.

Military Service Records

The state Office of the Adjutant General created a card index of all known Louisiana soldiers who fought for the Confederacy. On behalf of the state, Andrew B. Booth, using the data found on those cards, compiled a four-volume work entitled *Records of Louisiana Confederate Soldiers*. Some additional names came to light after this index was published. Although the index inevitably contains some errors, as does any large work of this kind, it remains the most convenient quick source of names of the state's Confederate soldiers.

The State Library, referred to above, has the following microfilmed series which contain lists of Louisianians who served in the state's military units:

Louisiana Commissioner of Military Records. *Records of Louisiana Confederate Soldiers and Louisiana Confederate Commands.* (2 rolls).

United Confederate Veterans, Louisiana Division. *Collective Records of General LeRoy Stafford, Camp Number 3, United Confederate Veterans in Shreve Memorial Library, Shreveport, Louisiana.* (2 rolls).

Miscellaneous State Records

This archives has other material which may aid you in your search. Staff will bring any of it to you. The card catalog shows the following which may interest you:

Records of the Adjutant General, 1850-1865. These consist of thirty-seven reports pertaining to the Louisiana militia and the state guards.

Letters to the Executive Office, 1860-1865. Much of this correspondence refers to state military units and their soldiers.

Civil War Pension Applications from Florida, Who had been Louisiana Soldiers. This is a computer printout prepared and furnished as a service by the Florida State Archives.

The "Rebel Archives." This is a collection of official papers from the Office of the Adjutant General. They cover the years 1855 through 1863. They contain records of some of the state regiments such as the "Louisiana Volunteers" and some militia units. This collection is on twelve rolls of microfilm.

Confederate Burials

Mr. Raymond W. Watkins, a resident of Virginia, has been collecting data for several years pertaining to burial places of all Confederate soldiers. As a service, he furnishes his findings to many of the Southern archives. The material which has been received by the Louisiana archives may be found in a black, loose-leaf notebook. His lists are inserted there as they arrive. Included are names of soldiers from Louisiana and also from any other states. Although there is no index to this material, each list of names is in alphabetical order.

LOUISIANA'S ROLE IN THE WAR

Before the war, Louisiana was prosperous, fast-growing, and rich in agriculture. It was populated by farmers and plantation owners previously living in Georgia, Alabama, and Mississippi, as well as by those with backgrounds in France, Germany, and Ireland. Almost forty-seven percent of the population were slaves; this did not include a substantial group of free Negroes, some of whom also owned slaves. Thirty-one of the forty-eight parishes had more slaves than free persons. New Orleans was a shipping center and the only city of any size in the state. Shreveport, Baton Rouge, and Alexandria were still classified as small towns, despite the fact that Baton Rouge was the capital. Any election of a president who represented a threat to the sanctity of their most valuable property--slaves--struck fear and anger in their hearts.

After the presidential election, Louisiana's governor called a special session of the legislature for 10 December 1861. In his message to the group, he concluded with the words, "I do not think that it comports with the honor and self-respect of Louisiana, as a slave-owning state, to live under the Government of a Black Republican President."[8]

The legislature agreed to call a convention on 23 January 1861 to decide the question of secession. Delegates were to be elected 7 January. At the same time, it created a military board with the governor as its chairman to purchase arms and ammunition for volunteers who would form up into companies from each parish. As in the sister states, there was a vocal minority who pleaded for patience and hoped to keep the state in the Union. When the delegates had been chosen, there were forty-four "cooperationists," eighty "secessionists," with six classified as "doubtful." On 26 January, after voting down several resolutions in favor of moderation, the majority voted to secede. The final vote on the question was 113 to seventeen. At that point Louisiana became a free, sovereign state--until it became one of the Confederate States of America.

Even before secession, the federal arsenals at Baton Rouge, Fort Jackson, and Fort St. Philip on the Mississippi south of New Orleans, were seized by Louisiana troops. The governor hastened to send huge amounts of supplies and guns to Mississippi, that state unable to defend itself against a possible Union invasion. The governor also issued a call to all able-bodied males aged eighteen to fifty-five to become part of the newly organized state militia. Those over age forty were to serve only in their own parishes.

The new Confederate army called upon Louisiana to send 1,700 men and shortly thereafter called for 3,000 more. After Fort Sumter was fired upon, Louisiana issued a call for 5,000. Those men were concentrated largely at New Orleans to await action wherever the need arose.

It was expected that New Orleans would soon be attacked because of its strategic position on the Mississippi. Located on opposite banks of the river, Fort Jackson and Fort St. Philip were fortified, and a chain was strung across the river to prevent any unfriendly boats from passing. In April 1862, twenty-four ships, eighteen of them under the command of Adm. David C. Farragut, appeared at the mouth of the river; the attack came soon after. On 24 April, thirteen of the craft sailed right past the two forts and steamed toward New Orleans. Within a few days the forts had surrendered to the Union land forces, and Farragut took New Orleans without a shot being fired. With the forts gone, it would have been folly for New Orleans to try to fight back, especially since most of its troops had been sent to other locations in the South. The fall of the forts caused chagrin and fault-finding, but the damage had been done. New Orleans was ruled by hostile military forces and continued to be so ruled until the close of the war. General Benjamin F. Butler was placed in charge of the city, and he proceeded to "teach the rebels a lesson." He ruled the city with harsh and unyielding military discipline and incurred the hatred and wrath of its citizens. He was replaced by the more liberal Gen. Nathaniel Banks in December.

Following the fall of New Orleans, the city of Baton Rouge was taken without opposition. Before Union General Thomas Williams marched his troops in, the citizens of the town burned its storehouses of cotton and emptied its liquor to prevent the Union soldiers from getting it. As the soldiers moved in, they plundered and pillaged at will, with or without orders from their superiors. A few months later, on 5 August, the Confederate troops struck back at Baton Rouge. Both sides claimed a victory after the battle. To concentrate its strength at New Orleans, the Union did evacuate the city two weeks later. As they left, they took the state library with them and established it at New Orleans. With the abandonment of Baton Rouge, the Confederates retained control of the Mississippi, at least between there and Vicksburg, Mississippi.

During all of 1862, there were many skirmishes and raids into the bayou areas of the state which caused the citizens in those areas to become destitute even before the harsh winter set in. In 1863, Louisiana toughened up its conscription laws in an attempt to defend the Red River and other smaller streams from inroads by the Union boats which sailed up and down in search of supplies and freed Negroes, many of whom then served in Union military units. The boats sailed at will on the Mississippi below Vicksburg and near the mouth of the Red River, but the Confederates generally managed to maintain control northward. Then the Union began to move again. They retook Baton Rouge and took Opelousa after a major battle in which many lives on both sides were lost. The citizens, leaving their slaves behind to turn their property over to the invaders, became refugees and fled toward Texas.

General Banks, who had retaken Baton Rouge, was intent on conquering Port Hudson on the Mississippi and asked General Grant at Vicksburg for reinforcements. Grant, however, was intent on taking Vicksburg and asked Banks to reinforce him instead. Neither gave in, and the result was that both were victorious with the troops they had. After a siege, Port Hudson surrendered on 9 July 1863, and Vicksburg fell five days earlier. With those events, the entire Mississippi came under complete control of the Union armies. This effectively divided the Confederacy into two parts, with neither part able to help the other, and also kept it from moving supplies from the breadbasket of Texas to the eastern states. The Union troops then followed up by taking the cities of Donaldsonville and Brashear City. They also fought many battles along the Teche River in lower Louisiana, laying that area to waste as well.

Since the state government was allowed to function, even with parts of the state under federal control, a new governor was elected in January 1864. Henry W. Allen, a veteran of the battles of Shiloh and Baton Rouge, raised a state guard and revamped the militia. He turned the state troops over to the Confederate army. During his term the federal troops launched a three pronged campaign to take over Shreveport and thus open the path to the cotton lands in the West. The campaign failed when they were turned back at Mansfield, where 30,000 soldiers faced off against each other. As the federal troops retreated, they burned the buildings, destroyed everything in their path, and robbed any citizen who got in their way. As they forged ahead, the Confederate troops stationed in Alexandria evacuated as they approached. From that time on, both sides tended to withdraw from Louisiana to fight on other fronts in the South. The federal government created the Division of West Mississippi with Gen. E. R. S. Canby in charge. General Banks remained in New Orleans. The Confederates placed Gen. Simon B. Buckner in charge of the District of Western Louisiana, a part of the Department of the Trans-Mississippi.

After Lee surrendered in Virginia in April 1865, Gen. Kirby Smith, heading the Trans-Mississippi, with headquarters at Shreveport urged his troops to stand fast, to regroup, and to look to the day when they would hold out against the Union forces and eventually win the day for the South. Jefferson Davis, fleeing from the fallen capital at Richmond, hoped to reach Smith and his troops and fight on to save the Confederacy. When Smith was called upon to surrender, he refused. A conference of governors from Louisiana, Texas, Arkansas, and Missouri (the latter being a governor in exile) met together and urged Smith to capitulate since the cause appeared to be hopeless. The soldiers decided the issue for themselves by leaving by the hundreds each day. Smith left General Buckner at Shreveport and moved to Houston to rally his troops, but when he got there he had no troops to lead-- his army had dissolved. Buckner and two other Confederate generals met with General Canby at New Orleans and agreed to terms of surrender on 26 May 1865. The terms allowed the soldiers to go home on parole after taking a pledge to fight no more. It was not until 2 June that Smith approved the terms while aboard the USS *Fort Jackson* off Galveston Harbor. He was the last of the departmental commanders to surrender.

Louisiana's Governor Allen gave up his office and pleaded with the citizens to be patient and adapt to their new circumstances without rancor or hatred.

The National Archives has compiled service records for the personnel who served in Confederate units from Louisiana, as listed below. They may be found in Microcopy 320, consisting of 414 rolls. See chapter four for a complete description of this series.

First Cavalry
First Battalion, Cavalry (State Guards)
Second Cavalry
Second Battalion, Cavalry (State Guards)
Third Cavalry
Third (Harrison's) Cavalry
Third (Wingfield's) Cavalry
Fourth through Eighth Cavalry
Thirteenth Battalion (Partisan Rangers)
Eighteenth Battalion, Cavalry
Ogden's Cavalry
Cavalry Squadron (Independent Rangers of Iberville) Militia
Squadron Guides d'Orleans, Militia
Mounted Rangers of Palquemines, Militia
Captain Benjamin's Company, Cavalry
Captain Bond's Company, Mounted Partisan Rangers

Captain Borge's Company (Garnet Rangers), Militia
Captain Cagnolatti's Company, Cavalry (Chasseurs of Jefferson), Militia
Captain Cole's Company, Cavalry
Captain Delery's Company, (St. Bernard Horse Rifles), Militia
Captain Dreux's Cavalry, Company A
Dubecq's Company, Cavalry
Captain Greenleaf's Company (Orleans Light Horse), Cavalry
Captain Lott's Company (Carroll Dragoons), Cavalry
Captain Millaudon's Company (Jefferson Mounted Guards)
Captain Miller's Independent Company, Mounted Rifles
Captain Norwood's Company (Jeff Davis Rangers), Cavalry
Captain Nutt's Company (Red River Rangers), Cavalry
Captain Webb's Company, Cavalry
First Heavy Artillery
Second Battalion, Heavy Artillery
Eighth Battalion, Heavy Artillery
First Field Battery, Artillery
Second Field Battery, Light Artillery
Third Battery (Benton's), Light Artillery
Fifth Field Battery (Pelican Light Artillery), Light Artillery
Sixth Field Battery (Grosse Tete Flying Artillery), Light Artillery
Beauregard Battalion Battery, Artillery
Bridge's Battery, Light Artillery
Captain Castellanos' Battery, Artillery
Captain Fenner's Battery, Light Artillery
Captain Green's Company (Louisiana Guard Battery), Artillery
Captain Guyol's Company (Orleans Artillery), Artillery
Captain Holmes' Company, Light Artillery
Captain Hutton's Company (Crescent Artillery, Company A), Artillery
Captain Kean's Battery (Orleans Independent Artillery), Artillery
Captain King's Battery, Artillery
Lafayette Artillery, Militia
Captain Landry's Company (Donaldsonville Artillery), Artillery
Captain Le Gardeur, Jr.'s Company (Orleans Guard Battery), Light Artillery
Captain McPherson's Battery (Orleans Howitzers), Militia
Captain Moody's Company (Madison Light Artillery), Artillery
Ordnance Detachment

Pointe Coupee Artillery
Siege Train Battalion
Watson's Battery, Artillery
Washington Battalion, Artillery
First Infantry
First (Nelligan's) Infantry
First (Strawbridge's) Infantry
First Reserves
First Regiment, Second Brigade, First Division, Militia
First Regiment, Third Brigade, First Division, Militia
First Regiment, European Brigade, Militia
First Regiment, French Brigade, Militia
First Native Guards, Militia
First Chasseurs a pied, Militia
First Battalion Infantry (State Guards)
First (Rightor's) Special Battalion, Infantry
First (Wheat's) Special Battalion, Infantry
Second Infantry
Second Regiment, Second Brigade, First Division, Militia
Second Regiment, Third Brigade, First Division, Militia
Second Reserve Corps
Second Regiment, French Brigade, Militia
Third Infantry
Third Regiment, European Brigade (Garde Francaise), Militia
Third Regiment, French Brigade, Militia
Third Regiment, First Brigade, First Division, Militia
Third Regiment, Second Brigade, First Division, Militia
Third Regiment, Third Brigade, First Division, Militia
Fourth Infantry
Fourth Regiment, European Brigade, Militia
Fourth Regiment, French Brigade, Militia
Fourth Regiment, First Brigade, First Division, Militia
Fourth Regiment, Second Brigade, First Division, Militia
Fourth Regiment, Third Brigade, First Division, Militia
Fourth Battalion, Infantry
Fifth Infantry
Fifth Regiment, European Brigade (Spanish Regiment), Militia

Sixth Infantry
Sixth Regiment, European Brigade (Italian Guards Battalion), Militia
Seventh Infantry
Seventh Battalion, Infantry
Eighth Infantry
Ninth Infantry
Ninth Battalion, Infantry
Tenth Infantry
Tenth Battalion, Infantry
Eleventh Infantry
Eleventh Battalion, Infantry
Twelfth Infantry
Thirteenth Infantry
Thirteenth and Twentieth Infantry
Fourteenth Infantry
Fourteenth (Austin's) Battalion, Sharp Shooters
Sixteenth Infantry
Sixteenth Battalion, Infantry
Seventeenth Infantry
Eighteenth Infantry
Consolidated Eighteenth Regiment and Yellow Jacket Battalion, Infantry
Nineteenth Infantry
Twentieth Infantry
Twenty-first (Kennedy's) Infantry
Twenty-first (Patton's) Infantry
Twenty-second Infantry
Twenty-second (Consolidated) Infantry
Twenty-fifth Infantry
Twenty-sixth Infantry
Twenty-seventh Infantry
Twenty-eighth (Gray's) Infantry
Twenty-eighth (Thomas') Infantry
Thirtieth Infantry
Thirty-first Infantry
Algiers Battalion, Militia
Assumption Regiment, Militia
Battalion British Fusileers, Militia

Battalion French Volunteers, Militia
Bonnabel Guards, Militia
Beauregard Regiment, Militia
Beauregard Battalion, Militia
Bragg's Battalion, Militia
British Guard Battalion, Militia
Catahoula Battalion
Cazadores Espanoles Regiment, Militia
Chalmette Regiment, Militia
Claiborne Regiment, Militia
Confederate Guards Regiment, Militia
Consolidated Crescent Regiment, Infantry
Continental Cadets, Militia
Continental Regiment, Militia
Crescent Cadets, Militia
Crescent Regiment, Infantry
Fire Battalion, Militia
Irish Regiment, Militia
Jackson Rifle Battalion, Militia
Jeff Davis Regiment, Infantry
La Fourche Regiment, Militia
Leeds' Guards Battalion, Militia
Lewis Regiment
Lewis Guards, Militia
Louisiana and Government Employees Regiment
Maddox's Regiment, Reserve Corps
Mechanics Guard, Militia
Miles' Legion
Orleans Fire Regiment, Militia
Orleans Guards Regiment, Militia
Pelican Regiment, Infantry
Pointe Coupee Regiment, Militia
Provisional Regiment, Louisiana Legion
Red River Sharp Shooters
Reserve Corps
Sabine Reserves
St. James Regiment, Militia

St. John the Baptist Reserve Guards, Militia
St. Martin's Regiment, Militia
Terrebonne Regiment, Militia
Vermillion Regiment, Militia
Watkins' Battalion, Reserve Corps
Weatherly's Battalion, Infantry
C. S Zouave Battalion, Volunteers
Captain Barr's Independent Company (Blakesley Guards), Militia
Captain Bickham's Company (Caddo Militia)
Captain Brenan's Company (Company A, Shamrock Guards), Militia
Conscripts, Louisiana
French Company of St. James, Militia
Captain Herrick's Company (Orleans Blues)
Captain Knap's Company (Fausse River Guards), Militia
Captain Lartigue's Company (Bienville Guards), Militia
Captain McArthur's Company (Sabine Rifles)
Captain McLean's Company (Ben McCulloch Rangers)
Captain Mooney's Company (Saddlers Guards), Militia
Moreau Guards, Militia
Captain Noble's Company (Planche Guards), Militia
Captain O'Hara's Company (Pelican Guards, Company B)
Captain Otero's Company (Titterton's Guards), Militia
Stanley Guards, Company B, Militia
Captain Sugi's Company (Sappers and Miners), Militia
Vinson's Company, Scouts
Miscellaneous, Louisiana
Miscellaneous Organizations, Officers

MISSISSIPPI
DEPARTMENT OF ARCHIVES AND HISTORY
P.O. Box 571, Jackson 39205
(Capitol Green--South of the Old Capitol)

HOURS: 8:00 a.m.-5:00 p.m., Monday-Friday
8:30 a.m.-4:30 p.m., Saturday
closed: state holidays, including New Year's Day, Lee's Birthday (third
Monday in January), Washington's Birthday (third Monday in

February), Confederate Memorial Day (last Monday in April), Davis' Birthday (first Monday in June) Independence Day, Labor Day, Veterans' Day, Thanksgiving Day, Christmas Day.

This is a combined archives and library. You are not allowed to take briefcases or similar packages into the room, and your papers are subject to inspection as you leave. As you register you will be assigned a number for identification. Your first step in using the resources of the search room is to consult a series of finding aids to be found in several black notebooks which the staff will point out. Found opposite each entry in these notebooks are a "record group number" and a "document number." These must be placed on a green call slip and submitted to the staff who will bring the material to you. Only one box (volume) of records will be brought to you at a time. Some of the entries in the notebooks have an "MF" (microfilm) number opposite them. In those cases, help yourself to the appropriate roll in the adjoining microfilm room.

National Archives Microfilm

The following microfilm series have been purchased from the National Archives and are available in the microfilm room. See chapter four for a complete description of these series.

Index to Compiled Service Records of Confederate Soldiers Who Served in Organizations From the State of Mississippi. M269 (427 rolls).

Compiled Service Records of Confederate Soldiers Who Served in Organizations Raised Directly by the Confederate Government. M258. Only the following rolls in this series are available:

Lay's Regiment (rolls 34, 35)
Woods' Regiment (rolls 40-46) various infantry units (rolls 64-66)

Selected Records of the War Department Relating to Confederate Prisoners of War, 1861-1865. M598 (145 rolls).

Index and Register for Telegrams Received by the Confederate Secretary of War, 1861-1865. M618. Only rolls 11-19 in Series L (July 1862-April 1865) are available.

Records Relating to Confederate Naval and Marine Personnel. M260 (7 rolls).

Register of Confederate Soldiers, Sailors, and Citizens Who Died in Federal Prisons and Military Hospitals in the North. M918 (1 roll).

Pensions

Mississippi's first Confederate pension law was enacted in 1888. It provided for an annual award of $30 for soldiers or sailors of the Confederacy who had lost a limb or had become incapacitated by wounds received in action. Only those with no adequate means of support were eligible. In addition to the survivor himself, widows of those who were killed in action could also qualify if they were indigent. Apparently, some Mississippi soldiers took a servant with them as they went into battle. If such servant had lost a limb or had become incapacitated and was indigent, he could also receive a pension. Amendments to the law in 1890 broadened the qualifications for eligibility to allow pensions to indigent Mississippi residents who had served in the Confederate army or navy. Widows of such veterans were also eligible.

The amount of the awards was dependent upon the size of the annual appropriations by the legislature. Although a maximum amount was specified, the small appropriations usually resulted in some lesser amount. Pensioners were classified into groups according to the degree of disability and their financial status. For instance, in 1895, those in one group were awarded $25, another group $50, and those in yet another group $100. In 1904, the number of groups was reduced to two, with maximum awards of $75 or $125. After all the persons in those two special groups were paid, the other pensioners divided up equally what was left of the appropriation.

The state auditor, serving as the pension commissioner, was given almost arbitrary powers. By 1916, however, those powers had been transferred to county pension boards. They purged the existing rolls of those receiving pensions and examined all the current files as they created new rolls. Those who had been wrongfully placed in disability groups as well as those who no longer qualified under the law were struck from the rolls. A rule was added that disabled persons must have become disabled because of wounds received in action. Persons living in a state or county institution were barred from receiving a pension, and they could own no property valued at more than $600. Widows qualifying for a pension who were blind, infirm, or were permanent invalids were given awards roughly twice the amount given to other widows.

The pension applications, in addition to routine information about military service and wounds received, asked for names of any sons aged sixteen to twenty-one or any "relations whose legal or moral duty it is to provide for you." The applicant's occupation was listed and whether he held any public office. Names of comrades-in-arms were sometimes given to verify military service. A widow's application added data about her marriage and her husband's death. The group she was placed in sometimes depended upon how long she had been married before her husband died. All the applications have been microfilmed, and you may help yourself to them in the microfilm room. There is no index since they are arranged in alphabetical order by name of the veteran or widow.

Military Service Records

Mississippi took great pains in 1863, before Jackson fell to the Union, to prevent their records from falling into enemy hands. A few men who lived in that city packed three boxes of military records, told no one what they were doing, and hid them in the basement of the Jackson Masonic fraternity building. They did not reveal to anyone where the records were, but as the years passed they began to die with their secret. Eventually, only one of the group, a Col. E. E. Baldwin, remained alive. When the Mississippi Department of Archives and History was created, Colonel Baldwin hastened to divulge the existence of the papers. A state delegation hurried to the Masonic building and retrieved the boxes. Soon thereafter, they were loaned to the United States War Department for use in its nationwide project to compile service records of Confederate soldiers. As soon as the records had served that purpose, the head of the Mississippi archives personally traveled to Washington, D. C., to claim the documents and return them to his state.

These records, consisting mainly of muster rolls and payrolls, have been classified and put into sixty different boxes. To preserve them, a program of conservation including paper deacidification and lamination is under way. The contents of the sixty boxes are listed in the black notebooks described earlier. They are arranged by regiment, regiments number one through forty-eight having been classified so far. These include units which served both in the Army of Northern Virginia and the Army of the Tennessee. The material is being further sub-divided by subject matter, and the first thirty-three boxes have been so sub-divided at this writing. The finding aids notebooks list all the sub-classifications. So far, none of these records are on microfilm.

Beginning on page nine of the finding aids notebooks (following the descriptions of the sixty boxes) are titles of other military service records which may aid you in your search. To inspect them, fill out and submit a call slip and the staff will bring them to you. Some examples of the titles are shown below:

> Roll of Mississippi Confederate Soldiers, 1861-1865
> Indigent and Disabled Soldiers and Dependents, 1864-1868
> Paroles of Honor: Prisoners of War
> Deceased Soldiers' Claims
> Cbstracts and Receipts and Disbursement by Colonel Clark
> Requisitions for Supplies
> Clothing Books, First Marine Brigade
> General and Special Orders, Wither's Artillery
> Proceedings of Courts-martial
> Petitions for Exemptions from Military Duty and for Furlough
> Military Service Discharges, 1862-1864
> Register of Commissions, Army of Mississippi, 1861-1865

In contrast to the above material which has not been microfilmed, there is other military service material which has been microfilmed. Those are in "records group nine" and the "MF" number for each is shown below. You may find these in the microfilm room. These records have been extracted from the War Department collections at the National Archives.

> Confederate Military Records, Historic and Descriptive Rolls, Final Statement and Records of Various Types. MF 20, 21.
> Letters and Telegrams Sent--Ordnance Offices, Nashville and Atlanta, 1861-1862. MF 34.
> Records of Stores Purchased, Nashville and Atlanta--Invoices; Letters Received, Ordnance at Richmond, Virginia. M35.
> Records of Ordnance and Ordnance Stores Received, Nashville and Atlanta, 1861-1862. MF 36.

Invoices, Orders, Time Books, etc., Virginia State Armory, Richmond, Virginia. MF 37.

Miscellaneous State Records
Confederate Soldier's Home

In 1903 the United Sons of Confederate Veterans and the Daughters of the Confederacy joined together to raise funds to establish a home for indigent Confederate veterans. On 10 December of that year, the home was opened in the family home of Jefferson Davis and called "The Beauvoir Veterans' Home." The State of Mississippi assumed the financial support by legislation enacted 15 March 1904 and stipulated that the board of directors must include members from each of the two organizations responsible for its creation. On 30 March 1955, the state relinquished its support of the home, and it reverted to the two organizations. They operated it for only a brief period and then closed it down. It stands today as a shrine to Jefferson Davis.

Information about the residents of this home may be obtained in two sources available at the state archives. The first is a copy of a bound volume containing the names of the residents and their dates of admission and departure (either to their own homes or by death). The regiment and company of each resident is listed. Those buried at the home are included in the "Cemetery Register." The second source is a copy of an admissions register for the period 2 December 1903 to 19 February 1957. A "Cemetery Register" in this volume covers the period 21 March 1907 through 10 December 1951. These records are on microfilm and may be found in "record group seventy-seven." The original volumes remain at the home.

WPA Collection

Listed in the finding aids notebooks as "record group sixty" are various collections of index cards prepared by clerks employed by the Works Projects Administration (WPA). These cover various subjects, and the following are a few which may be helpful in locating something about your ancestor. All are arranged by county.

County Rosters of Civil War Veterans. No. 641.
Confederate Regiments and Companies. No. 648.

Partial Burial Lists of Confederate Veterans, Headstone Applications, Out-of-State Burials. No. 685.

Graves Registration

Listed in the finding aids notebooks as "record group fifty-eight" are copies originally prepared by the United States War Department Graves Registration Unit. They have been microfilmed onto six rolls and contain the reference number MF 1. Most of the names on these cards are for Confederate veterans, but they also include a few veterans from the American Revolution, the War of 1812, the Indian Wars, and the Mexican War.

Military Units

The National Archives has the compiled service records for the personnel who served in units from Mississippi as listed below. They may be found in Microcopy 269, consisting of 427 rolls. See chapter four for a complete description of this series.

First Cavalry
First Cavalry Reserves
First (McNair's) Battalion, Cavalry (State Troops)
First (Miller's) Battalion, Cavalry
First (Montgomery's) Battalion, Cavalry (State Troops)
First Choctaw Battalion, Cavalry
Second Cavalry
Second State Cavalry
Second Cavalry Reserves
Second Partisan Rangers
Second (Harris') Battalion, State Cavalry
Second Battalion, Cavalry Reserves
Third Cavalry
Third Cavalry Reserves
Third Cavalry (State Troops)
Third (Ashcraft's) Battalion, Cavalry
Third (Cooper's) Battalion, State Cavalry
Fourth Battalion, Cavalry Reserves

Fourth Cavalry
Fourth Cavalry, Militia
Fourth Battalion, Cavalry
Fifth Cavalry
Sixth Cavalry
Sixth Battalion, Cavalry
Seventh through Tenth Cavalry
Eleventh (Perrin's) Cavalry
Eleventh (Ashcraft's) Cavalry
Eleventh (Consolidated) Cavalry
Twelfth Cavalry
Seventeenth Battalion, Cavalry
Eighteenth Cavalry
Twenty-fourth Battalion, Cavalry
Twenty-eighth Cavalry
Thirty-eighth Cavalry
Jeff Davis Legion, Cavalry
Davenport's Battalion, Cavalry (State Troops)
Captain Abbott's Company, Cavalry
Captain Armistead's Company, Partisan Rangers
Captain Bowen's Company (Chulahoma Cavalry)
Captain Brown's Company (Foster Creek Rangers), Cavalry
Captain Buck's Company, Cavalry
Butler's Company, Cavalry Reserves
Captain Drane's Company (Choctaw County Reserves), Cavalry
Captain Duncan's Company (Tishomingo Rangers), Cavalry
Captain Dunn's Company (Mississippi Rangers), Cavalry
Captain Foote's Company, Mounted Men
Captain Gamblin's Company, Cavalry (State Troops)
Gardland's Battalion, Cavalry
Captain Gartley's Company (Yazoo Rangers), Cavalry
Captain Gibson's Company, Cavalry
Captain Grace's Company, Cavalry
Captain Grave's Company, Cavalry (State Troops)
Captain Hamer's Company (Salem Cavalry)
Ham's Regiment, Cavalry
Hughes' Battalion, Cavalry

Captain Knox's Company (Stonewall Rangers), Cavalry
Captain Maxey's Company, Mounted Infantry (State Troops)
Captain Maxwell's Company (State Troops) (Peach Creek Rangers)
Mitchell's Company, Cavalry Reserves
Captain Montgomery's Independent Company (State Troops)
Captain M (Herndon Rangers)
Captain Montgomery's Company of Scouts
Captain Morphis' Independent Company of Scouts
Captain Nash's Company (Leake Rangers)
Perrin's Battalion, State Cavalry
Captain Polk's Independent Company (Polk Rangers), Cavalry
Power's Regiment, Cavalry
Captain Rhodes' Company, Partisan Rangers, Cavalry
Captain Russel's Company, Cavalry
Captain Semple's Company, Cavalry
Captain Shelby's Company (Bolivar Greys), Cavalry
Captain Smyth's Company, Partisan Rangers
Captain Stewart's Company (Yalobusha Rangers)
Stockdale's Battalion, Cavalry
Street's Battalion, Cavalry
Stabb's Battalion, State Cavalry
Terrell's Unattached Company, Cavalry
Captain Vivion's Company, Cavalry
William's Company, Cavalry
Captain Wilson's Independent Company, Mounted Men (Neshoba Rangers)
Yerger's Regiment, Cavalry
First Light Artillery
Fourteenth Battalion, Light Artillery
Captain Bradford's Company (Confederate Guards Artillery)
Byrne's Battery, Artillery
Captain Cook's Company, Horse Artillery
Culbertson's Battery, Light Artillery
Captain Darden's Company, Light Artillery (Jefferson Artillery)
Captain English's Company, Light Artillery
Captain Graves' Company, Light Artillery (Issaquena Artillery)
Captain Hoole's Company, Light Artillery (Hudson Battery)
Captain Hoskin's Battery, Light Artillery (Brookhaven Light Artillery)

Captain Kittrell's Company (Wesson Artillery), Artillery
Captain Lomax's Company, Light Artillery
Captain Merrin's Battery, Light Artillery
Captain Richards' Company, Light Artillery (Madison Light Artillery)
Captain Roberts' Company (Seven Stars Artillery), Artillery
Captain Stanford's Company, Light Artillery
Captain Swett's Company, Light Artillery (Warren Light Artillery)
Captain Turner's Company, Light Artillery
Captain Yates' Battery, Light Artillery
First (Foote's) Infantry (State Troops)
First (Johnston's) Infantry
First (King's) Infantry (State Troops)
First (Patton's) Infantry (Army of 10,000)
First (Percy's) Infantry (Army of 10,000)
First Battalion, Infantry (Army of 10,000)
First State Troops, Infantry (1864)
First Battalion, State Troops, Infantry (12 months, 1862-63)
First Battalion, State Troops, Infantry (30 days, 1864)
First Battalion, Sharp Shooters
First Infantry
Second Infantry
Second Mississippi Infantry (Army of 10,000)
Second Battalion, Infantry
Second (Davidson's) Infantry (Army of 10,000)
Second (Quinn's) Infantry (State Troops)
Second Battalion, Infantry (State Troops)
Second State Troops, Infantry (30 days, 1864)
Third Infantry (State Troops)
Third Infantry
Third Infantry (Army of 10,000)
Third Battalion, Infantry
Third Battalion, Infantry (State Troops)
Third Battalion, Reserves
Fourth Infantry
Fourth Infantry (State Troops)
Fifth Infantry
Fifth Battalion, Infantry

Fifth Infantry (State Troops)
Sixth Infantry
Seventh Infantry
Seventh Battalion, Infantry
Eighth Infantry
Eighth Battalion, Infantry
Ninth Infantry
Ninth Battalion Sharp Shooters
Tenth through Fourteenth Infantry
Fourteenth (Consolidated) Infantry
Fifteenth Cavalry
Fifteenth (Consolidated) Infantry
Fifteenth Battalion, Sharp Shooters
Sixteenth through Twenty-seventh Infantry
Twenty-ninth through Thirty-seventh Infantry
Thirty-ninth through Forty-sixth Infantry
Forty-eighth Infantry
Captain Adair's Company (Lodi Company)
Captain Adams' Company (Holmes County Independent)
Captain Applewhite's Company (Vaiden Guards)
Captain Barnes' Company of Home Guards
Captain Barr's Company
Captain Berry's Company, Infantry (Reserves)
Blythe's Battalion (State Troops)
Captain Burt's Independent Company (Dixie Guards)
Camp Guard (Camp of Instruction for Conscripts)
Captain Clayton's Company (Jasper Defenders)
Captain Comfort's Company, Infantry
Conscripts, Mississippi
Captain Condrey's Company (Bull Mountain Invincibles)
Captain Cooper's Company, Infantry
Captain Drane's Company (Choctaw Silver Greys)
Captain Fant's Company
Captain Gage's Company
Captain Gage's Company (Wigfall Guards)
Gillenland's Battalion (State Troops)
Captain Gordon's Company (Local Guard of Wilkinson County)

Captain Grace's Company (State Troops)
Captain Griffin's Company (Madison Guards)
Captain Hall's Company
Captain Henley's Company (Henley's Invincibles)
Captain Hightower's Company
Hinds County Militia
Captain Hudson's Company (Noxubee Guards)
Captain Lewis' Company, Infantry
Captain McCord's Company (Slate Springs Company)
Captain McLelland's Company (Noxubee Home Guards)
Captain T. P. Montgomery's Company
Captain Moore's Company (Palo Alto Guards)
Captain Morgan's Company (Morgan Riflemen)
Moseley's Regiment
Captain Packer's Company (Pope Guards)
Captain Page's Company (Lexington Guards)
Captain Patton's Company (State Troops)
Capt. D. J. Red's Company, Infantry (Red Rebels)
Capt. S. W. Red's Company (State Troops)
Captain Roach's Company (Tippah Scouts)
Captain Roger's Company
Captain Shield's Company
Captain Standefer's Company
Lieutenant Stricklin's Company (State Troops)
Captain Taylor's Company (Boomerangs)
Captain Terry's Company
Captain Walsh's Company (Muckalusha Guards)
Wilkinson County Minute Men
Capt. Kershaw Williams' Company (Gray Port Greys)
Capt. Thomas William's Company
Captain Wilson's Company (Ponticola Guards)
Captain Withers' Company, Reserve Corps
Captain Yerger's Company (State Troops)
Miscellaneous, Mississippi

MISSISSIPPI'S ROLE IN THE WAR

The States' Rights Party had its beginning as early as 1830, when John A. Quitman of Mississippi began to speak out in favor of separation from the Union. He felt the federal government was intent on destroying the social system of the South--meaning the slavery system. Even the poor farmers with no hope of ever owning a slave were defensive about any talk of abolishing the practice because that would put the Negro on his own level. When Quitman was elected governor of Mississippi in 1850, he called a special session of the legislature to place the state "in an attitude to assert her sovereignty."[9] A convention was called to act on the question of secession, but the people, not having some explosive spark to solidify their thinking, were split on the issue. After Quitman's attempt failed, the more conservative ones of the population began to refer to him and his followers as "fire-eaters." When the violence broke out in Kansas and Harper's Ferry over the slavery issue, the fire-eaters were addressed with more respect. Although Quitman died in 1858, he had established the groundwork for his successor, John J. Pettus, who also called for a convention to decide the question of secession. This time the spark was present--the election of Abraham Lincoln and his "Black Republicans." Despite a flurry of opposition by the "cooperationists" who spoke out for delay to facilitate cooperating with their sister states, a majority of the delegates voted for immediate secession, and on 9 January 1861, Mississippi became the sovereign state once envisioned by Quitman.

With the action of the convention, Jefferson Davis, a United States senator from Mississippi, resigned his position. On 21 January, in his last speech to the Senate, he pleaded for peace between the North and the South but warned that the North should not attempt to interfere with the South's decision to form its own nation. He was given the post of Major General of the Army of Mississippi, a post he was soon to resign in favor of the presidency of the Confederate States of America.

Governor Pettus sent a battery of men to defend Vicksburg, seven companies to Fort Pickens, and one unit to Ship Island. The convention had authorized a division of volunteer soldiers to serve for a twelve month period. It established a military board under the chairmanship of the governor to create a state army. No funds were provided, however, to equip or arm it. Authorization to borrow funds for that purpose was made, but this was a gesture of futility. The patriotic and emotional fervor in the state made it easy to enlist men by the thousands, and within a few months there were dozens of companies of recruits waiting for guns. Without the means to pay or train his men, the governor tried to have as many as possible transferred to the Confederate army, but most of them simply lay around their own towns waiting for orders.

Belatedly, the governor agreed to purchase arms from Belgium and from a firm in Philadelphia, but both shipments were intercepted before they could reach Missisippi. This left the troops armed only with their own shotguns. Worse, the farmers had continued to plant cotton for a cash crop rather than food crops. This caused both soldiers and civilians to suffer in the coming months. Further, since the state operated only two cotton mills, one at the penitentiary, the cotton could not even be converted into uniforms, clothes, or blankets to any significant degree. The baled cotton sat around waiting to be sold.

Twenty-three companies were sent to Pensacola to help defend that port in Florida, and fifteen hundred others were transferred to the Confederate army unwanted because the Confederates also lacked sufficient supplies. When Pettus appointed Reuben Davis as his assistant to take charge of the war effort, the military organization in the state was accelerated. Then the people objected to the high costs involved and resisted the call for higher taxes. These objectors included the plantation owners--the very people for whom the state had chosen to fight. After the fall of Memphis, New Orleans, and then Corinth, Mississippi, Pettus began to reinforce Vicksburg. An attack on that vital port city was sure to come, sooner or later.

Pettus and his successor Charles Clark, spent the balance of the war disagreeing with Jefferson Davis and the Confederacy over whose soldiers should be stationed at Vickburg. Davis usually won the dispute. They also argued over who should pay the soldiers and over the exemptions each of them were granting to certain selected groups of persons. They also argued over the proper use of the state militia--whether it should be used as a military force under the governor or possibly transferred to the Confederate forces. The many issues were eventually settled by the Mississippi High Court which ruled in favor of the Confederacy. After that, the only duty performed by the state militia was the rounding up of Confederate deserters. Fighting was under the control of the Confederacy.

As the Confederacy decided to add fortifications to Vicksburg in 1863, it demanded Negroes work on the construction. The Mississippi planters objected that they were not receiving sufficient remuneration for the use of their slaves. Confederate impressment officers began to seize the slaves, food, and even houses, to support the military. The state itself also impressed supplies from its citizens, often competing with Confederate agents.

In early 1862, Union Generals Don Carlos Buell and Ulysses S. Grant arrived at Pittsburg Landing, Tennessee, just a few miles from the Mississippi state line. They fought at Shiloh on 6 April, forcing the Confederate armies to retreat to Corinth, Mississippi, from which they also withdrew in the path of the oncoming Union troops. The Confederates then moved back to Tupelo after putting up a fight at Holly Springs. Later that month Grant took Port Gibson. Then Gen. William T. Sherman, split off from the main forces with Grant, took a body of troops to the capital city of Jackson. Confederate General Joseph E. Johnston, rather than subject his fifteen thousand troops and the entire city to certain devastation, withdrew his men from the city on 14 May 1863. The Union troops marched in, but then left it three days later in order to concentrate their strength at Vicksburg--the prime objective of Grant in Mississippi. Sherman took three thousand slaves left behind in Jackson to augment his forces. Confederate General John C. Pemberton moved toward Vicksburg to defend it against the pending onslaught by Grant. On the way he had to fight at Champion's Hill, on 17 May, where he suffered almost thirty-nine hundred casualties.

In 1862, Admiral Farragut had tried in vain to take Vicksburg by combined naval and land advances. The location of the city atop a three hundred foot bluff made it impossible for Farragut's guns in the river to fire on it, and defenses against land forces were successful. For a while, the city was safe. In the spring of 1863, after the floods had subsided, Grant made several passes at the city but could not break through the defenses by indirect routes. In early May, Grant and several of his other units began to march on the city to launch a frontal attack. They were thrown back on 19 May and 22 May, convincing Grant to use other tactics. A siege of the city was begun with Union troops slowly tightening a circle around the city to prevent those inside from receiving any reinforcements, ammunition, or food. After much starvation and learning of a new planned attack by Grant, General Pemberton asked for terms for capitulation. Grant answered by reminding him that his previous terms of unconditional surrender still held. On 4 July, the next day,

Pemberton and his 29,511 troops marched out and laid their arms down before a respectful and admiring army of Union soldiers. The Mississippi River was then open to navigation without Confederate interruption.

Less than two weeks after the fall of Vicksburg, General Johnston again evacuated the city of Jackson and set up a camp at Enterprise. He moved from there to Macon, to Columbus, and then to Meridian which was serving as the state's temporary capital. Meanwhile, the Union had taken over the naval yard at Yazoo City. By the close of 1863, a large part of Mississippi was in Union hands.

As early as 1862, after Shiloh and the fall of Corinth, pro-Union sentiment within the state began to be more vocal. Many were more interested in saving their own hides and in finding a way to profit from their cotton stores than in defending an army that seemed certain to lose anyway. They went to Memphis and New Orleans and dealt with cotton traders there. The state itself even traded there to gain money to buy salt, the scarce commodity essential for the preservation of their meat. Many of the poor farmers, angry over the exemptions given to the wealthy planters, signed loyalty oaths proferred by the federal government as a means to go to such places as Biloxi, then in Union hands, to sell cotton. Others were eager to join in rebellion against the Confederacy for other reasons. These were the army deserters who had become disenchanted with Pemberton's leadership at Vicksburg. They left in droves, set up camps, and lived off the land, striking terror in the hearts of the citizens who dared oppose them. The most notable rebellion was in Jones County, a pro-Union county even before the war began. It was there that a man named Nate Knight led a band of renegades against anyone still professing loyalty to the Confederacy. Jones County became a haven for deserters and "Unionists" during the last year of the war.

In 1864, General Sherman continued his march to the sea, leaving a sixty-mile swath of burnt land across Mississippi and Georgia. General Forrest, in northern Mississippi, fought at Brice's Crossroads and then in Georgia and the Carolinas, but there was no stopping Sherman. At the very end, Gen. Richard Taylor, leading the remnants of the Alabama and Mississippi regiments, surrendered to General Canby at Meridian. The date was 4 May 1865, a month following Lee's surrender in Virginia.

NORTH CAROLINA
ARCHIVES AND HISTORY--STATE LIBRARY BUILDING
109 East Jones Street, Raleigh 27611

ARCHIVES HOURS: 8:00 a.m.-5:30 p.m., Tuesday-Friday
    8:30 a.m.-5:30 p.m., Saturday
LIBRARY HOURS: 8:00 a.m.-5:30 p.m., Monday-Friday
    8:30 a.m.-5:30 p.m., Saturday (Genealogy Branch)
closed: Both the archives and the library are closed on state holidays,
including the Saturday following a Friday holiday or preceding a Sunday holiday. The holidays include: New Year's Day, Easter Monday, Memorial Day, Independence Day, Labor Day, Veterans' Day, Thanksgiving Day and the day following, Christmas and the days before and after. The archives (but not the library) are also closed two days in January--usually the second Tuesday and Wednesday--to verify its holdings.

Free parking is available in a lot southwest of the building with an entrance on Edonton Street. The genealogy branch of the library is on the mezzanine just below the archives search room which is on the second floor.

If you choose to write for a record rather than make a personal visit, be sure to enclose a legal size, self-addressed, stamped envelope. If you write from outside the state you must also enclose a fee of $5.00. Any copies required will be billed to you separately. Written requests must be restricted to only one source and refer to only one person.

If you visit personally, you will find that security for the search room is very tight. Before you enter, you will be required to place your wraps, briefcases, folders with pockets, books, bound notebooks, and envelopes in a locker provided for that purpose. An identification card will be issued to you by an attendant in the entrance lobby just outside the search room. This must be used inside the room when requesting material and must be shown when you leave or reenter the room. Television cameras continually scan the search room and are monitored by staff in the entrance lobby.

Once inside the search room acquaint yourself with the card catalogs and bound indexes on the shelves adjacent to the card catalog cabinets. You must become familiar with the series of finding aids in the many black notebooks found there. Some of those notebooks are labeled "State Agencies" and one of them is sub-labeled "Military Collections." The agencies include the auditor, adjutant general, and the secretary of state. The material is grouped according to county. Each entry in these notebooks has a box number opposite it. Using the title of the material you desire and its box number, you may complete a call slip and submit it to one of the staff at the front counter. The material will then be procured and handed to you at that counter. Before receiving it you must turn in your identification card. It will be kept until you leave the room. Material brought to you may be examined at any of the tables in the search room and must be returned to the counter when you are finished with it. Only one box of materials will be handed to you at a time.

National Archives Microfilm

In the microfilm room adjoining the search room are the following microfilm series which have been purchased from the National Archives. See chapter four for a complete description of these series.

Index to Compiled Service Records of Confederate Soldiers Who Served in Organizations From the State of North Carolina. M230 (43 rolls).
Compiled Service Records of Confederate Soldiers Who Served in Organizations From the State of North Carolina. M270 (580 rolls).

Not a National Archives series but helpful as a reference is a roll of microfilm entitled "North Carolina Synonym File of Confederate Units." This gives both local and official designations of the state's military units.

Pensions

Prior to 1885, veterans who had lost arms or legs or who were blinded during their military service, were provided either artifical limbs or compensation by the state. The pension law of 1885 provided for pensions to veterans or widows of veterans who had become disabled by loss of an arm, leg, or an eye, or were otherwise incapcitated as a result of military action while serving in the Confederate forces. Barred from pensions were those who owned property valued at $500 or more or who received an annual salary of $300 or more. Widows were barred from receiving a pension if they had remarried. In 1887, an amendment made it possible for a widow to receive a pension if her veteran husband had died of disease while in service regardless of whether he had received a wound.

In 1889, a new pension law was enacted nullifying the old one. That law, as amended in 1901, required the applicant to have been a North Carolina resident for twelve months. Widows must have married the veteran prior to 1 April 1865. A schedule of awards was created based on the extent of the disability. The first class received $72 annually, and the fourth and lowest class received $30. Other features of the older law were retained for the most part. Subsequent amendments revised the allowable marriage dates for widows. For instance, they eventually were eligible if they had been married for as short a time as ten years, provided the veteran had died before 1899. Later, widows were permitted to remarry without loss of their pensions. These and other minor amendments, especially in the payment rates, were made frequently until 1953. In more modern times, applicants might have been declared eligible without regard to indigency.

Applications for a pension were submitted to the local county pension board which passed on their acceptability. When approved, the application was forwarded to the state auditor for payment. Each year the auditor sent reports to the county clerks listing the pensioners on the rolls. The clerks examined the lists for accuracy, making changes as needed, and returned them to the auditor. Those annual lists will be brought to you if you submit a call slip for the years when your ancestor might have appeared on a list.

The applications were standard forms on which the applicant provided information relative to the legal requirements for eligibility. The widow's form repeated the information on the veteran's application and added data concerning her marriage to him and his death. Since a person might have filed more than one application in the state, there may be more than one application in his or her file. All the applications, both those approved and disapproved, have been indexed by name of the veteran or widow and are listed in two black notebooks kept by the staff at the front desk. You must ask to see these. One of them lists the names of those who applied under the original law, and the other lists those who applied under the 1901 law. After you find the name you need in one of these notebooks, the staff will bring you the pension file containing the original application. Neither the indexes nor the approximately 45,000 files have been microfilmed.

In addition to the pension files themselves and the annual lists prepared by the state auditor, there are other sources related to pensions listed in the finding aids notebooks. You may inspect them by submitting a call slip with the title and code number shown below.

Lists of Approved Pensions, 1886. Aud P11.
Lists of Approved Pensions, 1887. Aud P12 and Aud P13.
Private Pension Bills (those introduced in the legislature). Aud P15.
Pension Office Correspondence. Aud P110 and Aud P114.

Military Service Records

Various collections of military service records of North Carolina men in the Confederate forces are to be found in the "Civil War Collection." Reference to this source, identified as "CWC," may be found in the finding aids notebook. Some of the groups of records in this collection are described below:

Roll of Honor

In 1862, the state Adjutant General's Office began to compile a roster of the state's regiments from North Carolina. It was called the "Roll of Honor." Names in this roster are arranged by the military units as they were called at that time. It is important to realize that by the end of the war the designations were modified by new titles and by reorganization. Each unit lists its personnel by rank and then alphabetically. This material was sent to the War Department in Washington, D.C., to form the basis of the compiled service records which are now on National Archives film. Because of this duplication, all the information in this "Roll of Honor" is more easily found in the compiled service records.

Muster Rolls and Military Unit Records

As with the names on the "Honor Roll," the large number of muster rolls, payrolls, and other descriptive rolls from North Carolina were turned over to the War Department and used in the compiled service records. Thus, the material in these 210 rolls will also merely duplicate the information in the compiled service records. These records are cited as CWC 42-46 in the finding aids notebooks.

Bounty Payrolls

Most soldiers who enlisted from North Carolina received enlistment bounties. The rolls of those who received such payments have been arranged either by county, or, where more than one county furnished troops to the same unit, by regiment. A search in the finding aids notebooks will lead you to the collection which might include your ancestor. These are cited as CWC 9-12 and CWC 13-19. These rolls were prepared from muster rolls and include the signatures of the soldiers receiving money for their service. Their counties and the amounts paid are shown.

Bounty Pay and Allowances Due Deceased Officers and Soldiers

There are a few instances of a record of a payment made by the Confederate government to an heir of an officer or soldier when he died. These are arranged by county. They include the name of the person who made the claim, describe the service history of the deceased, the date and place of death, and other miscellaneous information.

Roster of the Militia Officers of North Carolina, 1862-1865

Many persons served in local militia units and never fought with a regular state or Confederate unit. Their records probably never were included in the compiled service records, and this source may be the only place you may find his name--but only if he was an officer. The state Adjutant General's Office prepared a list of the officers of those units and arranged them by county. The numbering of the units was changed soon after the list was compiled, and pen and ink changes sometimes show the new titles. Historical research is needed to reconcile the changing unit designations with the original designation made at the time of your ancestor's service. There is no index to these lists.

Moore's Roster

John W. Moore published four volumes in 1882 which listed 104,498 North Carolina Confederate soldiers. These are believed to comprise approximately seventy percent of the total. There is a card for each person listed in Moore's volumes, and they may be inspected in a special card catalog found in the southwest corner of the search room. Moore's works have been updated by similar publications by Manarin and Jordan (see chapter five).

Miscellaneous State Records
Confederate Soldiers' Home

North Carolina established a Confederate soldiers' home at Raleigh for white veterans and at the state hospital at Goldsboro for Negro veterans. Indexes of names of residents at both homes may be found in the same notebook described earlier which contains an index of pension applications under the 1901 pension law. There are three records pertaining to soldier's home residents, and they may be examined after submitting a call slip showing the title and code number as shown below.

Confederate Soldiers' Home, Roll Book, 1890-1911. Aud 7.3.
This is an alphabetical list of 803 residents with accompanying papers containing personal information.
Confederate Soldiers' Home, Inmates' Records, 1911-1936. Aud 7.5.
This record consists of 138 questionnaires which were completed by the residents themselves and often contain names of their next of kin.
Confederate Soldiers' Home. Inmates' Register, 1890-1917. Aud 7.4.
This is a three part record and includes a record of deaths at the home.

Petitions for Pardon

After the war ended, the president issued pardons to certain qualifying Southern citizens who applied for them. The applications are part of the War Department's so-called "amnesty papers." See chapter four for a complete description of this process. North Carolina has photocopies of the nearly two thouand applications from the state, and they are available for inspection. These are cited as CWC 1-18. Also, there is a card index to the names in this collection. It may be found in the search room.

Artificial Limbs

The state auditor kept a record of veterans who received artificial prostheses to replace arms or legs lost in the war. There is also a record of those who chose to receive monetary compensation in lieu of a prosthesis. Information includes the county of residence, the military unit, a description of the loss and the date when the claim was honored. This is in the Civil War collection, and cited as CWC 41.

Gravestone Records

In the ten year period between 1956 and 1966, the United Daughters of the Confederacy conducted a survey of North Carolina graveyards to locate and identify burial places of the Confederate dead. A survey form was used to record information such as the military unit, birth and death dates, and other facts inscribed on the gravestone. These forms fill thirteen volumes (black notebooks) which may be found on the shelves in the southeast corner of the search room. There are approximately eight thousand forms and they have been indexed. The index cards are in a card catalog adjacent to the shelf housing the thirteen volumes.

NORTH CAROLINA'S ROLE IN THE WAR

In 1860 the paramount sentiment in North Carolina was in favor of remaining in the Union, but as developments unfolded the mood changed. The firing on Fort Sumter and the failure of a "peace conference" to bring about accomodations agreeable to the South led to a feeling that North Carolina should join with the other Southern states against the Union. Secessionists began to organize meetings to galvanize public opinion. These groups were strong in Wilmington, the most radical city of the state. When Governor Ellis was informed that the federal government wanted two regiments of troops from his state, he replied, "Your dispatch is received, and if genuine (which its extraordinary character leads me to doubt), I have to say in reply that I regard a levy of troops for the purpose of subjugating the states of the South, is in violation of the Constitution and a usurpation of power. I can be no party to this wicked violation of the laws of the country, and to this war upon the liberties of a free people. You can get no troops from North Carolina."[10] As a defensive measure, Ellis seized Forts Caswell, Macon and Johnston, as well as the arsenal at Fayetteville and the Branch Mint at Charlotte. On 20 May, the state convention passed its ordinance of secession. North Carolina was the last state to secede. It was welcomed by the Confederate States on 27 May, and the citizens of North Carolina ratified the new constitution on 6 June.

A month before the state seceded, the governor had sent a regiment of troops to Virginia and had established a training camp at Raleigh, in anticipation of the need to raise a force of thirty thousand volunteers. After Lincoln received the rejection from the governor, he sent federal troops to occupy the coastal ports at Hatteras, Roanoke Island, and then New Bern.

Being a fairly prosperous and modernized state compared to its southern neighbors, North Carolina tooled up to help supply the material of war to the Confederacy. It turned out cloth from its textile mills and grew crops for food. It maintained its own state government and its own system of laws. It rejected any hint of martial law within its borders from the Confederacy, and it railed against any attempt to bypass its civil law. The newly elected governor, Zebulon B. Vance, insisted that the Confederacy exempt from military service any North Carolinian necessary to the operation of the state government and objected to Confederate agents impressing supplies within its borders. To its credit, North Carolina made strong efforts to feed its own poor, especially the families of fighting men, all during the war.

Opposing Vance were the many avowed Unionists in the state and their bands of outlaws called "buffaloes" who terrorized those who favored the South. Such groups instituted a "peace movement" to challenge Vance when he ran for reelection in 1864, but were unable to unseat him because of his prior support for the poor. Thus, even though the war was going badly for the South by that time, North Carolina was able to stand by its early decision.

North Carolina provided approximately 125,000 men for the battles, most of which occurred outside the state. This was a much larger amount than any other Confederate state provided. Of the first twenty-one regiments formed in North Carolina by the close of August 1861, sixteen were sent to Virginia, leaving only the more recently formed six regiments inside the state. The more pressing problem was obtaining sufficient clothing, arms, and equipment to support the hordes of volunteers.

In addition to the significant manpower contribution, North Carolina was of tremendous help to the Confederacy by its large scale running of the coastal blockade imposed by the Union navy. This was especially true out of Wilmington, a port which stayed out of Union hands until the very end. Europeans were eager to get the cotton and tobacco from America, and the Confederate states were happy to oblige--in return for gold and war material. Private ship owners and investors reaped millions in profits by buying cotton at a few cents a pound and selling it to European traders for ten or more times what they paid for it. After two or so successful runs through the blockade to trade in the Bahamas and Bermuda, a ship owner could become financially secure for the rest of his life. The state of North Carolina, realizing the potential for profit, owned its own blockade running ship, the *Advance,* and had part interest in three other such vessels. It has been estimated that these types of activities brought sixty-five million dollars to the coffers of the Confederacy through the port of Wilmington alone.

The first use of North Carolina troops was in a battle eight miles across its border, in Virginia, at a village called Big Bethel Church. Confederate troops were stationed there, and Union General Benjamin Butler sent thirty-five hundred of his men to take the town. Reinforced by fourteen hundred more, the Confederates fought the attackers to a draw. The date was 10 May 1861. This battle inspired the lines inscribed on a monument to the Confederate soldiers located on capital square at Raleigh:

"First at Bethel
Farthest to the front at Gettysburg and at Chickmauga,
Last at Appomattox."

The only really heavy fighting in North Carolina occurred when six thousand Union troops moved in from Tennessee, and under Gen. George F. Stoneman overran the western Piedmont section of the state. In February, 1862, the town of Winston was burned after being attacked by six Union gunboats and a group of volunteers from Rhode Island. Its sister town, Salem, although defenseless, was spared for some unknown reason. The next month, on 14 March, the town of New Bern surrendered. Edward Stanley, a former North Carolinian, was named by President Lincoln as the state's military governor, but he resigned the following January convinced that the task was an impossible one. The New Bern takeover was part of the campaign by Union vessels to close the coastal ports. They were opposed by the seventh and the tenth North Carolina regiments supported by seven small naval vessels dubbed the "mosquito fleet." They were unsuccessful and the tiny naval force was destroyed.

Later in the war, after Gen. William T. Sherman had completed his march to the sea and the taken Charleston, South Carolina, he moved into North Carolina with sixty thousand troops; against which no Confederate army could stand. Sherman fought defenders at Bentonville and Goldsboro and headed toward Raleigh. General Joseph E. Johnston surrendered his army at Durham on 26 April 1865 and the war in the East was over, thus saving Raleigh from destruction.

An estimate shows that the 125,000 North Carolina troops were in seventy-two regiments composed of 111,000 men, eight regiments composed of 10,000 reserves, and a home guard composed of 4,000. It also lists 14,673 North Carolinians killed in action, more than one-quarter of all Confederate soldiers killed in the war.[11]

Military Units

The National Archives has the compiled service records for the personnel who served in units from North Carolina as listed below. They may be found in Microcopy 270, consisting of 580 rolls. See chapter four for a complete description of this series.

First Cavalry (Ninth State Troops)
Second Cavalry (Nineteenth State Troops)
Third Cavalry (Fourty-First State Troops)
Fourth Cavalry (Fifty-Ninth State Troops)
Fifth Cavalry (Sixty-Third State Troops)
Fifth Battalion, Cavalry
Sixth Cavalry (Sixty-fifth State Troops)
Seventh Battalion, Cavalry
Eighth Battalion, Partisan Rangers
Twelfth Battalion, Cavalry
Fourteenth Battalion, Cavalry
Fifteenth Battalion, Cavalry, State Reserves
Sixteenth Battalion, Cavalry
Captain Howard's Company (Local Defense), Cavalry
McRae's Battalion, Cavalry

Captain Swindell's Company, Partisan Rangers
First Battalion, Heavy Artillery
First Artillery (Tenth State Troops)
Second Artillery (Thirty-sixth State Troops)
Third Artillery (Fortieth State Troops)
Third Battalion, Light Artillery
Tenth Battalion, Heavy Artillery
Thirteenth Battalion, Light Artillery
Captain Moseley's Company (Sampson Artillery)
First Infantry
First Infantry (six months, 1861)
First Junior Reserves
First Detailed Men
First Battalion, Junior Reserves
First Regiment, Militia
Second Infantry
Second Battalion, Infantry
Second Detailed Men
Second Junior Reserves
Second Conscripts
Second Battalion, Local Defense Troops
Third Infantry
Third Junior Reserves
Third Battalion, Senior Reserves
Fourth Infantry
Fourth Senior Reserves
Fourth Battalion, Junior Reserves
Fifth Infantry
Fifth Senior Reserves
Sixth Infantry
Sixth Senior Reserves
Seventh Infantry
Seventh Senior Reserves
Seventh Battalion, Junior Reserves
Eighth Infantry
Eighth Senior Reserves
Eighth Battalion, Junior Reserves

Ninth (First) Battalion, Sharp Shooters
Eleventh (Bethel Regiment) Infantry
Twelfth Infantry
Thirteenth Infantry
Thirteenth Battalion, Infantry
Fourteenth through Sixteenth Infantry
Seventeenth Infantry (First Organization)
Seventeenth Infantry (Second Organization)
Eighteenth Infantry
Twentieth through Thirty-third Infantry
Thirty-third Militia
Thirty-fourth Infantry
Thirty-fifth Infantry
Thirty-seventh through Thirty-ninth Infantry
Forty-second through Fifty-first Infantry
Fifty-first Militia
Fifty-second through Fifty-eighth Infantry
Sixtieth through Sixty-second Infantry
Sixty-fourth Infantry (Eleventh Battalion, Allen's Regiment)
Sixty-sixth Infantry (Eighth Battalion, Partisan Ragners; Thirteenth
    Battalion)
Capt. J. W. Whitman's Company, Sixty-sixth Battalion, Militia
Sixty-seventh Infantry
Sixty-eighth Infantry
Clark's Special Battalion, Militia
Cumberland County Battalion, Detailed Men
Hill's Battalion, Reserves
Mallett's Battalion (Camp Guard)
McCorkle's Battalion, Light Duty Men
Thomas' Legion
Captain Allen's Company (Local Defense)
Captain Bank's Company (Currituck Guard)
Captain Bass' Company
Captain Brown's Company
Conscripts, Unassigned
Captain Cox's Company, Local Defense (Provost Guard,Kingston)
Captain Croom's Company, Local Defense (Kingston Guards) Kingston
    Provost Guard

Captain Doughton's Company (Allegheny Grays)
Captain Galloway's Company, Coast Guards
Captain Gibb's Company (Local Defense)
Captain Giddins Company (Detailed and Petitioned Men)
Captain Griswold's Company, Local Defense (Provost Guard, Goldsboro)
Home Guards
Captain Hoskins' Company (Local Defense)
Captain Howard's Company, Prison Guards
Captain Jones' Company (Supporting Force)
Captain Lawrence's Company, Volunteers (Wilson Partisan Rangers)
Captain Lee's Company, Local Defense (Silver Grays)
Captain Mallett's Company
Captain McDugald's Company
Captain McMillan's Company
Captain Nelson's Company (Local Defense)
Captain Snead's Company (Local Defense)
Captain Townsend's Company (State Troops)
Captain Wallace's Company (Wilmington Railroad Guard)
Miscellaneous, North Carolina

SOUTH CAROLINA
DEPARTMENT OF ARCHIVES AND HISTORY
1430 Senate Street, Columbia 29211
(P.O. Box 11679)

HOURS: 9:00 a.m.-9:00 p.m., Monday-Friday
       9:00 a.m.-6:00 p.m., Saturday
       1:00 p.m.-9:00 p.m., Sunday
closed: New Year's Day, Easter Sunday, Independence Day,Labor Day,
       Thanksgiving Day, Christmas and theday following (and sometimes
       the day before).

Free parking is available on the lot entered from Bull Street. You must obtain a permit from the archives reference desk and display it on your car while it is parked. After 5:00 p.m., you must use the Bull Street entrance to the archives.

As you register at the reference desk, you will be required to place your briefcase, outer clothing, and packages in a locker provided for that purpose. Your belongings are subject to search as you leave the building. You may wish to purchase a booklet entitled "The South Carolina Archives; A Temporary Summary Guide" which lists the archives holdings in detail.

Except for the microfilm and the use of the indexes, you must ask for any records you wish to examine by submitting a call slip to the reference desk. No more than three records will be brought to you at one time. When you are finished with them, return them along with the yellow slip which came with them to the reference desk.

This archives has only a few publications. You are urged to visit the nearby South Caroliniana Library at the University of South Carolina located just a few blocks away. That historic library has an extensive collection of genealogical and historical works which should prove helpful to you.

National Archives Microfilm

On the west wall of the search room are several gray boxes which contain microfilm which was purchased from the National Archives. Select one roll at a time and register it on a sheet provided for that purpose. After you finish using it, place it on a nearby credenza and the staff will refile it. Available here are the following National Archives microfilm series related to Confederate personnel. See chapter four for a complete description of these series.

Consolidated Index to Compiled Service Records of Confederate Soldiers (all states). M253 (535 rolls).
Compiled Service Records of Confederate Soldiers Who Served in Organizations From the State of South Carolina. M267 (392 rolls).
Compiled Service Records of Confederate General and Staff Officers and Nonregimental Enlisted Men. M331 (275 rolls).

Pensions

The first South Carolina pension law for Confederates was enacted about 1888. It provided that those who had served in a Confederate military unit during the war and who were indigent might qualify for a pension. In later years, widows and other heirs were also eligible for a pension if they were indigent. Successive amendments to the law, up to 1919, gradually eased the requirements for eligibility. The application is a one page form which asked for identifying information, military history, and financial status. In many instances, statements from comrades-in-arms were included to testify to the claimed military service. On the reverse of the form, the reviewing officials made notations concerning the applicant's income, the value of his property, and whether the application was approved or disapproved.

The pension applications and related material are arranged by county. Therefore, the simplest way to obtain it is to submit a call slip to the reference desk on which is included the name of the veteran and his county of residence. Staff will bring you any pension data which is found in their records of that county. For ready reference, the pension material available for each of the counties is listed below:

County	Material
Anderson	Applications (undated)
	Applications, 1919
	Checks, 1892-1929
	Rolls, 1896, 1962 (3 vols.)
Cherokee	Pension records, 1901-11 (2 vols.)
	Approved pension rolls, 1897-1915 (2 vols.)
Edgefield	Pension checks, 1922-27
Fairfield	Roll book, 1919
	Distribution of state pension funds, 1930-43
Horry	Applications, 1901-19
	Roll books, 1889-1916 (2 vols)
Laurens	Roll books, 1898-1930 (10 vols)
	Distribution of state funds, 1933-68 (the roll for 1896 is incorporated with the Common Pleas Sales, 1891-97
	Papers, 1915-28
	Camp Garlington Ledger, 1912-25
	Enrollments for Jack's Township (undated)
Lee	(see Sumter County)

Lexington	Pension record, 1888
	Roll books, 1896-1923
	Distribution of state pension fund, 1916-18
Marlboro	Applications, 1898-1900
	Check stubs, 1919-20 (2 vols.)
	Roll book, 1895
	Distribution of state pension fund, 1916-18
Newberry	Distribution of state pension fund, 1916-18
Spartanburg	Roll books, 1889-96 (2 vols)
	Distribution of state pension fund, 1916-19
	Papers, ca 1899-1925
Sumter	Pension records, 1901-05 (Lee County pension records of 1902 included)
Union	Pension stubs, 1906
	Pension roll, 1901-13
	Applications, 1910-19
	Records of pension earners, 1906-12
York	Application papers, 1919-64
	Roll book, 1896-1962

If the staff is not able to locate any pension material for your ancestor in the counties you have named, and if you believe he received a pension any time after 1919, you should turn to the computer printout entitled "Applications Index, 1919-1925." All persons, including veterans, widows, comrades-in-arms, and witnesses whose names appear in the applications are listed here in alphabetical order. Each entry in this printout gives the name of the veteran, the applicant, town and county of residence, military unit, date of application, and a cross-reference to other applications where the veteran's name might also appear. The entry number shown for each listing is needed to request the pension file from the staff.

Military Service Records

There are several separate collections which may mention your ancestor. When requesting them, note the office which compiled them as indicated on the next page:

Office of the Confederate Historian

Roster of Officers. This is a book listing the names of the officers from South Carolina during 1861-1862.

Roll of Troops. This is a book listing the troops from South Carolina who served in the war. There is also a series of drawers in a wooden file cabinet near the reference desk which contain index cards of South Carolina men who served in the war. This index was prepared many years ago and is known to be very incomplete.

Memory Roll of the Gist Rifles. This is a roll of Company D, Hampton Legion, A. N. V. Gist Rifles.

Gettysburg Soldiers. These are stubs of checks drawn on the Legislature Fund to transport Confederate soldiers to Gettysburg, Pennsylvania.

Deceased Soldiers. These are three volumes listing names of deceased Confederate soldiers from South Carolina.

Office of the Adjutant and Inspector General

Draft Substitutes. This book, dated 1862, lists names of persons who were drafted into service but who arranged for a substitute to serve in their place. The names of the substitutes are also listed as well as their military unit and the appropriate dates. In those cases where the draftee possessed a certificate of British citizenship or was an alien from some other country, there is a special notation to that effect.

Overseers' Roll. This book, dated 1862, lists names of persons who employed overseers who were exempted from service. The names of the overseers and the place of residence and dates are shown. The employers' names are in alphabetical order but not the overseers' names.

SOUTH CAROLINA'S ROLE IN THE WAR

As in Mississippi and for more than a decade, the leaders of South Carolina had objected to the treatment accorded it by the federal government. This conflict raised the question of separation. Without a doubt, the prime issue in the discussions was the right to own and protect their property--slaves. The issue of states' rights was a subject of public oratory, but this was a secondary issue created to rationalize the true issue of slavery. The only real differences of opinion was the issue of whether the state should go it alone as a separate nation or wait until other southern states, especially Alabama, Mississippi, and Georgia, were also ready to take the same step. The members of the first group were called "separate state actionists" and the second "cooperationists." All of them believed that the federal government might become more accomodating to the needs of the South if sufficient pressure were placed on it. But if not, they were prepared to secede and govern themselves and throw off the yoke of bias and ill treatment from Washington, D.C., and the Northern "abolitionists."

As soon as Lincoln, the "Black Republican," was elected to the presidency, the South Carolina legislature called for a state convention to be held 17 December, before Lincoln was inaugurated. The purpose was to secede from the Union without delay. After conferring with several neighbor states who urged it to take the lead with the understanding that they would follow, the convention, sitting at the Hall of St. Andrew's Society in Charleston, adopted an ordinance which said simply that the "union now subsisting between South Carolina and other States, under the name of 'The United States of America' is hereby dissolved."[12] Thus, the so-called "Palmetto Republic" was born. At this same convention, it was decided to call another convention to meet at Montgomery, Alabama, on 4 February to form a confederation of Southern states that intended to secede. At that convention, a constitution was drafted, and South Carolina officially ratified it on 3 April 1862, becoming part of the Confederate States of America.

Anticipating that the federal government might well object to secession, South Carolina began to strengthen its military defenses. Its obsolete militia laws were overhauled and a system of volunteer fighting units was overlaid on the militia organization. Various companies were transferred from the existing militia units for twelve month terms. New units were also organized and stationed at strategic places within the state. By 6 March there were 104 companies comprising 8.835. Of that number, 3,027 were stationed at Charleston under the command of Gen. Pierre Beauregard. A move was made to seize cannon, guns, and powder from federal establishments within the state. A complex plan was devised to take over Fort Sumter guarding the harbor at Charleston. This plan was rushed into completion after Lincoln stated in his inaugural speech that he would "hold, occupy, and possess the property and places belonging to the Government."

Before moving on Sumter, South Carolina took over the forts abandoned by the federal troops at Fort Moultrie (on Sullivan's Island opposite Charleston) and the small fort called Castle Pinckney in the Charleston harbor. Union Major Robert Anderson had moved from those two locations to concentrate his troops on Fort Sumter. The state troops moved in on 27 and 28 March 1861 to take the two abandoned forts. By that action, the first actual acts of war took place--though without gunfire or force.

When General Beauregard sent a letter to Major Anderson on 11 April, demanding a surrender, the major replied that he would not surrender but that he would be starved out within a few days anyway because of Beauregard's siege and the failure of the federal government to bring in supplies or food. Another message from the general prompted a reply from the major that he would evacuate the island at noon, on 15 April, unless he received differing orders or unless he was attacked before then. This reply was deemed to be ambiguous. Beauregard, without checking with higher officials, decided to attack. He informed Anderson that he would fire after waiting only one more hour. He ordered the first shot fired from nearby James Island at 4:20 a.m. After thirty hours of cannon fire, with the federal troops holed up in underground tunnels and rooms, Anderson surrendered the fort with full military honors. Not one man had been killed, but during a salute to the flag at the surrender ceremonies, a cannon prematurely went off causing explosions among loose cartridges nearby. This killed one federal soldier and fatally wounded another. The South Carolina military and civilians were jubilant; they fully expected that the war now started would end after a few battles and within a matter of a few months, lasting certainly not longer than a year.

South Carolina began to prepare for war in earnest. It raised several companies and turned them over to the Confederate army or sent them to Virginia where there was a greater need at the time. This generosity was to diminish later on during the war. Disputes between the state and the Confederacy became more frequent; fewer men were sent to Virginia. With financial assistance from the Confederacy, construction of boats was begun. Railroads were upgraded, and guns and equipment were obtained to outfit the enlarging army of volunteers. In December 1861, the militia law was amended again to provide for twelve month terms for all males between the ages of eighteen and forty-five, for service either inside or outside the state. Governor Pickens called for twelve thousand volunteers and threatened a state draft if they were not forthcoming. When his term ended, he was succeeded by Milledge L. Bonham, and the legislature passed a conscription act providing for certain occupational exemptions. These laws were amended again in 1864 in a desperation move to draft all those aged sixteen to fifty, with those up to age sixty to serve only within the borders of the state.

South Carolina did not exempt overseers of the troublesome slaves, however, and this problem was debated until the Confederate government settled it when it passed its own conscription act on 11 October 1862. It provided for exemptions of overseers or owners at the rate of one white man for every twenty slaves on two or more plantations within five miles of each other. This provision was generally objected to by the poor farmers who saw the rich man exempted while he had to fight. Also, there was a provision for purchasing a substitute for a person called up--another advantage for the rich man. To the credit of South Carolina's citizens, though, the ratio of exemptions and substitutes by this state was far lower than the ratio in all the other Confederate states. For instance, South Carolina had only 791 substitutes compared to 2,040 in North Carolina, 7,050 in Georgia, and 15,000 in Virginia. Also, other figures showed that the desertion rate by South Carolina troops was lower than in other states.

After Sumter was taken, there was a lull in military action of several months insofar as South Carolina was concerned. On 7 November 1861, the Union, with twelve thousand troops, took the weakly fortified Forts Walker and Port Royal. The invading troops rounded up all the cotton and Negroes they could for use by the North. The Negroes were organized into the First Regiment of South Carolina Volunteers, later named the United States Colored Infantry, the first Negro military unit in the Union army. Charleston citizens were panicked by the overthrow of Beauregard at Port Royal. Believing their own city would surely be attacked sooner or later, they rushed to fortify it. Robert E. Lee was made commander of the Department of South Carolina and Georgia, and his mission was to defend the coastline. He had only 10,300 men to accomplish this impossible task and decided to abandon all the ports of South Carolina except Charleston.[13]

During 1862, minor battles were fought around Charleston that involved the various islands surrounding the city. In March 1863, these battles grew in intensity when the Union army launched the long expected attack on Charleston. They first surrounded Cole Island and Folly Island. Three thousand men then crossed over from Folly Island across Lighthouse Inlet to Morris Island. They bombed the fort there for fifty days, but the soldiers hidden in their "bombproofs" held out until the Union gave up the effort. They then attacked Fort Sumter in an attempt to retake it, but even though they reduced it to rubble with their shells, the Confederate troops there never capitulated. It remained in Southern hands throughout the war. It was a symbol of resistance only because its almost complete destruction had eliminated any military significance. Morris Island, however, did eventually capitulate, and there was heavy and continuous shelling of the fort at Sullivan's Island. Despite this, the Union ships were never able to put themselves into a position where they could run past the forts into Charleston Harbor.

Charleston remained a valuable base for the blockade runners. More goods were shipped out of that city to the European buyers and traders than any city except Wilmington, North Carolina. The operations involved the placing of cotton, tobacco, and other goods on fast, lightweight ships, racing by the heavy Union ships, and meeting the foreign traders from England or Scotland at rendezvous in the Caribbean. These commercial endeavors enriched the South, especially those private ship owners and investors who became fabulously wealthy after only two or three blockade runs. Fighting directly against the Union navy were several wooden ships and four ironclad vessels built at Charleston. The sea battles were never significant, however, as compared to the massive land battles along the coast and further inland.

Since there were few battles in South Carolina until the last few months, the state contributed manpower for use in other theaters of operation. In July 1863, South Carolina units were serving Lee's army at Gettysburg; under Generals Longstreet, Hill, and Stuart in Virginia; under General Johnston in Mississippi; and under General Bragg at Chattanooga. They were also stationed all along the South Carolina coast. Thousands of them saw action in many battles in Virginia and at Vicksburg, Mississippi.

During 1864, South Carolina lost some of its major cities. The Union accomplished the taking of Charleston on 17 February, aided by a detachment of Negro troops. The citizens and the local military troops evacuated the city ahead of the takeover, burning cotton to prevent it from falling into enemy hands. Then the Union troops made raids on the towns of Mannin, Sumter, and Camden before returning to their base at Georgetown. Wherever they went, they destroyed supplies as they found them.

The crushing end for South Carolina came in 1864 after General Sherman had completed his siege and capture of Atlanta. From there, he and his sixty thousand men marched to Savannah and took it also. They then split into two groups, one heading for Beaufort, and the other crossing the Savannah River at Two Sisters Ferry, plundering in South Carolina and on into Georgia. Their ultimate goal was Columbia, the capital of South Carolina. This city was considered the "hot bed of secessionism" and was the object of hatred by the entire North. The North blamed the war on South Carolina and their political leaders at Columbia. They entered that city with 65,000 soldiers, followed by 20,000 civilians who tagged along behind, intent on looting and pillaging as soon as they reached the city. These hangers-on included the so-called "bummers," deserters, and other renegades. Earlier, refugees from other parts of the state, running from the Union armies, had converged on the capital and were there before Sherman's men arrived. They, too, were caught up in the death and destruction which marked the arrival of the troops.

The governor and his legislature, assisted by what was left of the Confederate troops in the area, destroyed what military supplies they could and fled the city. Even before the Union soldiers arrived to loot, the Confederate soldiers before leaving did some looting of their own. The mayor surrendered the city on 17 February. The Union soldiers, believing General Sherman would appreciate it, initiated a mass burning of cotton and homes in revenge against their enemy. Contributing to their wild behavior that night was the large supply of liquor left behind. Sherman was later to say that he did not order the destruction of the city, but did not object to it after it had happened.

After they had razed Columbia, Sherman and his army headed north to North Carolina, where he was soon to accept the Confederate surrender of Gen. Joseph E. Johnston at Durham. The war had ended and South Carolina, so eager for battle four years before, lay dead and dying--unknowingly looking forward only to a regime of northern carpetbaggers and scalawags. Slavery, their main cause for fighting, had been outlawed by the Emancipation Proclamation and an amendment to the Constitution of the United States. They had no recourse but to accept that fact.

Military Units

The National Archives has the compiled service records for the personnel who served in Confederate units from South Carolina as listed below. They may be found in Microcopy 267, consisting of 392 rolls. See chapter four for a complete description of this series.

First Cavalry
First Mounted Militia
Second Cavalry
Second Battalion, Cavalry Reserves
Third Cavalry
Fourth Cavalry
Fourth Battalion, Cavalry
Fourth Regiment, Cavalry Militia
Fifth through Seventh Cavalry
Tenth Battalion, Cavalry
Twelfth Battalion, Cavalry (Fourth Squadron Cavalry)
Fourteenth Battalion, Cavalry
Seventeenth (Sixth) Battalion, Cavalry
Nineteenth Battalion, Cavalry
Capt. A. W. Cordes' Company, Cavalry (North Santee Mounted Rifles)
Capt. Theodore Cordes' Company, Cavalry Militia (German Hussars)
De Saussure's Squadron of Cavalry
Capt. A. C. Earle's Cavalry
Captain Kirk's Company, Partisan Rangers
Captain Rodger's Company, Cavalry (State Troops)
Captain Rutledge's Company, Cavalry Militia (Charleston Light Dragoons)
Captain Simon's Company, Volunteers (Etiwan Rangers)
Captain Trenholm's Company, Militia (Rutledge Mounted Riflemen)
Captain Tucker's Company, Cavalry
Captain Walpole's Company, Cavalry (Stono Scouts)
First Artillery
First Regiment Artillery, Militia
Second Artillery
Third (Palmetto) Battalion, Light Artillery
Manigault's Battalion, Artillery

Fifteenth (Lucas') Battalion, Heavy Artillery

Captain Bachman's Company, Artillery (German Light Artillery)

Captain Beauregard's Company, Light Artillery (Ferguson's Company, Light Artillery)

Captain Child's Company, Artillery

Captain Fickling's Company, Artillery (Brooks Light Artillery)

Captain Gaillard's Company, Light Artillery (Santee Light Artillery)

Captain Garden's Company, Light Artillery (Palmetto Light Battery)

Captain Gilchrist's Company, Heavy Artillery (Gist Guard)

Captain Gregg's Company, Artillery (McQueen Light Artillery)

Captain Hart's Company, Horse Artillery, Volunteers (Washington Artillery)

Captain Jeter's Company, Light Artillery (Macbeth Light Artillery)

Capt. J. T. Kanapaux's Company, Light Artillery (Lafayette Artillery)

Captain Kelly's Company, Light Artillery (Chesterfield Artillery)

Captain Lee's Company, Artillery

Captain Mathewes' Company, Heavy Artillery

Captain Melchers' Company, Artillery (Company B, German Artillery)

Captain Parker's Company, Light Artillery (Marion Artillery)

Captain Stuart's Company, Artillery (Beaufort Volunteer Artillery)

Captain Wagener's Company, Light Artillery (Company A, German Artillery)

Captain Walter's Company, Light Artillery (Washington Artillery)

Captain Mayham Ward's Company, Artillery (Waccamaw Light Artillery)

Captain Zimmerman's Company, Artillery (Pee Dee Artillery)

First (Butler's) Infantry

First (Hagood's) Infantry

First (McCreary's) Infantry (First Provincial Army)

First (Orr's) Rifles

First Infantry (six months, 1861)

First Regiment, Militia (Charleston Reserves)

First Regiment Charleston Guards

First State Troops (six months, 1863-64)

First (Charleston) Battalion, Infantry (Gaillard's Battalion)

First Battalion, Sharp Shooters

First Regiment Rifles, Militia (Branch's Rifle Regiment)

Second Infantry (Second Palmetto Regiment)

Second Rifles

Second State Troops (six months, 1863-64)
Second Reserves (ninety days, 1862-63)
Second Battalion Sharp Shooters
Third Infantry
Third (Lawren's and James') Battalion, Infantry
Third Reserves (ninety days, 1862-63)
Third Battalion Reserves
Third State Troops (six months, 1863-64)
Fourth Infantry
Fourth State Troops (six months, 1863-64)
Fourth Battalion, Reserves
Fifth Infantry
Fifth State Troops (six months, 1863-64)
Fifth Reserves (ninety days, 1862-63)
Fifth (Brown's) Battalion, Reserves
Fifth Militia
Sixth Infantry
Sixth Reserves (ninety days, 1862-63)
Sixth (Byrd's) Battalion, Infantry
Sixth (Merriwether's) Battalion, Reserves
Seventh Infantry
Seventh Reserves (ninety days, 1862-63)
Seventh (Ward's) Battalion, State Reserves
Seventh (Nelson's) Battalion, Infantry (Enfield Rifles)
Eighth Infantry
Eighth Reserves
Eighth (Stalling's) Battalion, Reserves
Ninth Infantry
Ninth Reserves (ninety days, 1862-63)
Ninth Battalion, Infantry (Pee Dee Legion)
Tenth Infantry
Eleventh Infantry (Ninth Volunteers)
Eleventh Reserves (ninety days, 1862-63)
Twelfth Infantry
Thirteenth Infantry
Thirteenth Battalion, Infantry (Fourth and Mattison's)
Fourteenth Infantry

Fifteenth Infantry
Sixteenth Infantry (Greenville Regiment)
Sixteenth Regiment, Militia
Seventeenth Infantry
Seventeenth Regiment, Militia
Eighteenth Infantry
Eighteenth Regiment, Militia
Nineteenth through Twenty-second Infantry
Twenty-third Infantry (Hatch's Regiment, Coast Rangers)
Twenty-fourth Infantry
Twenty-fourth Militia
Sixteenth and Twenty-fourth (Consolidated) Infantry
Twenty-fifth Infantry (Eutaw Regiment)
Twenty-fifth Militia
Twenty-sixth Infantry
Twenty-seventh Infantry (Gaillard's Regiment)
Battalion State Cadets, Local Defense Troops Charleston
Captain Carbonnier's Company, Militia (Pickens Rifles)
Charleston Arsenal Battalion
Conscripts, South Carolina
Captain Estill's Company, Infantry, Local Defense (Arsenal Guard, Charleston)
Captain Hamilton's Company, Provost Guard
Hampton Legion
Holcombe Legion
Manigualt's Battalion, Volunteers
Ordnance Guards (Captain Dotterer)
Palmetto (First Palmetto) Sharp Shooters (Jenkins Regiment)
Captain Rhett's Company (Brooks Home Guards)
Captain Senn's Company, Post Guard
Captain Shiver's Company
Captain Simon's Company
South Carolina (Walker's) Battalion, Infantry
Captain Symons' Company, Sea Fencibles
Miscellaneous, South Carolina

TENNESSEE
STATE LIBRARY AND ARCHIVES
403 Seventh Avenue North, Nashville 37219
(just south of the Capitol)

HOURS: 8:00 a.m.-8:00 p.m., Monday-Saturday
    12:30 p.m.-9:00 p.m., Sunday
closed: national holidays, Good Friday and election days (primary and general). Closed on the weekend when a holiday falls on Friday or Monday. Open on most state holidays.

This is a combined archives and library, and Confederate records may be found in both. The archives contains microfilmed records and has an extensive manuscript section also. The library contains published Confederate records as well as some burial records. Although you must register in the outer lobby as you enter and your belongings are subject to search as you leave the building, security generally is relaxed with few inner controls. The lobby of the building houses the card catalog to the library holdings. Indexes of microfilmed records are found on a shelf just inside the archives section, and guides to the manuscript section are in a room at the far end of the archives section. You should ask staff to point out those particular guides. You may help yourself to the rolls in the microfilm room which is adjacent to the archives section.

If you write from outside the state, the staff will make no searches for you in the records which pertain to Confederate military service. Rather they will refer you to the National Archives. If you ask specifically for pension material, however, they will assist you since the National Archives does not have that type of material. Do not send any money in advance; you will be billed after the material is located. At that time you will be charged only for copying. At this writing, a copy of a pension application costs $3.00. The supporting papers found in a pension file will be copied for an additional $3.00. Copies of military records (available to Tennessee residents or those who visit the archives in person) are copied for a fee of $5.00. Other material found in any of the various record groups will be copied for $1.00 per page.

National Archives Microfilm

This archives has purchased the following microfilm from the National Archives, and it is available in the microfilm room. See chapter four for a complete description of these series.

Consolidated Index to Compiled Service Records of Confederate Soldiers (all states). M253 (535 rolls).

Index to Compiled Service Records of Confederate Soldiers Who Served in Organizations From the State of Tennessee. M231 (48 rolls).

Compiled Service Records of Confederate Soldiers Who Served in Organizations From the State of Tennessee. M268 (359 rolls).

Records Relating to Confederate Naval and Marine Personnel. M260 (7 rolls).

Pensions

In 1891, Tennessee enacted its first Confederate pension law and created a five member Board of Pension Examiners to administer the program. Three of the members were ex-Confederate soldiers. Eligible for a pension were those who had been honorably discharged from a Confederate military unit, were indigent to the point that they were incapable of "making a support," and had been a resident of Tennessee for at least one year. Widows also became eligible in 1905.

The pension applications contain detailed information about military service including wounds, a description of any property owned, and much family data. Often there is included a report of military service obtained from the War Department records or from affidavits from comrades-in-arms. Widows' applications had to show proof of marriage. Negroes were also eligible for a pension if they qualified. The information required on the application was the same as for whites, but it identified the applicant's owner in those cases where he had been a slave. The file also had to contain a statement from some resident who testified that the applicant's "habits are good and free of dishonor." Often, the former owners or their family provided such statements. Parenthetically, the applications for white applicants inquired into the use of intoxicants, but no such question was asked of Negro applicants.

The applications are separated into three groups: "soldiers," "colored soldiers," and "widows." In 1964, when these applications were indexed, there were 16,693 in the first category, 285 in the second category, and 11,180 in the third category. This published index may be found on the shelf just inside the archives section. After each name are notations about the military unit, if he had served in some unit organized outside Tennessee.

In 1903, the legislature did not appropriate enough funds to enable the payment of all the approved applications, so a program was initiated to purge the rolls of those who were either no longer eligible under the law or whose needs were less severe than others. To accomplish this screening, a questionnaire was sent to all pensioners then on the rolls. The questionnaire inquired about the person's physical condition, financial status, size and members of his family, and occupation.

The pension applications and the supporting papers are in fragile condition and are not available to the public. They have been microfilmed, however, and you may find them in the sixty rolls in the drawers labeled "Soldiers' Pension applications" and the three rolls labeled "Colored Soldiers' pensioners."

Military Service Records

It is suggested that when attempting to find some record of Confederate military service you first consult the two volume work published by the Civil War Centennial Commission, entitled *Tennesseans in the Civil War, a Military History of Confederate and Union Units, with Available Roster of Personnel.* This is divided into two sections, "Confederate Rosters" and "Federal Rosters." Names are in alphabetical order, and the name or number of the military units is shown. These rosters were obtained primarily from the compiled service records housed at the National Achives, but additional names were added as gleaned from such sources as newspaper items, regimental and other unit histories, county histories, personal letters, and graveyard inscriptions.

There are also three rolls in the microfilm room entitled "Confederate Muster Rolls." These are copies of the rolls loaned to the War Department when it created the compiled service records mentioned above. The original rolls are not available to the public.

In the manuscript room, at the far end of the archives section (described later), are "Commission Books" which list the names of officers of the state militia units for various time periods. Volume seven covers the years of the Civil War. It has two parts. The first covers the years 1861-1862, and the names are not in alphabetical order. The second covers the years 1862-1865, and the names are in alphabetical order. These lists are also available on microfilm and may be found on roll three in the series labeled "state militia."

Miscellaneous State Records
Manuscript Room

At the far end of the archives section is a small room devoted to manuscript material. Staff stationed there will assist you, but there are three primary aids which will enable you to locate the material you need without assistance. One of these is the card catalog along the wall. This lists the manuscripts available on microfilm. All the manuscripts have been placed on microfilm, but sometimes it is easier to locate a reference to a certain document in one of the two other finding aids to be found in this room. These are two pamphlets found on top of a file cabinet. One is labeled "Register No. 10--Civil War Collection, Confederate and Federal" and the other is a pamphlet labeled "Record Group Numbers . . . ." Each of these is discussed below.

Microfilm Catalog. First, find a heading "Civil War." Under this heading are cards which refer to specific titles and collections. The cards show the box number, accession number, folio number, or microfilm (Mf) number. These numbers are needed as you prepare a call slip whether you want the originals brought to you or whether you search for the rolls yourself in the microfilm room. One of the cards in this catalog is titled "Confederate Collection (Register 10)." At this point you may go directly to the pamphlet described below.

Register Number 10--Civil War Collection. In this green pamphlet you will find titles of material which may interest you along with references to box numbers, accession numbers, folio numbers, and microfilm numbers. The holdings described in this pamphlet are arranged in four parts:

1. Documents arranged by box number. A few examples of the types of papers found in this category are: casualty lists--Tennessee; diaries (by

name); letters (by name); military units (by state and regiment); hospital registers, Memphis (a separately wrapped volume); order books, fifth regiment, Tennessee Cavalry (a separately wrapped volume).

2. An alphabetical index of persons, places, military units, and various other subjects. A few examples of the types of papers found in this category are: Browning, Ben--mention of; Bryant, Jesse--sketch of; Eastman, E. G.--obituary; Seth, Henry--one letter; Jefferson County--Confederate veterans roster.

3. A name index of correspondence contained in boxes 24-30.

4. An index of clippings regarding military units (arranged by state and name or number of the regiment).

Record Group Numbers. This blue pamphlet lists the material available according to particular collections, each with its own "record group number." Examples are:

1. Adjutant General's Office--record group 21. These records cover the years beginning in 1796, although the bulk of them are concerned with the Civil War era. They are arranged by subject.

2. Civil War Centennial Commission--record group 22.

3. Confederate Soldiers' Home--record group 2.

4. Army of the Tennessee--Correspondence--record group 4. This collection is primarily concerned with the years 1861-65, and consists of letters, medical records, some muster rolls, quartermaster records, and some militia rolls.

Using the reference numbers on the microfilm card catalog or in the two above described pamphlets, you may request the original manuscript or go directly to the microfilm room and help yourself. There, you should locate the cabinets labeled "Manuscripts Collection." Then you will see thirty-three drawers labeled "Microfilmed Manuscripts." After you finish examining the rolls you select, leave them on a table in that room; do not refile them yourself.

Miscellaneous State Records
Census of Pensioners

A four page questionnaire was sent out in 1914 and 1915 to all known Tennessee Civil War soldiers, both Union and Confederate. A revised version was also sent out in 1920 (returned in 1922). There were 1,466 Confederate questionnaires, and they are stored in the manuscript room. Consisting of seven rolls, they are also available in the microfilm room under catalog number 484. An index is available at the front of each roll, and there is a printed index on the shelf just inside the archives section. The index lists the names in alphabetical order, and the county of residence and military unit is shown. An asterisk opposite some of the names indicates that the respondent voluntarily submitted additional material that is often of historical significance.

The questionnaires provide much valuable genealogical data. In addition to identifying personal and military history, they asked for a description of his occupation and the property he owned, including slaves, at the time of the war. Similar information was requested about his parents. Several questionnares asked for facts concerning the slave culture in the respondent's area at the time of the war. For example, the following were asked: "To what extent were the white men in your community leading lives of idleness and having others do their work for them?" and "Did slave owners mingle freely with non-slave holders?" There were also questions regarding education and religion. Inquiries also were made regarding how the veteran managed to return to his home after his discharge or release from military duty. Also, he was asked to give the names of the other soldiers in his unit, insofar as he could remember.

Confederate Home

A state Confederate Home was established in 1889 at the Hermitage, just outside Nashville. Records containing the names of residents of this home are retained and indexed in the manuscript room, both in the original and on microfilm. There are two file drawers of applications for admission and five columns of related correspondence and business papers. These are in record group 2, divided into five series. Series one consists of nine boxes of applications, alphabetically arranged. Series five is a register of inmates.

Records of Burials

Mr. Raymond W. Watkins, a Virginia resident, has been engaged for years in tracking down burial places of Confederate soldiers. He submits copies of his findings to some of the archives and libraries in Southern states. Those which have been received by Tennessee are found in the library in a "vertical file, labeled "Confederate Burials--(state)" or "Confederate Burials--Tennessee." The names are not indexed, but each of Mr. Watkins' submissions is in alphabetical order.

United Daughters of the Confederacy Applications

Six chapters of the United Daughters of the Confederacy were organized in Tennessee between 1894 and 1896. Applications for membership received during that period were turned over to the State Library in 1909. All subsequent applications were turned over to the archives section and may be found in the manuscript room. These applications were not indexed until two volumes were published as a bicentennial project. Volume one covers the years 1894-1924, and volume two covers the years 1924-1978. Names are arranged according to the Confederate veteran which was used as the basis for membership. Alongside are the names of the members with birthdates, and counties of residence. There are a few males included in these papers because the early applications included those from young persons desiring to become members of the Children of the Confederacy.

TENNESSEE'S ROLE IN THE WAR

In some of the Southern states prior to 1860, there was a pre-existing feeling that they must some day separate from the United States. Such was not the case in Tennessee. Despite the fact that much of its agricultural economy was based on the slave culture that Northern abolitionists and their "underground railroad" universally hated, an overwhelming number of the Tennessee citizens did not entertain the thought of secession. They believed that more could be achieved by working within the system than by bolting from it. They were reluctant to be stampeded. For example, the delegates to the Democratic National Convention held at Charleston, South Carolina, on 23 April 1860, refused to join with those who split and formed a "states' rights" branch of the party. Rather, all twenty-four of the Tennessee delegates remained and went on to a later convention held at Baltimore instead of to the one held at Richmond where the "states' righters" met. With them at Baltimore were the delegates from Virginia, North Carolina, Kentucky, and Maryland, all of whom also had rejected the "states' rights" group.

Events occurring before the Baltimore meeting served to change the minds of many Tennesseans including the delegates to the convention. Nineteen of them walked out to meet with their Southern colleagues in Richmond. Many delegates from the other border states followed them. The split in the party resulted in both Douglas and Breckenridge running as Democrats. The Republican candidate, Lincoln, although he received only forty percent of the nation's popular vote, earned enough electoral votes to be elected to the presidency. His election was enough to send most of the Southern states into hurried conventions for the purpose of officially withdrawing from the Union--not so in Tennessee.

When the Tennessee legislature initiated a referendum for the people to decide whether to hold such a convention, the idea lost by a four-to-one margin. Those in West-Tennessee, however, wanted the convention and were in favor of secession. Those in East-Tennessee, separated by a range of mountains and with economic needs wholly different from those of the western plantation owners, were heavily against the convention and were strongly pro-Union. Those in Mid-Tennessee were evenly split on the issue. An example of the widely different beliefs in one part of the state was the emotion displayed by the citizens of Franklin County. They petitioned to be moved out of Tennessee so they could join Alabama as full-fledged Confederates. After the first shot was fired at Sumter, the men of that county boarded trains and enlisted for military duty at Montgomery, Alabama. At the same time, those in East-Tennessee stole into Kentucky and enlisted in Union regiments.

Although Tennessee was not ready to secede, it did not believe that any action should be taken against the Southern states and felt that the federal government should let them go in peace. Governor Isham G. Harris spoke for his people when he replied to Lincoln's call for Tennessee troops to become part of the Union army. Harris replied, "Tennessee will not furnish a single man for purposes of coercion." Thereupon, he called the legislature into session on 25 April 1861. The legislature, sensing the drastically changed mood of the people, declared in favor of the South but agreed to a referendum by the people to be held 8 June. That vote went six to one in favor of secession. The exceptions were in strongly Unionist East-Tennessee.

To prepare for the inevitable, the governor permitted the Confederacy to establish a battery at Memphis as part of the move to fortify the various ports along the Mississippi River. He also bought arms from a New Orleans manufacturer to help defend his own state borders. On 2 July, he turned over all the Tennessee regiments with their horses, arms, and equipment, to the Confederate army with the understanding that the Confederacy would, in turn, defend the state against any invasion from the North.

The Confederate army appointed General Albert S. Johnston to head the operations in the entire area of Tennessee, Arkansas, and parts of Mississippi, Kentucky, Missouri, and the Arizona and Indian Territories. Johnston set up a "Line of the Cumberland" stretching from Columbus, Kentucky, on the Mississippi to the Cumberland Gap on the Virginia-Kentucky border. By November 1862, he had forty thousand troops, but most were ill-clothed and ill-equipped to do battle. Serving under him was General Leonidas Polk, commanding the Tennessee area with headquarters at Memphis.

During the many horrible battles which were to follow, only Virginia saw more bloodshed than did Tennessee. A part of the Union's overall strategy was to keep the pressure on Tennessee, to prevent a massing of the Confederate troops on the Atlantic Coast where the Union army hoped to conquer Richmond, and to crush the Confederate army in the East. The first Tennessee strongholds to fall were Forts Henry and Donelson on the Tennessee and Cumberland rivers near Nashville. Grant moved on those forts on 4 February 1862 before they could be strengthed sufficiently to withstand an attack. The men at Fort Henry were sent to Fort Donelson to make their stand. On 15 February, they were forced to surrender to Union naval troops. Grant's men had gotten mired in the mud and arrived late. When other Southern forts fell, the Line of the Cumberland collapsed, and Nashville was abandoned to the North. Union General Don Carlos Buell then rode in to panic the residents as he took control of the state capital.

General Johnston then decided to make a stand at Corinth, Mississippi, a supply line crossroad. With him were Generals Pierre G. T. Beauregard and Braxton Bragg. In order to surprise Grant and Sherman, who were also pushing to Corinth, Johnston met them at Shiloh Church, Tennessee, just north of the Mississippi state line, on 6 April 1862. A shocked Grant was pushed back all day, but after receiving ten thousand reinforcements, he initiated an attack of his own the next day forcing the Confederates to give up the fight. The losses on both sides were astronomical--more than thirteen thousand Union casualties and more than 10,600 Confederate casualties. The Confederate troops were so damaged that they could not mount another campaign for five months, and all the area of Tennessee, except the eastern portion, was controlled by the Union. After this battle at Shiloh, the Confederate army in that area was known as the Army of the Tennessee indicating the importance of this state in the war.

At Shiloh, General Johnston was twice wounded and finally bled to death from a gunshot to his thigh after he had ordered his physician to go forward to tend the other wounded. Replacing Johnston in the field was General Beauregard who had to take the brunt of Grant's attack on the second day of the battle. Later, at Corinth, Beauregard fell ill and General Bragg relieved him. He took the troops out of Corinth to fight again in Tennessee where he engaged the enemy in several victorious, but not really significant, battles in Mid-Tennessee. When Bragg met Buell in Kentucky, however, he had to fall back to Murfreesboro where he met Confederate General Forrest who had been engaged in Mid-Tennessee. For ineptitude in leadership while in Kentucky, apparently, General Buell was recalled to Nashville where he was criticised, faced a court-martial, and was replaced by Gen. William S. Rosecrans.

The next major battle in Tennessee took place on 1 January 1863, when Bragg fought Rosecrans to a standstill at Stone's River just outside Murfreesboro. He lost the battle the next day and on the third day retreated toward Chattanooga. Many felt that he had disgraced himself by having suffered 11,739 losses. Rosecrans, however, had lost 14,906 in his so-called victory, and his own troops were so weakened that they could not fight again for six months.

Bragg remained at Chattanooga until August 1863, when Union forces pushed him out of the city and into northern Georgia. He turned to face his enemy, General Rosecrans, on 18 September, on the banks of the Chickamauga River, a few miles southeast of Chattanooga. Bragg would have lost his entire army, but reinforcements by Gen. James Longstreet, with eleven thousand men, rushed at Rosecrans on the second day, sending Rosecrans reeling back to Chattanooga. The entire Union army would then have been lost had it not been for the troops under Gen. George H. Thomas, who refused to flee despite enduring many attacks. This stand gave Thomas his nickname, "The Rock of Chickamauga." Rather than pursue Rosecrans, Bragg decided to institute a siege of Chattanooga from the hills overlooking the city. In November, after having received supplies over the Tennessee River and with an augmented force of sixty thousand, the Union army moved out of the city toward Bragg who was in a dense fog at the base of Lookout Mountain. Thomas' troops scaled the mountain and took Missionary Ridge, above the city, and surprised the demoralized Confederate troops who fled into Georgia where they set up winter quarters. At the conclusion of this campaign and battle, the Union had secured the remaining part of Tennessee. It had cost the Union 5,824 troops, but the Confederates had lost 6,667.

In 1864, Sherman raced for Atlanta, pursuing General Joseph E. Johnston, who was charged with protecting that city. Becoming increasingly impatient, Jefferson Davis replaced Johnston with Gen. John B. Hood, who was given the command of the Army of the Tennessee. Hood, severely crippled from previous wounds, tried to surprise Sherman by making a quick dash across Northern Alabama and into Mid-Tennessee in an effort to cut his supply lines. With him marched thirty-eight thousand men. Sherman, intent on his "march to sea," dispatched his General Thomas to deal with Hood. They fought at Franklin, Tennessee, where Thomas lost approximately two thousand men. Hood lost three times that. They met again in December, and Hood lost so badly that he had to flee to the town of Pulaski and join up with General Forrest. The Union army was not interested in pursuing them any further because its supply lines had been saved intact and could now support Sherman in his drive eastward. This was the last major battle in Tennessee. Four months later, Lee and Johnston surrendered their troops in Virginia and North Carolina. The Tennessee soldiers who had fought at Nashville, reduced to about five thousand, joined Johnston at Durham to participate in the surrender.

When Governor Harris was chased out of Nashville early in 1862, he and the state officials set up a government in Mississippi. At the close of the war, when a Union controlled government was placed in charge of the state, it offered a reward for Harris' capture. He fled to Mexico. Replacing him at Nashville was a Lincoln appointee, Andrew Johnson. He assumed the post of military governor on 3 March 1862. His aggressive manner and strict control of the city met with disfavor and the citizens were relieved to see him go after two years of rule. During his regime he required loyalty oaths and sent those who refused to sign them to jail along with other Confederate sympathizers. A civil government made up of Unionist citizens was eventually established in December 1864. This move was taken by the federal government as a prelude to the state being taken back into the Union as quickly as possible. The new government amended the state constitution including a provision that slavery was abolished in the state. Thus, it was possible for Tennesee to become the first Confederate state to reenter the Union after the end of hostilities. Andrew Johnson, who had left the state to accept the nomination and election as vice-president of the United States, succeeded to the presidency after Lincoln was assasinated in April 1865. Tennessee and its citizens were left to cope with Johnson's reconstructionist agents.

The following year, in May 1866, a small group of educated men in Pulaski formed a harmless and amusing social club and named it Kuklos (Greek for "circle"). As a joke, they sometimes dressed up in white sheets and pretended to be ghosts of the Confederate dead. The Negro population became frightened at such shenanigans. The group became more encouraged to ride through the countryside scaring Negroes--just for the fun of it. With the excesses of radical Union reconstructionists, this group increasingly spoke out and were instrumental in lessening the burdens of the heavy hand of the conquerors. Eventually, as they formed into separate sub-groups, they referred to each local as Kucklos Klans--and later as Ku Klux Klans.[14]

Military Units

The National Archives has the compiled service records for the personnel who served in Confederate units from Tennessee as listed below. They may be found in Microcopy 268, consisting of 359 rolls. See chapter four for a complete description of this series.

First Cavalry
First (Carter's) Cavalry
First (McNairy's) Battalion, Cavalry
Second Cavalry
Second (Ashby's) Cavalry
Second (Smith's) Cavalry
Second (Biffle's) Battalion, Cavalry
Third (Forrest's) Cavalry
Fourth Cavalry
Fourth (McLemore's) Cavalry

Fourth (Murray's) Cavalry
Fourth (Branner's) Battalion, Cavalry
Fifth Cavalry
Fifth (McKenzie's) Cavalry
Fifth (McClellan's) Battalion, Cavalry
Sixth (Wheeler's) Cavalry
Seventh Cavalry
Seventh (Duckworth's) Cavalry
Seventh (Bennett's) Battalion, Cavalry
Eighth Cavalry
Eighth (Smith's) Cavalry
Ninth Cavalry
Ninth (Ward's) Cavalry
Ninth (Gantt's) Battalion, Cavalry
Tenth Cavalry
Tenth (De Moss') Cavalry
Tenth and Eleventh (Consolidated) Cavalry
Eleventh Cavalry
Eleventh (Gordon's) Battalion, Cavalry
Eleventh (Holman's) Cavalry
Twelfth Cavalry
Twelfth (Green's) Cavalry
Twelfth (Day's) Battalion, Cavalry
Thirteenth Cavalry
Thirteenth (Gore's) Cavalry
Fourteenth Cavalry
Fourteenth (Neely's) Cavalry
Fifteenth CavalryFifteenth (Consolidated) Cavalry
Fifteenth (Stewart's) Cavalry
Sixteenth Cavalry
Sixteenth (Logwood's) Cavalry
Sixteenth (Neal's) Battalion, Cavalry
Seventeenth Cavalry
Seventeenth (Sander's) Battalion, Cavalry
Eighteenth (Newsom's) Cavalry
Nineteenth (Biffle's) Cavalry
Nineteenth and Twentieth (Consolidated) Cavalry

Twentieth Cavalry
Twentieth (Russell's) Cavalry
Twenty-first Cavalry
Twenty-first (Carter's) Cavalry
Twenty-first (Wilson's) Cavalry
Twenty-first and Twenty-second (Consolidated) Cavalry
Twenty-second Cavalry
Twenty-second (Barteau's) Cavalry
Twenty-second (Nixon's) Cavalry
Twenty-eighth Cavalry
Allison's Squadron, Cavalry
Captain Clark's Independent Company, Cavalry
Cooper's Regiment, Cavalry
Cox's Battalion
Douglass' Battalion, Partisan Rangers
Greer's Regiment, Partisan Rangers
Holman's Battalion, Partisan Rangers
Captain Jackson's Company, Cavalry
Napier's Battalion, Cavalry
Newsom's Regiment, Cavalry
Nixon's Regiment, Cavalry
Capt. J. J. Parton's Company, Cavalry
Shaw's Battalion, Cavalry (Hamilton's Battalion)
Capt. Jeremiah C. Stone's Company A, Lyons Cavalry
Welcker's Battalion, Cavalry
Captain Williams' Company, Cavalry
Wilson's Regiment, Cavalry
Captain Woodward's Company, Cavalry
First Heavy Artillery (Jackson's Regiment)
Captain Barry's Company, Light Artillery (Lookout Artillery)
Captain Baxter's Company, Light Artillery
Captain Bibb's Company, Artillery (Washington Artillery)
Captain Browne's Company, Light Artillery
Captain Burrough's Company, Light Artillery (Rhett Artillery)
Caruther's Battery, Heavy Artillery
Captain Fisher's Company, Artillery (Nelson Artillery)
Captain Huggins' Company, Light Artillery

Captain Johnston's Company, Heavy Artillery (twelve months, 1861-62) (Southern Guards Artillery)
Captain Kain's Company, Light Artillery (Mabry Light Artillery)
Captain Lynch's Company, Light Artillery
Captain Marshall's Company, Artillery (Steuben Artillery)
McClung's Company, Light Artillery
Captain Morton's Company, Light Artillery
Captain Palmer's Company, Light Artillery (Reneau Battery)
Captain Phillips' Company, Light Artillery (Johnson Light Artillery)
Captain Polk's Battery, Light Artillery
Captain Ramsey's Battery, Artillery
Captain Rice's Battery, Light Artillery
Captain Scott's Company, Light Artillery
Captain Sparkman's Company, Light Artillery (Maury Artillery)
Captain Sterling's Company, Heavy Artillery
Captain Stewart's Company, Artillery
Captain Tobin's Company, Light Artillery (Memphis Light Battery)
Captain Weller's Company, Light Artillery
Captain Winson's Company, Light Artillery (Belmont Battery)
First Zouaves
First Light Artillery (First Battalion, Light Artillery) First Artillery (McCown's) Corps
First (Field's) Infantry
First (Turney's) Infantry
First (Field's) and Twenty-seventh (Consolidated) Infantry
First Consolidated Regiment, Infantry
First (Colms') Battalion, Infantry
Second (Robison's) Infantry (Walker Legion)
Second (Walker's) Infantry
Second Consolidated Regiment, Infantry
Third (Clack's) Infantry
Third (Lillard's) Mounted Infantry
Third Consolidated Regiment, Infantry
Third (Memphis) Battalion, Infantry
Fourth Infantry
Fourth Consolidated Regiment, Infantry
Fifth through Twelfth Infantry

Twelfth (Consolidated) Infantry
Thirteenth through Twenty-first Infantry
Twenty-second Infantry (Freeman's) Regiment
Twenty-second Battalion, Infantry
Twenty-third Infantry (Martin's) Regiment
Twenty-third (Newman's) Battalion, Infantry
Twenty-fourth Infantry
Twenty-fourth (Maney's) Battalion, Sharp Shooters
Twenty-fifth Infantry
Twenty-sixth Infantry (Third East Tennessee Volunteers)
Twenty-seventh Infantry
Twenty-eighth Infantry (Second Mountain Regiment Volunteers)
Twenty-eighth (Consolidated) Infantry
Twenty-ninth Infantry
Thirtieth Infantry
Thirty-first Infantry (Colonel A. H. Bradford)
Thirty-second Infantry
Thirty-third Infantry
Thirty-fourth Infantry (Fourth Confederate Regiment, Infantry)
Thirty-fifth Infantry (Fifth Regiment Provision Army, Mountain Rifle
    Regiment)
Thirty-sixth Infantry
Thirty-seventh Infantry (Seventh Regiment Provisional Army, First East
    Tennessee Rifle Regiment)
Thirty-eighth Infantry (Eighth Infantry, Looney's Regiment)
Thirty-ninth Mounted Infantry (Colonel W. M. Bradford's Regiment,
    Volunteers, Thirty-first Infantry)
Fortieth Infantry (Walker's Regiment, Volunteers, Fifth Confederate
    Infantry)
Forty-first Infantry
Forty-second Infantry
Forty-third Infantry (Fifth East Tennessee Volunteers, Gillespie's Regiment)
Forty-fourth Infantry
Forty-fourth (Consolidated) Infantry
Forty-fifth Infantry
Forty-sixth Infantry
Forty-seventh Infantry

Forty-eighth (Nixon's) Infantry

Forty-eighth (Voorheis') Infantry

Forty-ninth Infantry

Fiftieth Infantry

Fiftieth (Consolidated) Infantry

Fifty-first Infantry

Fifty-first (Consolidated) Infantry

Fifty-second through Fifty-fourth Infantry

Fifty-fifth (Brown's) Infantry

Fifty-fifth (McKoin's) Infantry

Fifty-ninth Mounted Infantry (Cooke's Regiment, First Easkin's) Battalion, Infantry

Sixtieth Mounted Infantry (Crawford's Regiment, Seventy-ninth Infantry)

Sixty-first Mounted Infantry (Pitts' Regiment, Eighty-first Infantry)

Sixty-second Mounted Infantry (Rowan's Regiment, Eightieth Infantry)

Sixty-third Infantry (Fain's Regiment, Seventy-fourth Infantry)

Eighty-fourth Infantry

One Hundred and Twenty-first Regiment, Militia

One Hundred and Fifty-fourth Senior Regiment, Infantry (First Volunteers)

Lieutenant Blair's Company (Local Defense Troops)

Conscripts, Tennessee

Crew's Battalion, Infantry

Detailed Conscripts, Tennessee (Local Defense and Special Service Troops, Nitre and Mining Bureau)

Engineers Corps, Tennessee

Harman's Regiment, Infantry

Captain McLin's Company, Volunteers (Local Defense Troops)

Captain Miller's Company (Local Defense Troops)

Nashville (Hawkins') Battalion, Infantry

Captain Park's Company (Local Defense Troops)

Captain Sowell's Detachment, Infantry

Captain Spencer's Company, Infantry

Sullivan County Reserves (Local Defense Troops)

Captain Tackitt's Company, Infantry

Miscellaneous, Tennessee

TEXAS
ARCHIVES DIVISION, STATE LIBRARY
1201 Brazos Street, Austin
P.O. Box 12927, Capitol Station, Austin 78711
(on the Capitol grounds)

HOURS: 8:00 a.m.-5:00 p.m., Monday-Friday
The genealogy section of the library is also open on Saturday.
closed: state holidays

As you register at the front desk of the search room you will be given an identification number, which must be placed on all request forms you submit during your visit. All briefcases, purses, camera cases, books, notebooks, writing pads, and outer clothing must be placed in a locker provided for that purpose. Paper and pencils are provided in the search room. All material taken out of the room is subject to search.

You will be assigned a specific table where you will notice a copy of *A Guide to Genealogical Resources in the Texas State Archives*. Document markers and order forms for copies will also be on the table. The pamphlet is available for sale at a nominal price and you may consider purchasing one for home study. An order form is used for each set of copies you wish to have made. Take the form and the material you want copied to a desk in a corner of the search room. If you have a box of material, do not take the papers you want copied out of the box--take the entire box to the desk. Should you want two or more copies of pension applications, only one will be made at a time to prevent misfiling.

To see any paper or collection of papers you must submit a request form on which you place the title and call number. Staff will then bring the material to your desk where you may examine it. The titles and call numbers are found in the many card indexes in the file cabinets on one wall of the room and in finding aids notebooks on a shelf near the center of the room or just adjacent to the front desk.

National Archives Microfilm

The State Library is located in the opposite wing of the building. There you will find a series of microfilm which was purchased from the National

Archives. See chapter four for a complete description of this series. It is titled *Index to Compiled Service Records of Confederate Soldiers Who Served in Organizations From the State of Texas.* M227 (41 rolls). In addition to this series, you will also find a seven-roll series of Texas muster rolls titled *Confederate Military Service Records.* A staff member will show you where to find these microfilm series.

Pensions

In 1881, Texas set aside 1,280 acres of land to be given to veterans or widows of veterans who were permanently disabled from wounds received in the service of either Texas or the Confederate States. In 1889, a pension law was enacted providing for cash awards to disabled veterans or their widows. Except for certain disabled persons, those who were under age sixty or had come to Texas after 1880 were not eligible. Any person who was disabled because of wounds received while in the Confederate forces for a period of at least three months, who had not deserted, and who was indigent was eligible. A widow who had married a qualifying veteran prior to 1 March 1866, who had been a Texas resident prior to 1 March 1880, and was indigent, was also eligible. "Indigency" was defined in the law as being "in actual want and destitute of property and means of subsistence."

In 1925, an amendment to the pension law enabled those who ad come to Texas before 1910 and widows born before 1861 to receive a pension. This amendment also blanketed in veterans of military actions against the Indians and Mexican raiders as well as those in state militia who saw active duty during the Civil War.

Applications and accompanying papers were submitted to the county judge, then to the county commissioners, and finally to the state Comptroller of Public Accounts for payment. The application asked questions concerning personal identification, occupation, military history, and county of residence. A widow's application also showed the husband's place and date of death, her own birthplace and age, and the date of her marriage.

In 1917, the law was amended again to provide payment for burial expenses provided the heirs filed within forty days of the pensioner's death. Such payments were made in the form of "Confederate Mortuary Warrants," and copies of those warrants were placed in the pension file. These warrants show the facts surrounding the death of the pensioner, the relationship of the person who petitioned for the payment, and the name of the person in whose home the pensioner died.

Many genealogy libraries have a copy of the publication *Index to Applications for Texas Confederate Pensions* (see chapter four), but this archives has a more complete index in which the errors found in the published version are corrected. The 1977 revision is titled *Index to Applications for Confederate Pensions, With Supplemental Indexes.* It may be found on the shelf in the center of the search room. It contains three parts: "Approved Applications," "Confederate Home Inmates," and "Rejected Applications for Pensions." The supplemental portion contains the names of those whose application had been missing, where positive identification had not been possible, or who were omitted for some other reason. As a further guide to the above, there is a green binder located near the front desk titled *Index to Rejected Pension Applications*. Since this list may not exactly match the other index of the same name, it may pay to check both of them. Given is the file number, county of residence, and the name of the widow's husband.

You will be permitted to examine a pension application after submitting a request form. The file number, or in the case of a rejected application the person's name, is to be used as the call number. The files have not been microfilmed.

Military Service Records
Muster Roll Cards

During the 1930s and 1940s, the Work Projects Administration (WPA) created a card index of names of persons who served in Texas military units. One part of that index includes seventy-seven thousand cards pertaining to men in the Texas militia during the Civil War years, whether or not they were eventually transferred to a regular state or Confederate unit. The cards also include names of some persons in Confederate units stationed in Texas. Information on the cards was taken from muster rolls but also from "returns of elections of officers." The original rolls and related papers are too fragile to permit public inspection, and they have not been microfilmed. Therefore, the only source of information concerning these men are the cards in this index. The cards may be found in a file cabinet along one wall of the search room.

Memorials and Petitions

Several persons filed claims in the state legislature for compensation for some kinds of military service during the Civil War, and these may give some information about the claimant's military history. There is a card index of the names of these persons, and it may be found in a file cabinet along one wall of the search room. The call number to request the actual document is shown on the index card.

Miscellaneous State Records
Confederate Soldiers' Home

Private donations supported the Texas Confederate Home between 1886, when it was opened, to 1891 when the state assumed responsibility for it. In 1963 it was turned over to the Austin State Hospital, and the veterans in residence at that time were transferred to the Kerrville State Hospital. A similar home for wives and widows of Confederate veterans plus other women who had contributed to the Confederate cause was established in 1908 under the auspices of the United Daughters of the Confederacy. The state took it over in 1911 and continued to support it until 1864 when it was closed.

A black notebook on a shelf near the center of the search room titled "Confederate Homes" gives some information about the residents. It is in three parts as described below.

Part One--the Men's Home. The names of the residents of this home are indexed on the first letter and according to the files which were kept at the home until they were turned over to the archives. Before a resident's file is brought to you, however, a staff member must review it and delete any medical type information which is considered to be of a confidential nature. This restriction applies to everyone including the resident's direct descendants.

Part Two--The Women's Home. This index is identical to the one pertaining to the men's home and the same restrictions apply.

Part Three--Roster Index. This index contains the names of the residents of both homes. Since they were taken from ledgers and journals maintained by the homes, there is no medical information. As noted earlier, there is also a section listing "Confederate Home Inmates" as a part of the *Index to Applications for Confederate Pensions.*

Lists of Confederate Indigent Families

Texas was careful to try to support needy families of men who were away from home serving in the Confederate forces or who were killed or disabled in such service. The chief justice of each county, on or before 1 March (in 1864 and 1865), submitted lists of dependents deemed eligible for financial relief. The county clerk then dispensed the state money provided for this purpose. The names of the recipients have been indexed and are available in a green binder located in a rack near the front desk of the search room. The files may be requested and examined. In preparing the call slip, use the number "304-186" for those persons from the counties of Anderson through Hunt. Use number "304-187" for those persons from the counties of Jackson through Wood.

Graves of Civil War Veterans

As part of the Civil War Centennial, the Texas State Historical Commission undertook a project to locate as many Civil War veterans' graves in Texas as possible. Their findings were turned over to the archives and are available for inspection. In addition to the purely identifying data found on the stones, there is considerable biographical information and military history.

Supplementing the above collection are lists of Confederate graves found by a Virginia resident, Mr. Raymond W. Watkins. He has spent several years locating Confederate graves wherever they may be found. As a courtesy, he submits lists of his findings from time to time to certain Southern archives. An index card is prepared and placed in a file cabinet known as the "Raymond W. Watkins Collection." That cabinet may be found on one wall of the search room. A call number on each card will refer you to the specific list submitted by Mr. Watkins.

TEXAS' ROLE IN THE WAR

If such had been possible, Texas should never have entered the Civil War at all, either as a Confederate or a Union state. But heavy and unrelenting propaganda and fear seduced most of the state's leaders and its citizens into joining with the Southern states. Plantations and the use of slaves was just beginning to gain a foothold in the state, and withdrawal from the Union was much too high a price to pay for the miniscule benefits to be gained from such action. Large scale agriculture in Texas at that time would have been unprofitable because the railroads had just barely nudged across its borders and transporting large crops would have been a problem. Texas had only recently been an independent republic--split off from Mexico--and accepted into the United States. The people were proud to be called Americans, but the overwhelming pressure on them from subversive elements convinced them that an abolitionist government would mean their ruination. Most of all, fear of Negro rebellion panicked the citizens, and the threat of "Africanization" scared all classes, rich and poor.

Fanning the flames of fear and dissension was an expanding organization called The Knights of the Golden Circle. It organized units throughout the state preaching the doctrine of "White Supremacy" and seeking out any whites who "tampered with" the Negro, such as teaching him to read and write or engaging him in any efforts of self-help. Often such persons as well as the Negro who had been "tampered with" were beaten or even hanged from a tree and left to dangle as an example to others. It was this far-right group that insisted that Governor Sam Houston call a special convention for the purpose of secession. He refused to be pushed because of his strong belief that leaving the Union would be a grave mistake. In reply, he pointed out that when Texas agreed to enter the Union, it agreed it would not enter into a compact with any other state without the express authority of the federal government. Soon, though, he was compelled to call the legislature into session to deal with the problem. That group, on 28 January 1861, voted to call a convention with power to act in behalf of the people of Texas--without regard, apparently, to the wishes or authority of the governor. At the same time, a Committee of Public Safety was established to prepare for defense against any resistance by Union troops stationed within the state.

Since the matter to be settled at the convention was to be submitted to a final vote of the people on 23 February, the Knights of the Golden Circle stepped up its campaign of terror to stifle any resistance. They beat up and killed anyone who dared speak out against secession. During this waiting period, a West Point graduate from Virginia, Robert E. Lee, came to San Antonio for a visit. Commenting on the politics of the day, he said, ". . . I can anticipate no greater calamity for the country than a dissolution of the Union. It is folly to talk of secession."[15]

Governor Houston, confronted with a plan to have federal troops come into Texas to put down the rebellion, reluctantly declined to ask for or to accept them.

The convention met at Austin on 28 January boycotted largely by the counties which were leaning toward Unionism. The delegates who were present passed an ordinance of secession on 1 February by an almost unanimous vote. When the people of the state voted, there were 46,129 for secession as opposed to 14,697 for staying in the Union. Of course, this did not include the thousands who probably were too frightened to go to the polls. Propaganda and personal pressure were the easy winners. The legislature amended the state constitution and included provisions for the signing of oaths of loyalty to the new government. When Houston and his secretary of state refused to sign, they were removed from office. Lieutenant Governor Edward Clark assumed the governorship. Houston went to his home at Huntsville and stayed. Despite the fact that he was known as the father of the state and was the one who dreamed of leading Texas to even greater glory, he remained in virtual exile until he died 26 July 1863.

When Texas geared up to fight, the Confederate States declined the state's offer, stating that the war would probably end soon and that the fighting would take place in the East anyway--too far away for Texans to travel. Later, of course, the Confederacy became desperate for manpower and welcomed them. When the Confederacy passed conscripton laws with their exemptions of slave owners and overseers and also enacted the "Act for Confiscation of Property," the Texans were far from enthusiastic. The latter law specified that all "alien property" was to be taken over by the Confederacy. Included in the definition of "alien property" was any asset for which a citizen was still in debt to a Northerner (thus partially owned by the Northerner). Many Texans, heavily in debt, lost everything as a result of that legislation. Recent immigrants, especially those with German backgrounds, objected to those measures, but when they spoke out in favor of the Union, the bands of the Knights of the Golden Circle burned them out or killed them--forcing the others to flee from the state.

The first act of war in Texas was a massive act of treason by David E. Twiggs, a general in the United States army in command of all the forts and troops in Texas. Rather than resign his post with honor, as did the other federal officers who chose to side with the Confederacy, Twiggs maneuvered his troops together, abandoned nineteen federal forts in the state to the

Confederacy, and moved to San Antonio with his army. He dallied there two weeks until Confederate General Ben McCulloch, with only a handful of soldiers, came to town to recruit troops and procure ammunition and arms. As soon as he took over the Alamo, then being used as a military storehouse, he called on Twiggs and suggested he surrender. He immediately accepted the suggestion. Since Texas was not yet offically at war, Twiggs and his men with their arms were permitted to leave the city--flying their colors. Before they reached their port of embarkation, however, Fort Sumter had been fired upon. Twiggs was called upon to surrender his troops then comprising about one-tenth of the Union army with about three million dollars in arms and equipment. Twiggs was officially dismissed from the Union army because of his treason, but he was rewarded with a generalcy by the Confederate army.

Early in 1861, a Texas unit, the Second Texas Mounted Rifle Regiment led by Col. John Baylor, moved to El Paso (then named Franklin) and took control of Fort Bliss after the federal troops left without resisting. Baylor then proceeded to Mesilla in the Territory of New Mexico where he proclaimed the territory to be under control of the Confederacy. He then proclaimed that all the Territory of New Mexico south of the 34th parallel was henceforth to be known and governed as the Territory of Arizona and established himself as its military governor. There was no one to dispute him.

The next Texas campaign was led by Gen. Henry H. Sibley. He went to San Antonio to raise a brigade on behalf of the Confederacy and then secured New Mexico, enlarging upon Baylor's previous successes. He did not leave San Antonio until November 1861. By January 1862, he was fighting troops led by Union General Edward R. Canby. He lost to Canby at Valverde but counterattacked. The battle ended with no clear cut victory but with heavy losses on both sides. They met again at Albuquerque before Sibley, having outrun his supply lines, began to retreat back to Texas. Rather than confront him directly, Canby merely trailed alongside him while his situation became precarious because of lack of food and supplies. By the time Sibley's men entered El Paso, they came in groups of two or three rather than in any kind of formation.

On 16 August 1862, with a group of soldiers from California, Canby took Fort Bliss for the Union. When he arrived, he found the place abandoned except for twelve wounded soldiers and their surgeon. They fed the men, paroled them and escorted them to San Antonio. Canby was content to remain at Fort Bliss rather than try to invade the other parts of Texas and risk the long, extended supply lines that had been the undoing of General Sibley.

Although the Union had moved early to take over forts along the Atlantic to establish a naval blockade, it was not until October 1862 that it moved to Galveston. The Confederates moved out before the Union came in. The following January, the Confederates launched attacks by land and by water to recapture the port. This attack by General Magruder was successful and kept Galveston in Confederate hands until the close of the war. There was relatively little foreign trade through the port, though, since most of the blockade running was out of the ports of Wilmington, Savannah, and Charleston.

Early in 1862, Gen. Nathan B. Forrest fought with Texas troops alongside other Confederate troops at Corinth, Mississippi. This was only one of the many major battles engaged in by Texas units outside their own state. They fought at Gettysburg, Antietam, Bull Run, and Chickamauga, as well as several other battle sites. The Texas Brigade was taken over by Gen. Thomas Hood, and although he was in command of it for only six months, the fame which came to the unit during that period caused it thereafter to be referred to as "Hood's Brigade." This unit outshone other illustrious Texas units including Gen. B. F. Terry's Texas Rangers who fought well at Shiloh, Tennessee. Altogether, approximately sixty to eighty thousand men from Texas were supplied to the Confederate army with approximately twenty thousand of them engaged east of the Mississippi.

Probably the most adventuresome engagement by Confederate troops was at Fort Griffin, at Sabine Pass, Texas. In September 1863, five thousand troops with five gunboats, twenty-one personnel boats, and eight sport boats were sent from New Orleans to capture the small fort occupied only by Lt. Dick Dowling and forty-seven men. Despite the overwhelming odds, this handful of men not only held off the attackers but captured two of their five gunboats and captured 350 soldiers. None of Dowling's men were killed.

There were sporadic invasions into Texas, but the numbers of men involved ran into the hundreds rather than the thousands who fought in the more easterly battles. It did require six thousand Union troops, however, to capture Brownsville, said to be the last battle fought in Texas, in November 1863. Colonel John S. Ford captured 800 federal soldiers at Palmetto Ranch near Brownsville. The federal force consisted of twelve regiments of Negro troops and a company of Texas Unionists. This battle took place 13 May 1865, a month after Lee had surrendered in Virginia.

With the end at hand, Texas soldiers, now waiting for official orders, began to desert in droves. They lived off the land as they trudged wearily either toward their own homes or toward Mexico to help Maximilian in his dream of setting up a Mexican empire. Among those who fled to Mexico to save their lives from a revengeful Northern administration was Pendelton Murrah, the recently elected governor of Texas. The state government then collapsed, and anarchy reigned until the United States established a provisional government on 15 July.

Military Units

The National Archives has the compiled service records for the personnel who served in Confederate units from Texas as listed below. They may be found in Microcopy 323, consisting of 445 rolls. See chapter four for a complete description of this series.

First Cavalry, State Troops (six months, 1863-64)
First (McCulloch's) Cavalry (First Mounted Riflemen)
First (Yager's) Cavalry (First Mounted Rifles)
First Battalion, Cavalry, State Troops (six months, 1863-64)
Second Cavalry (Second Mounted Rifles)
Second Cavalry, State Troops (six months, 1863-64)
Second Battalion, Cavalry, State Troops (six months, 1863-64)
Third Cavalry (South Kansas-Texas Mounted Volunteers)
Third Cavalry, State Troops (six months, 1863-64)
Third Battalion, Cavalry, State Troops (six months, 1863-64)
Third (Yager's) Battalion, Cavalry (Third Battalion, Mounted Rifles; Yager's Battalion, Mounted Volunteers)
Fourth Cavalry (Fourth Mounted Volunteers, First Regiment, Sibley's Brigade)
Fourth Cavalry, State Troops (six months, 1863-64)
Fifth Cavalry (Fifth Mounted Volunteers, Second Regiment, Sibley's Brigade)
Sixth Cavalry (Stone's Regiment, Second Cavalry)
Sixth Battalion, Cavalry (Gould's Battalion; Third Battalion, Cavalry)
Seventh Cavalry (Seventh Mounted Volunteers; Third Regiment, Sibley's Brigade)
Eighth (Taylor's) Battalion, Cavalry (Taylor's Battalion, Mounted Rifles)
Ninth Cavalry (Sims' Regiment, Fourth Cavalry)

Tenth Cavalry (Locke's Regiment)

Eleventh Cavalry (Young's Regiment, Third Cavalry)

Twelfth Cavalry (Parson's Mounted Volunteers, Fourth Dragoons)

Thirteenth Cavalry (Burnett's Regiment, Thirteenth Mounted Volunteers)

Fourteenth Cavalry (Johnson's Mounted Volunteers, First Regiment, Johnson's Brigade)

Fifteenth Cavalry (Second Regiment, Johnson's Brigade)

Sixteenth Cavalry (Fitzhugh's Regiment; Third Regiment, Johnson's Brigade)

Seventeenth Cavalry (Moore's Regiment)

Seventeenth (Consolidated) Dismounted Cavalry

Eighteenth Cavalry (Darnell's Regiment)

Nineteenth Cavalry (Burford's Regiment)

Twentieth Cavalry (Bass' Regiment)

Twenty-first Cavalry (First Lancers; First Regiment, Carter's Brigade)

Twenty-second Cavalry

Twenty-third Cavalry (Gould's Regiment, Twenty-seventh Cavalry)

Twenty-fourth Cavalry (Wilkes' Regiment; Second Lancers; Second Regiment, Carter's Brigade)

Twenty-fourth and Twenty-fifth (Consolidated) Cavalry

Twenty-fifth Cavalry (Gillespie's Regiment; Third Lancers; Third Regiment, Carter's Brigade)

Twenty-sixth Cavalry (Debray's Regiment, Davis' Mounted Battalion)

Twenty-seventh Cavalry (Whitfield's Legion; First Legion

Twenty-eighth Cavalry (Randall's Regiment, First Lancers)

Twenty-ninth Cavalry (De Morse's Regiment)

Thirtieth Cavalry (Gurley's Regiment, First Partisans)

Thirty-first Cavalry (Hawpe's Regiment)

Thirty-second Cavalry (Fifteenth Cavalry, Crump's Battalion, Mounted Volunteers)

Thirty-third Cavalry (Duff's Partisan Rangers, Fourteenth Battalion, Cavalry)

Thirty-fourth Cavalry (Alexander's Regiment, Second Partisan Rangers)

Thirty-fifth Cavalry (Brown's Regiment)

Thirty-fifth Cavalry (Likens' Regiment)

Thirty-sixth Cavalry (Woods' Regiment, Thirty-second Cavalry)

Thirty-seventh Cavalry (Terrell's Regiment, Thirty-fourth Cavalry)

Baird's Cavalry (Fourth Regiment, Arizona Brigade; Showalter's Regiment)
Baylor's Cavalry (Second Regiment, Arizona Brigade)
Benavides' Cavalry
Border's Cavalry (Anderson's Regiment)
Border's Battalion, Cavalry
Bourland's Cavalry (Bourlands "Border" Regiment)
Chisum's Cavalry (Dismounted), (Second Partisan Rangers; Stone's
    Regiment)
Crump's Cavalry (Lane's Cavalry, First Partisan Rangers)
Frontier Battalion, Cavalry
Gano's Squadron, Cavalry
Gidding's Battalion, Cavalry
Good's Battalion, Cavalry
Granbury's Consolidated Brigade (First Consolidated Regiment)
Hardeman's Cavalry (First Regiment, Arizona Brigade; Thirty-first Cavalry)
Madison's Cavalry (Third Regiment, Arizona Brigade; Phillips' Regiment)
Mann's Cavalry (Bradford's Regiment)
Martin's Cavalry (Fifth Partisan Rangers)
McCord's Frontier Cavalry
Morgan's Cavalry
Ragsdale's Battalion, Cavalry
Saufley's Scouting Battalion, Cavalry
Steele's Command, Cavalry
Terry's Cavalry
Waller's Cavalry
Wells' Cavalry
Wells' Battalion, Cavalry
Captain Bone's Company, Cavalry
Captain Coopwood's Spy Company, Cavalry
Captain Doughty's Company, Cavalry, State Troops ("Refugio Spies")
Captain Durant's Company, Cavalry (Local Defense)
Lavaca County Minutemen
Captain Lilley's Company, Cavalry (Pardoned Deserters)
Captain McDowell's Company, Cavalry (Lockhart Volunteers)
Captain Nolan's Mounted Company (Local Defense)
Captain Pearson's Company, Partisan Rangers (Local Defense)
Captain Ragsdale's Company, Cavalry (Red River Dragoons)

Capt. W. H. Randolph's Company, Cavalry
Captain Sutton's Company, Cavalry (Graham Rangers)
Captain Terry's Mounted Company (State Troops)
Captain Thomas' Company, Partisan Rangers (four months, 1862-63)
Capt. L. Trevenio's Company, Cavalry
Captain Trevenio's Squad, Partisan Mounted Volunteers
Captain Upton's Company, Cavalry (Local Defense)
First Heavy Artillery
First Field Battery (Edgar's Company, Light Artillery)
Second Field Battery
Fourth Field Battery (Van Dorn Light Artillery)
Fourth (Shea's) Battalion, Artillery
Fifth Field Battery
Sixth Field Battery
Seventh Field Battery (Moseley's Company, Light Artillery)
Eighth Field Battery
Ninth Field Battery (Lamar Artillery)
Tenth Field Battery
Eleventh Field Battery (Captain Howell's Company, Light Artillery)
Twelfth Field Battery
Fourteenth through Seventeenth Field Battery
Dege's Battalion, Light Artillery
Captain Douglas' Company, Artillery
Captain Good's Company, State Troops, Artillery (Dallas Light Artillery)
Captain Greer's Rocket Battery
Captain Hughes' Company, Light Artillery
Captain Jones' Company, Light Artillery
Lt. H. van Buren's Company, Light Artillery
First Infantry (Second Infantry)
First State Troops
First State Troops, Infantry (six months, 1863-64)
First (Burnett's) Battalion, Sharp Shooters
First Battalion, State Troops, Infantry
Second Infantry (First Infantry, Moore's Regiment; Galveston Regiment;
    Van Dorn's Regiment)
Second State Troops, Infantry (six months, 1863-64)
Third Infantry (First Infantry, Luckett's Regiment)

Third State Troops, Infantry (six months, 1863-64)
Third (Kirby's) Battalion (Infantry and Cavalry, six months, 1861-62)
Fourth Infantry
Fourth Infantry, State Troops (six months, 1863-64)
Fourth (Oswald's) Battalion, Infantry (German Battalion; six months, 1861-62)
Fifth Infantry
Fifth Infantry, State Troops (six months, 1863-64)
Sixth Infantry (Third Infantry)
Sixth and Fifteenth (Consolidated) Volunteers, Cavalry and Infantry)
Seventh (Greeg's) Infantry
Eighth (Hobby's) Infantry
Ninth (Nichols') Infantry (Fifth Infantry, six months, 1861-62)
Ninth (Young's) Infantry (Eighth Infantry, Maxey's Regiment)
Tenth (Nelson's) Infantry
Eleventh Infantry (Roberts' Regiment)
Eleventh (Spaight's) Battalion (Cavalry, Artillery, and Infantry)
Twelfth Infantry (Eighth Infantry, Yount's Regiment)
Thirteenth Volunteers (Cavalry, Artillery, and Infantry)
Fourteenth (Clark's) Infantry
Fifteenth Infantry
Sixteenth Infantry (Seventh Infantry; Flournoy's Infantry)
Seventeenth Infantry (Allen's Regiment)
Eighteenth (Ochiltree's) Infantry
Nineteenth Infantry
Twentieth Infantry (Elmore's Regiment)
Twentieth Battalion, State Troops
Twenty-first Infantry (Spaight's Regiment)
Twenty-second (Hubbard's) Infantry
Twenty-fourth Battalion, Infantry (State Troops)
Bean's Battalion, Reserve Corps
Chambers' Battalion, Reserve Corps, Infantry
Griffin's Battalion, Infantry (Griffin's Regiment, Infantry; Twenty-first Regiment or Battalion, Infantry)
Houston Battalion, Infantry (Detailed Men)
Timmons' Infantry
Waul's Legion (Infantry, Cavalry, and Artillery)

Captain Arnold's Company, Infantry Riflemen, Militia
Captain Atkins' Company, State Troops (The Galveston Coast Guards)
Captain Benton's Company, Volunteers
Brazoria County Minutemen
Capt. Watts Cameron's Company, Infantry
Carter's Company, Infantry (Austin City Light Infantry)
Captain Cotton's Company, Infantry (Sabine Volunteers)
Captain Cunningham's Company, Infantry (The Mustang Grays)
Captain Currie's Company, Infantry
Captain Duke's Company, Volunteers (Jefferson Guards)
Captain Edgar's Company, State Troops (Alama City Guards)
Captain Gould's Company, State Troops (Clarksville Light Infantry)
Captain Graham's Company, Mounted Coast Guards, State Troops
Captain Hampton's Company, State Troops (Victoria Blues)
Captain Killough's Company, Home Guards (Wheelock Home Guards)
Captain Maxey's Company, Light Infantry and Riflemen (Lamar Rifles,
    State Service)
Captain McMinn's Company
Captain McNeel's Company, Local Defense Troops (McNeel Coast Guards)
Captain Merriman's Company, Local Defense Troops (Orange County Coast
    Guards)
Captain Perry's Company, Local Defense Troops (Fort Bend Scouts)
Captain Rainey's Company, Volunteers (Anderson County Invincibles)
Captain Rutherford's Company, Infantry (Unattached)
Captain Simms' Company, Home Guards
Captain Teague's Company, Volunteers (Southern Rights Guards)
Captain Teel's Company, State Troops (six months, 1861)
Captain Townsend's Company, Infantry (Robertson Five Shooters)
Captain Whaley's Company, Infantry
Captain Yarbrough's Company, Infantry (Smith County Light Infantry)
Miscellaneous, Texas
Conscripts, Texas

VIRGINIA
ARCHIVES BRANCH, STATE LIBRARY
11th Street at Capitol Square, Richmond 23219

HOURS: 8:15 a.m.-5:00 p.m., Monday-Saturday
closed: state holidays, including the combination King's Birthday and Lee-
Jackson Day (third Monday in January), Confederate Memorial Day
(27 May) and election day. Also New Year's Day, Washington's
Birthday (but open if the legislature is in session), Columbus Day,
Veterans Day,Thanksgiving Day, Christmas.

This archives is in one wing and the library is in the other wing of the
main floor of the building. As you enter the archives search room, you are
required to register at the staff desk. When you request that documents be
brought to you, by filling out and submitting a "stack service slip," they will
be brought to you at that desk. You may examine them at one of the tables
unless the material consists of original documents. In those cases, staff will
escort you to a special viewing room. Return the material to the staff desk
after you are finished examining it. If you plan to use a microfilm reader, ask
that one be assigned to you. At times of heavy usage, you may be placed on a
waiting list. When your turn comes up, a limit of two hours will be imposed
after which your name will be returned to the waiting list.

National Archives Microfilm

In the microfilm area you will find two series of microfilm which have
been purchased from the National Archives. See chapter four for a complete
description of these series.

*Index to Compiled Service Records of Confederate Soldiers Who Served
in Organizations From the State of Virginia.* M382 (62 rolls).
*Compiled Service Records of Confederate Soldiers Who Served in
Organizations From the State of Virginia.* M324 (1,075 rolls).

Pensions

Virginia enacted a pension law for Confederate veterans in 1888. It was restricted to those who were residents of the state as of April 1861 and who had resided in the state for at least five years prior to filing an application. This restriction is unique among other states which uniformly permitted pensions for qualifying Confederate veterans regardless of their residence at the start of the Civil War. All applicants must have been indigent to the extent that they did not earn more than $200 per year and owned no property valued at more than $1,000. A veteran must also have been disabled due to wounds or disease suffered while in service. No one receiving a pension from any other state or the federal government could receive one from Virginia. Along with the veterans, women who had served as matrons in a Confederate hospital for at least twelve months were eligible for a pension.

Applications were submitted to a three-person pension board in each county. Final approval was given by the county judge, and payments were made by the state auditor, whose office also maintained the record keeping for the program. The applications were standard forms asking questions relative to the applicant's residence, military history, and financial status including a description of any property owned and income received. Often there are statements from comrades-in-arms attesting to the claimed military service. Where appropriate, doctors' statements were also submitted.

The applications have not been microfilmed, but an index of the names has been prepared and it is available on microfilm. You may find that index in a steel file cabinet in the microfilm area. Look for a top drawer labeled "Confederate Pension Index." When you locate the name of your ancestor in the index, take down his name, his county (or independent city), and the act under which his pension was approved. Give that information to the staff at the desk and the pension file will be brought to you. The applications have been separated into three series according to the act under which they were granted. The first was in 1888, the second in 1900, and the third in 1902, extending through 1934.

As a part of the pension law enacted in more recent years, funeral expenses not to exceed $25 were also allowed. There is a roll book for the years 1926-1930, listing the names for whom those payments were made. They are not in alphabetical order, but since there are only a few names for each county or city, it is not difficult to search the lists. Given is the date of death, the date a claim was made, and the date the payment was made. You may examine this book by requesting it on a stack service slip.

Military Service Records
Muster Rolls

This archives has compiled a group of "simulated" muster rolls based on newspaper clippings, names found in journals, and other sources. The name and material for each person has been placed on large sheets. There are columns on those sheets for name, unit, and "remarks." In that latter column are listed such things as wounds, deaths, and other pertinent information. These sheets are bound into twenty large volumes. They may be found on a shelf in the west wall of the search room. Before you use these volumes, consult the card index of Confederate veterans to be found in a wooden file cabinet in the search room. Those cards will show the volume and page number for each name. Since the volumes are not labeled and are difficult to identify without staff assistance, go to the desk and ask for direction to the correct volume based on the data from the index card.

Military Records Guide

At the staff desk you will find a black notebook titled "Military Records Guide." This is a finding aid for many types of military records covering many years and including the Civil War period. The documents and collections of papers housed in this archives which pertain to military data are listed in that notebook. Each entry has a five digit code number opposite it. If you wish to examine any of the material listed there, include that code number on a stack service slip and staff will bring it to you. Typical of the material listed in that notebook are the following examples:

1. Prisoners of War
2. Men Killed in Battle (listed by name of battle)
3. Vouchers
4. Unit lists (for various military units including muster rolls, payrolls, returns, and rosters).

VIRGINIA'S ROLE IN THE WAR

If your ancestor lived in Virginia during the years of the Civil War, you may well hypothesize that he was a soldier or a sailor. If he did not don a uniform, he almost certainly saw something of the fighting that went on in his state. It would have been difficult to escape it because Virginia was the chief battleground of the war for four long years. Fighting was especially heavy in the Shenandoah Valley and in the 150 mile stretch between Petersburg and Washington, D.C. When the Confederate capital was moved to Richmond in June 1861, it became the chief objective of the Union's military campaign. At that same time, Washington, D.C. became the chief objective of the Confederacy's military campaign. Thousands of lives were lost in the fields and forests between these two capital cities.

Virginia, considered a border state rather than a part of the deep South, wavered for a while after its sister states rushed into secession. It hoped that some accommodation could be reached between North and South, and thus the question of where its loyalties would lie would be moot, although it was a foregone conclusion that if the choice had to be made, it would go with the South. The majority of the delegates to the first state convention voted to remain in the Union, preferring to wait to see if the federal government would protect the slave economy and enforce the Runaway Slave Act. Even after John Brown's raid on Harper's Ferry, and even after Lincoln called for troops to put down Southern insurrection, a second convention still resisted a move to secede. A majority of the delegates to the third convention, on 17 April, were in favor of leaving the Union, subject to a vote of the people in an election to be held 23 May 1861. The largest state east of the Mississippi (before West Virginia left it), Virginia was populous, wealthy, and strategically located. It was a prize wanted both by the Confederacy and the Union, and the entire country waited for the momentous vote in May. The decision of the people was overwhelming for secession, and the federal government knew it was in for a long and costly war.

The people in the counties of the northwestern part of the state were strongly pro-Union, and they took this opportunity to move toward their long held belief that they should not be a part of Virginia, anyway. Immediately, they began holding conventions until they eventually created a "Reorganized Government" and elected their own senators to replace the Virginia senators who had resigned in Washington when the state seceded. The majority of the men in that area enlisted in Union military units, but thousands of them headed south to become part of Virginia's Confederate units. Family splits were numerous with relatives later finding themselves facing each other in battle on opposite sides.

Long before Virginia's vote, the state legislature had authorized the governor to call up military volunteers. Units were already being formed throughout the state, and the governor accepted them along with their officers and their equipment. Robert E. Lee was called upon to assume the command of the state troops. A West Point graduate who had earlier stated that to secede would be folly, Lee had become persuaded to support his native state and accepted the post on 23 May 1861. Before the war was over he was to become the supreme commander of all the Confederate armies. Three days before Lee took charge, Virginia troops had already seized the federal arsenal at Harper's Ferry and the navy yard at Portsmouth and Norfolk.

The troops raised by Virginia were turned over to the Confederate government. When their twelve month terms were about to expire, the Confederacy offered a bounty of $50 and a sixty-day furlough if they would reenlist for two more years. On 23 January 1862, the Confederacy called for troops to serve for three years, and no longer accepted state soldiers for periods of less than three years.

Of all the theaters of war, the Virginia campaigns were the most extensive both in terms of numbers of fighting men and the numbers and severity of the battles. The numbers of troops fighting battles in the west were huge in individual battles such as those at Shiloh and Chickamauga, but generally those lasted only a day or two with longer periods of inactivity between. In Virginia, on the other hand, there was a continuous campaign of massive proportions going on almost constantly with fighting over the same terrain time after time. Losses mounted into the many thousands at each major confrontation. For the ancestor hunter with Virginia lines or lines to soldiers who fought in Virginia, the main campaigns and battles which occured within the state are described below in capsule form arranged by the year in which they took place.

1861. Early fighting broke out at Bethel Church, on 6 June near North Carolina just west of Yorktown, Virginia. Confederate troops pushed the advancing federal troops back to Hampton Roads. A month later the federal forces moved to Manassas (Bull Run) to try to seize the railroad there. The

Confederate forces under Gen. Thomas J. "Stonewall" Jackson pushed them back indicating that it was to be a long war.

1862. After raising his army to one hundred thirty thousand men, General McClellan was ordered by President Lincoln to make a move on Richmond. Using his naval forces, he proposed to move his army by boat to the Virginia peninsula between the York and the James Rivers. The campaign began with the famous naval duel between the ironcald ships, the *Monitor* and the *Merrimack* (rechristened the *Virginia*), at Hampton Roads. Neither ship won a victory in this first-ever clash between ironclads.

This concluded, McClellan moved his men into position, but the Confederate General Joseph E. Johnston, with sixty thousand troops, moved to defend Richmond. When McClellan was within nine miles of the city, Johnston rushed his lines. After two days of indecisive fighting and after Robert E. Lee took over for Johnston who was seriously wounded, McClellan withdrew to fight another day. While the Richmond battled raged, General Jackson was holding Union troops out of the Shenandoah Valley. His mission was to hold the valley and to prevent Gen. Nathaniel P. Banks from moving toward Richmond to help McClellan. Although he fought and ran, his aggressiveness contributed to a high level decision to hold Banks in the valley as a buffer between the South and Washington, D.C. The Union then sent three separate armies into the valley against Jackson. With reinforcements on hand, Jackson began to attack each of the armies before they could join together in a concerted attack. In every assualt, he was successful. He fought at McDowell, Fort Royal, Winchester, Cross Keys, and Port Republic. All the Union armies then retreated from the area, leaving the agricultural supplies and the communication lines open to the Confederacy. Jackon and his men had fought for forty-eight successive days and had covered 676 miles.

Pleased by Jackson's successes, General Lee decided to order his General "Jeb" Stuart to join with Jackson and attack McClellan's flank. They all met in what was known as the Seven Days Campaign at Mechanicsville, Gaines' Mill, Malvern Hill, and points between. McClellan ran north in an attempt to escape the onslaught. He safely reached the James River by using the firepower from his gun boats. He had lost 15,849 men and Stuart and Jackson had lost 20, 614 men during that seven days in May.

Jackson and Lee were soon to meet another challenge by the Union army under Gen. John Pope. First, Jackson met Pope in August and won at

Cedar Mountain. Then, under Lee's orders, Jackson swept around Pope's army at Manassas. On the first day, 29 August, of this Second Battle of Manassas (Bull Run), Pope dominated; but on the second day Lee counterattacked and drove Pope back to Washington, D.C. Pope's troops had suffered approximately 9,000 casualties, compared to approximately 16,000 by Lee's troops.

Lee now felt the time was right to invade the North. In September he launched a campaign through Maryland by way of Harper's Ferry which fell to Jackson on 15 September. Taken there were 10,000 troops and 30,000 small arms. The battles at Sharpsburg (Antietam) and at other Maryland towns are described in the section dealing with Maryland and will not be repeated here--except to note that Lee had to run back to Virginia to save his army.

1863. This was the year when Confederate General John S. Mosby with his semi-legal "rangers" made several raids into Northern Virginia. On a larger scale, the Union armies sought to crush Lee by placing one wing of their forces near Frederickburg while the other wing crossed the Rappahannock. The two wings planned to join and then head toward Richmond. Lee decided to send his General Jubal A. Early to Fredericksburg while he went to Chancellorsville to meet Union General Joseph Hooker. He again used Jackson and Stuart as part of his battle plan. Unfortunately, during a reconnaissance, Jackson was accidentally shot by one of his own men and died soon afterward from complications of the wound. Stuart and lee pressed on to push the Union back north and were successful in pushing Hooker's force back across the Rappahannock.

Although he was winning battles, the immense loss of manpower and the dwindling stores of supplies made Lee's situation increasingly desperate. While he still had enough men and arms, he decided once more to invade the North. This time he went up the Shenanodoah Valley and all the way into Pennsylvania to a small town named Gettysburg. After three days of fighting there, causing a total of 51,000 casualties on both sides, Lee managed to get his army out and back once more to Virginia. For the balance of the year, while a process of rebuilding and equipping went on, there were only sporadic confrontations in Virginia.

1864. During this year the most intense fighting took place in the West, most of which were Union victories over undermanned Confederate armies in Tennessee, Mississippi, Georgia, and the Carolinas. The Union armies in the East turned their attention to Virginia once more when they began their grand strategy to crush Lee once and for all. Three main offensives were launched at the same time. One went up the Shenandoah Valley, another up the peninsula toward Richmond, and the other, led by the newly appointed supreme commander, General Ulysses S. Grant, crossed the Rapidan River to confront Lee head on. Grant met him in an area called "The Wilderness" where it was too thickly wooded for large guns or horses to penetrate. Fighting was hand to hand, and the woods were set on fire by the shelling. Many soldiers burned to death on the spot. This carnage continued for two days until Grant, on 7 May, broke off, permitting Lee to race for Spotsylvania Court House where he waited for Grant to follow him. After thousands of casualties on both sides, including the death of Jeb Stuart, Grant was able to continue southward while Lee fell back to Cold Harbor where they fought again. There, on 3 June, Grant made fourteen separate assaults but failed to dent Lee's lines although he lost 7,200 Union soldiers in just one-half hour.

Like a man possessed and realizing that Lee was losing as many men as he was, Grant pressed on. Marching around Richmond rather than going in directly, he concentrated on Petersburg. After failing to take that city by a four-day direct attack, he settled down to a siege to starve it into surrender. Meanwhile, Union and Confederate forces attacked and counterattacked all along the Shenandoah Valley. General Early once got so close to Washington, D.C. that President Lincoln was able to personally view the fighting in nearby Silver Spring, Maryland. In the end, General Sherman drove down the valley and took complete control, burning and destroying as he went.

1865. Finally, on 1 April, Grant made a massive push forcing Lee not only to evacuate Petersburg but also Richmond. Although the Union had suffered 42,000 casualties during these sieges, the Confederates had suffered 28,000 casualties. What was left of its army was hardly enough to wage a major battle. In a desperate attempt, Lee retreated into the western part of the state, vainly hoping to receive supplies and to escape on a train expected between Danville and Richmond. Unable to obtain supplies from the local citizenry and when the train missed him, Lee knew the end was at hand. Racing madly away from their pursuers, one-third of his remaining troops were caught by Sheridan's forces near Lynchburg, at Sayler's Creek. Lee and the others continued to march on until it became apparent that Grant had blocked all avenues of retreat. On 9 April, Lee agreed to meet with Grant in a private home at Appomattox, Virginia, where he agreed to Grant's terms of surrender. On 12 April, there was a formal surrender ceremony; the war in Virginia was over, and other armies of the Confederacy outside the state were quick to follow in the weeks to come.

Military Units

The National Archives has the compiled service records for the personnel who served in Confederate units from Virginia as listed below. They may be found in Microcopy 324, consisting of 1,075 rolls. See chapter four for a complete description of this series.

First Cavalry
First Battalion, Cavalry
Second Cavalry
Third Cavalry (Second Virginia Cavalry)
Fourth Cavalry
Fifth Cavalry
Fifth Cavalry (12 months, 1861-62) (Fourth Virginia Cavalry, Mullins'
    Regiment)
Fifth (Consolidated) Cavalry
Sixth Cavalry
Seventh (Ashby's) Cavalry
Eighth Cavalry
Ninth Cavalry (Johnson's Regiment)
Tenth Cavalry
Eleventh Cavalry
Twelfth Cavalry (Tenth Virginia Cavalry)
Thirteenth Cavalry (Sixteenth Battalion, Cavalry; Fifth Cavalry; 12 months,
    1861-62)
Fourteenth Cavalry
Fourteenth Battalion, Cavalry (Burroughs' Battalion)
Fifteenth Cavalry
Fifteenth Battalion, Cavalry (Northern Neck Rangers; Critcher's Battalion,
    Virginia Cavalry)
Sixteenth through Twentieth Cavalry
Twenty-first Cavalry (Peters' Regiment)
Twenty-second Cavalry (Bowen's Regiment, Virginia Mounted Riflemen)

Twenty-third Cavalry
Twenty-fourth Cavalry
Twenty-fourth Battalion, Partisan Rangers (Scott's Battalion)
Twenty-fifth Cavalry
Twenty-sixth Cavalry
Thirty-second Battalion, Cavalry
Thirty-fourth Battalion, Cavalry (First Battalion, Virginia Mounted Rifles; Witcher's Battalion, Virginia Mounted Rifles)
Thirty-fifth Battalion, Cavalry
Thirty-sixth Battalion, Cavalry
Thirty-seventh Battalion, Cavalry (Dunn's Battalion, Partisan Rangers)
Thirty-ninth Battalion, Cavalry (Richardson's Battalion of Scouts; Guides and Couriers; Thirteenth Battalion, Cavalry)
Fortieth Battalion, Cavalry
Forty-first (White's) Battalion, Cavalry
Forty-sixth Battalion, Cavalry
Forty-seventh Battalion, Cavalry
Caldwell's Battalion, Cavalry
Ferguson's (Guyandotte) Battalion, Cavalry
Hounshell's Battalion, Cavalry (Partisan Rangers)
O'Ferrall's Battalion, Cavalry
Swann's Battalion, Cavalry (Carpenter's Battalion)
Captain Balfour's Company (Mounted Riflemen)
Captain Jourdan's Company (Rockbridge Rangers)
Captain McFarlane's Company, Cavalry
Captain Moorman's Company, Cavalry (Partisan Rangers)
Mounted Guard, Fourth Congressional District, Virginia
Patrol Guard, Eleventh Congressional District, (Mounted)
Captain St. Martin's Company, Mounted Riflemen
Captain Sale's Company, Mounted Reserves, Rappahannock District, Virginia
Captain Thurmond's Company, Cavalry (Partisan Rangers)
Captain Young's Company, Cavalry (Howitzers, Marine Artillery)
First Artillery (Second Virginia Artillery)
First Light Artillery (Pendleton's Regiment)
First Battalion, Light Artillery (Hardaway's Battalion, Moseley's Battalion)
Second Artillery

Third Light Artillery (Local Defense)

Tenth (Allen's) Battalion, Heavy Artillery

Twelfth Battalion, Light Artillery

Thirteenth Battalion, Light Artillery

Eighteenth Battalion, Heavy Artillery

Nineteenth (Atkinson's) Battalion, Heavy Artillery

Twentieth Battalion, Heavy Artillery

Thirty-eighth (Read's) Battalion, Light Artillery

Captain Allen's Company, Heavy Artillery (Lunenberg Artillery)

Captain E. J. Anderson's Company, Light Artillery

Captain R. M. Anderson's Company, Light Artillery (First Company, Richmond Howitzers)

Captain Ancell's Company, Light Artillery

Captain Armistead's Company, Light Artillery (Matthew's Light Artillery)

Captain Barr's Company, Light Artillery

Captain Binford's Company, Volunteers (Fourth Company, Richmond Howitzers)

Captain Bowyer's Company, Heavy Artillery (Botetourt Artillery)

Captain Brander's Company, Light Artillery (Letcher Artillery)

Capt. G. W. Brown's Company, Horse Artillery

Capt. J. S. Brown's Company, Light Artillery (Wise Artillery)

Captain Bryan's Company, Artillery (Bryan Artillery; Monroe Artillery)

Captain Carpenter's Company, Light Artillery (Allegheny Rough Artillery)

Captain Carrington's Company, Light Artillery(Charlottesville Artillery)

Capt. J. W. Carter's Company, Horse Artillery

Capt. W. P. Carter's Company, Light Artillery

Captain Cayce's Company, Light Artillery (Purcell Artillery)

Capt. G. B. Chapman's Company, Light Artillery (Monroe Battery)

Capt. W. H. Chapman's Company, Light Artillery (Capt. J. K. Booton's Company, Dixie Artillery)

Captain Clutter's Company, Light Artillery

Captain Coffin's Company, Heavy Artillery

Captain Coleman's Company, Heavy Artillery

Captain Cooper's Company, Light Artillery

Courtney Artillery (Henrico Artillery)

Captain Curtis' Company, Artillery (Fredericksburg Artillery)

Captain Cutshaw's Company, Light Artillery (Jackson Artillery)

Captain Dane's Company, Artillery (Powhatan Artillery)
Captain Donald's Company, Light Artillery
Captain Douthat's Company, Light Artillery (Botetourt Artillery)
Capt. J. W. Drewry's Company, Artillery (South Side Artillery)
Captain Ellett's Company, Light Artillery (Crenshaw Battery)
Captain Epes' Company, Heavy Artillery (Johnston Artillery)
Captain Fleet's Company, Artillery (Middlesex Artillery)
Captain Forrest's Company, Artillery (Chesapeake Artillery)
Captain French's Company, Light Artillery (McComas Battery, Light
    Artillery; Giles Light Artillery)
Captain Fry's Company, Light Artillery (Orange Artillery)
Captain Garber's Company, Light Artillery (Staunton Artillery)
Goochland Light Artillery
Capt. Archibald Graham's Company, Light Artillery (Rockbridge Artillery)
Capt. Edward Graham's Company, Horse Artillery (Petersburg Artillery)
Captain Grandy's Company, Light Artillery (Norfolk Light Artillery Blues)
Captain Giffin's Company, Light Artillery (Salem Flying Artillery)
Captain Hankins' Company, Light Artillery (Surry Light Artillery)
Captain Hardwicke's Company, Light Artillery (Lee Battery)
Captain Huckstep's Company, Light Artillery (Fluvanna Artillery)
Captain Jackson's Company, Horse Artillery (Second Organization, 1863-
    65)
Captain Jeffress' Company, Light Artillery (Nottoway Light Artillery)
Capt. J. R. Johnson's Company, Light Artillery
Capt. C. F. Johnston's Company, Artillery (Albemarle Artillery, Everett
    Artillery)
Capt. A. J. Jones' Company, Heavy Artillery (Pamynky Artillery)
Capt. L. F. Jones' Company, Artillery (Second Company, Richmond
    Howtizers)
Captain King's Company, Light Artillery (Saltville Artillery)
Captain Devill's Company, Artillery (United Artillery)
Captain Kirkpatrick's Company, Light Artillery (Amherst Artillery)
Captain Kyle's Company, Heavy Artillery
Captain Lamkin's Company, Light Artillery
Captain Lowry's Company, Light Artillery (Centreville Rifles)
Captain Lanier's Company, Artillery
Captain Leake's Company, Light Artillery (Turner Artillery)

Captain Lurty's Company, Horse Artillery

Captain McClanahan's Company, Light Artillery

Captain Moore's Company, Light Artillery

Captain Motley's Company, Light Artillery (Pittsylvania Artillery)

Captain Nelson's Company, Light Artillery

Captain Otley's Company, Light Artillery (Local Defense)

Captain Page's Company, Light Artillery (Magruder Light Artillery)

Captain Paris' Company, Artillery (Staunton Hill Artillery)

Captain Parker's Company, Light Artillery

Captain Patteson's Company, Heavy Artillery (Campbell Battery)

Captain Pegram's Company, Light Artillery (Branch Field Artillery)

Captain Penick's Company, Light Artillery

Captain Pollock's Company, Light Artillery (Fredericksburg Artillery)

Capt. B. F. Price's Company, Light Artillery (Danville Artillery)

Capt. W. H. Rice's Company, Light Artillery (Eighth Star Artillery; New Market Artillery)

Captain Richardson's Company, Artillery (James City Artillery)

Captain Rives' Company, Light Artillery (Nelson Light Artillery)

Captain Rogers' Company, Light Artillery (Loudoun Artillery)

Capt. Daniel Shank's Company, Horse Artillery

Captain Shoemaker's Company, Horse Artillery (Beauregard Rifles, Lynchburg Beauregards)

Capt. B. H. Smith's Company, Artillery (Third Company, Richmond Howitzers)

Capt. J. D. Smith's Company, Light Artillery (Bedford Light Artillery)

Captain Snead's Company, Light Artillery (Fluvanna Artillery)

Captain Sturdivant's Company, Light Artillery

Captain Taylor's Company, Light Artillery

Captain Thompson's Company, Light Artillery (Portsmouth Light Artillery)

Captain Thornton's Company, Light Artillery (Caroline Light Artillery)

Captain Turner's Company, Light Artillery

Captain Utterback's Company, Light Artillery

Captain Waters' Company, Light Artillery

Captain Weisiger's Company, Light Artillery

Captain Wilkinson's Company, Heavy Artillery (Company A, Marion Artillery, Company A, Richmond Local Guards)

Wise Legion, Artillery

Captain Wimbish's Company, Light Artillery (Long Island Light Artillery)
Captain Woolfolk's Company, Light Artillery (Ashland Light Artillery)
Captain Wright's Company, Heavy Artillery (Halifax Artillery)
Captain Young's Company, Artillery (Halifax Light Artillery)
First Infantry (Williams Rifles)
First (Farinholt's) Reserves
First Battalion, Reserves
First State Reserves (Second Class Militia)
First Reserves
First Battalion, Infantry (First Battalion, Virginia Regulars; Irish Battalion)
First Battalion, Infantry, Local Defense (Ordnancy Battalion, Armory
    Battalion)
Second Infantry
Second Infantry, Local Defense
Second State Reserves
Second Battalion, Infantry, Local Defense (Waller's Battalion, Quartermaster
    Battalion)
Second Battalion Reserves
Third Infantry
Third Kanawha Regiment, Infantry
Third Infantry, Local Defense
Third Reserves (Booker's Regiment, Reserves)
Third (Archer's) Battalion, Reserves
Third Battalion, Valley Reserves (Augusta County Reserves)
Fourth Infantry
Fourth Reserves (Preston's Regiment; Fifth Regiment, Reserves)
Fourth Battalion, Reserves
Fourth Battalion, Infantry, Local Defense (Naval Battalion; Navy Depart-
    ment Battalion)
Fifth Infantry
Fifth Battalion, Infantry (Wilson's Battalion, Archer's Battalion)
Fifth Battalion, Infantry, Local Defense (Arsenal Battalion)
Fifth Battalion, Reserves (Henry's Reserves)
Sixth Infantry
Sixth Battalion, Reserves (Thirteenth Battalion, Reserves; Smith's Battalion,
    Reserves)
Sixth (Tredegar) Battalion, Infantry, Local Defense

Seventh Infantry
Seventh (First Nitre) Battalion, Infantry Local Defense
Seventh Battalion, Reserves (Fifth Battalion, Valley Reserves)
Eighth Infantry
Eighth Battalion, Reserves (First Battalion, Valley Reserves)
Ninth Infantry
Ninth Battalion, Reserves (Second Battalion, Valley Reserves)
Ninth (Hansbrough's) Battalion, Infantry
Ninth Militia
Tenth Infantry
Tenth Battalion, Reserves (Fourth Battalion, Valley Reserves)
Eleventh Infantry
Eleventh Battalion, Reserves (Fourth Battalion Reserves; Wallace's Battalion, Reserves)
Twelfth through Fourteenth Infantry
Fourteenth Militia
Fifteenth Infantry
Sixteenth Infantry (Colston's Regiment, Infantry; Twenty-sixth Regiment, Infantry)
Seventeenth through Twenty-first Infantry
Twenty-first Militia
Twenty-first Battalion, Infantry (Pound Cap Battalion, Thompson's Battalion, Special Service Battalion)
Twenty-second Infantry (First Kanawha Regiment)
Twenty-second Battalion, Infantry (Second Battalion Infantry)
Twenty-third Infantry
Twenty-third Battalion, Infantry (First Battalion, Infantry; Hounshell's Battalion, Infantry; Derrick's Battalion, Infantry)
Twenty-fourth Infantry
Twenty-fifth Infantry (Heck's Regiment)
Twenty-fifth Battalion, Infantry (Richmond Battalion, Infantry, City Battalion, Infantry)
Twenty-fifth Militia
Twenty-sixth Infantry
Twenty-sixth (Edgar's) Battalion, Infantry
Twenty-seventh Infantry (Sixth Infantry)
Twenty-eighth Infantry

Twenty-eighth (Tabb's) Battalion, Infantry
Twenty-ninth Infantry
Thirtieth Infantry
Thirtieth Battalion, Sharp Shooters (First Battalion, Sharp Shooters; Clarke's
    Battalion, Sharp Shooters)
Thirty-first Infantry
Thirty-first Militia
Thirty-second through Thirty-fourth Infantry
Thirty-fourth Militia
Thirty-sixth Infantry (Second Kanawah Infantry)
Thirty-seventh Infantry
Thirty-seventh Militia
Thirty-eighth Infantry (Pittsylvania Regiment)
Thirty-ninth Infantry
Thirty-ninth Militia
Fortieth Infantry
Forty-first Infantry
Forty-first Militia
Forty-second Infantry
Forty-third Militia
Forty-fourth Infantry
Forty-fourth Battalion, Infantry (Petersburg City Battalion)
Forty-fifth Infantry
Forty-fifth Battalion, Infantry
Forty-sixth Infantry (First Regiment, Infantry, Wise Legion; Second Regi-
    ment, Wise Brigade)
Forty-sixth Militia
Forty-seventh Infantry
Forty-seventh Militia
Forty-eighth through Fifty-first Infantry
Fifty-first Militia
Fifty-second Infantry
Fifty-second Militia
Fifty-third Infantry
Fifty-fourth Infantry
Fifty-fourth Battalion, Infantry
Fifty-fourth Militia

Fifty-fifth Infantry

Fifty-sixth through Fifty-eighth Infantry

Fifty-eighth Militia

Fifty-ninth Infantry (Second Regiment, Infantry, Wise Legion)

Fifty-ninth Militia

Sixtieth Infantry (Third Regiment, Infantry, Wise Legion)

Sixty-first Infantry (Wilson's Regiment, Infantry, Seventh (Wilson's) Battalion, Infantry

Sixty-first Militia (Matthew's Battalion)

Sixty-second Mounted Infantry (First Partisan Rangers, Sixty-second Partisan Rangers, Sixty-second Infantry, Sixty-second Cavalry, Imboden's Partisan Rangers)

Sixty-third Infantry (McMahon's Regiment)

Sixty-fourth Mounted Infantry (Sixty-fourth Infantry; Sixty-fourth Cavalry; Slemp's Regiment, Infantry)

Sixty-fourth Militia

Sixty-seventh Militia

Seventy-second Militia (Russell County Militia)

Seventy-fourth Militia

Seventy-seventh Militia

Seventy-ninth Militia

Eighty-second Militia

Eighty-sixth Militia

Eighty-seventh Militia

Eighty-eighth Militia

Eighty-ninth Militia

Ninety-second Militia

Ninety-fourth Militia

Ninety-seventh Militia (Colonel Mann Spitler's Militia; Second Regiment; Seventh Brigade, Militia)

One Hundred and Eighth Militia

One Hundred and Ninth Militia

One Hundred and Eleventh Militia

One Hundred and Eleventh Militia

One Hundred and Fourteenth Militia

One Hundred and Fifteenth Militia

One Hundred and Twenty-second Militia

One Hundred and Twenty-ninth Militia
One Hundred and Thirty-fifth Militia
One Hundred and Thirty-sixth Militia (Third Regiment, Seventh Brigade, Militia)
One Hundred and Forty-sixth Militia (First Regiment, Seventh Brigade, Militia)
One Hundred and Fifty-first Militia
One Hundred and Fifty-seventh Militia
One Hundred and Sixty-second Militia
One Hundred and Sixty-sixth Militia
One Hundred and Eighty-eighth Militia
One Hundred and Eighty-ninth Militia
One Hundred and Ninetieth Militia
One Hundred and Ninety-eighth Militia
Averett's Battalion, Reserves
Burk's Regiment, Local Defense
Carroll County Militia
Cohoon's Battalion, Infantry (Sixth Battalion, North Carolina Infantry)
French's Battalion, Infantry
Grayson County Militia
Montague's Battalion, Infantry
Breckenridge County Reserves
Scott County Militia
Tomlin's Battalion, Infantry
Tuttle's Battalion, Local Defense
Virginia State Line
Wade's Regiment, Local Defense
Washington County Militia
Wythe County Militia
Captain Avis' Company Provost Guard
Lieutenant Bosher's Company, Local Defense
Captain Chappell's Company, Local Defense (Pickett Guard)
Captain Clark's Company, Reserve Forces
Captain Cooper's Company, Local Defense
Captain Delany's Company, Local Defense (Home Guards)
Captain Durrett's Company, Local Defense
Captain Earhart's Company, Local Defense (Blacklich Home Guards)

Captain Ezell's Company, Local Defense
Captain French's Company, Local Defense
Captain Gregory's Company, Infantry (High Hill Greys)
Guards and Scouts, Rockingham County, Virginia
Captain Hamilton's Company, Local Defense
Captain Henerson's Company, Local Defense
Captain Hobson's Company, Second Class Militia
Hood's Battalion, Reserves
Captain Hutter's Company, Infantry (The Southern Guard)
Captain Jordan's Company, Local Defense
Captain Keyser's Company, Reserves
Captain Lyneman's Company, Infantry
Captain Mallory's Company, Local Defense (Provost Guard)
Captain Mileham's Company, Infantry
Lieutenant Morehead's Company, Local Defense
Captain Murphy's Company
Captain Neff's Company, Local Defense (Mount Airy Home Guard)
Captain Patterson's Company, Local Defense (Home Guard First District,
    Bland County)
Captain Scott's Company, Local Defense (Company A, Greensville County
    Home Guard)
Captain Stowers' Company, Militia
Captain Sutherland's Company, Local Defense
Captain Taylor's Company, Local Defense
Captain Taylor's Company, Volunteers (Young Guards)
Captain Thurston's Company, Reserves Forces
Westmoreland County, Reserves
Wise's Battalion, Volunteers
Captain Wolff's Company, Second Class Militia
Captain Wood's Company, Local Defense
Virginia Military Institute
Miscellaneous, Virginia
Conscripts, Camp Lee, Virginia

CHAPTER 3

Searching in the Border States

ARIZONA

When the Civil War began Arizona was a part of the New Mexico Territory but welcomed the arrival of Texas troops representing the Confederacy and aligned itself with the Confederacy as a separate territory. Confederate General Henry H. Sibley (then a colonel) had organized a force of four thousand men at Fort Bliss at the site of present day El Paso, Texas. They marched up the Rio Grande into the New Mexico Territory. He defeated Union General Edward R. S. Canby (then a colonel) at Valverde and went on to occupy Alburquerque and Santa Fe, the capital of the territory. Canby was relieved of command, and James H. Carleton, with his California Volunteers, augmented with troops sent from Colorado and Missouri, was given the mission of removing the Confederate troops from the area. Sibley, with supply lines outrun, and his troops starving, turned back to Fort Bliss, thus putting the New Mexico Territory in Union hands where it remained.

When the leaders of the Arizona area passed a resolution in March 1861 in favor of joining the Confederacy, Confederate troops led by Gen. John R. Baylor with his Texas Mounted Rifles moved in to fill the void. He proclaimed that all the territory south of the thirty-fourth parallel was the Arizona Territory. He proclaimed himself military governor of all that area. He organized a group which he called the Arizona Guards. Its primary function was the killing of hostile Indians. Indians were becoming a menace since the federal troops once stationed there to provide protection had moved out. Chased out of the territory by Carleton, Baylor's reign was short-lived. Carleton took over and proclaimed himself the new military governor and also set about killing Apaches, Navaho, and other hostile Indians. The Arizona

Territory remained in Union hands throughout the balance of the war although the Confederacy had officially accepted it early in 1862.

In 1862, Arizona formed three independent companies, by order of General Sibley, consolidated later into Herbert's Battalion. Other troops who operated in the territory were almost entirely Texans, and when Herbert's Battalion broke up in 1863 some of its men moved into Texas units. The National Archives has the compiled service records for this unit, and they are available on the one roll of Microcopy 318. See chapter four for a complete description of this series.

INDIAN TERRITORY (OKLAHOMA)

Inhabiting the Indian Territory at the time of the Civil War were the Five Civilized Tribes: Cherokee, Creek, Seminole, Choctaw, and Chickasaw. These tribes had been removed from the Southeast by the United States government. In their new land they developed an agricultural society, much like that which they had left, that included the possession and use of Negro slaves. In the territory, they raised crops and shipped them to New Orleans for cash and fared reasonably well. They had embraced the Christian religion and had established a school system. The Seminoles even governed themselves in accordance with their own constitution.

In March 1861, Major Emery of the Union Army took command of the troops stationed in the territory, but they were soon ordered to relocate in Kansas. The Confederate troops in Texas immediately moved in and pursued the Union troops as they left. This allowed the Confederate representatives to deal with the Indians and try to gain their loyalty. Although there were some serious splits in philosophy within each of the tribes, generally they sided with the Confederacy. A generous treaty was arranged by the Confederate States of America, and the tribes agreed to it. Under its terms, the Indians would no longer be required to make payments for their lands and would be permitted to continue to own slaves. They also would be assured of self government. In return, they would furnish fighting men to the Confederate army. Several military units composed partially or entirely of Indians were organized. The factions of the tribes which dissented formed their own military units and joined with the Union units to fight their brother Indians in the Confederate units. The Choctaw and the Chickasaw were almost completely Southern in their allegiance, but the Cherokee, Creek, and the Seminole were divided among themselves. At one point, Confederate General Cooper, with fourteen hundred troops composed of both Texans and "lower Creeks" fought the "upper Creeks" but without a clear-cut victory for either side. Eventually, the Indians who sympathized with the Union were forced to flee into the Kansas territory, thus leaving the Confederates in control of the Indian Territory.

Early in 1862, Gen. Albert Pike was sent by the Confederacy to command the military forces in the Indian Territory. He took thirty-five hundred Indians to Pea Ridge, Arkansas, where they fought alongside Missourians and Arkansans. After that battle he took his troops back to the territory. Pike later resigned because of lack of support from the Confederate government. During the balance of the war there was constant shifting of leadership in the territory, not only by the Confederates, but also by the Union. Slow and steady inroads into the territory were made by the Union, and many Indians had to flee to refugee camps. At Honey Springs, Union General James G. Blunt, using a regiment of Negroes and other troops, fought the largest battle in the Territory and saved it for the Union. From that time on, Cherokee General Stand Watie engaged in guerilla warfare in several successful raids on Union supply lines. At the close of the war, Watie was the last Confederate general to surrender. As part of the reconstruction program after the war, the Indians were forced by the victorious United States to live on lands one-half the size of their original lands, had to forego slavery, and were governed from Washington, D.C.

Although the Territory did not become the State of Oklahoma until 1907, it did provide for pensions for those who had fought with the Confederacy from any state or territory. Legislation enacted on 5 January 1915 enabled any Confederate veteran who had been an Oklahoma resident for at least one year to receive a pension if he had served in a Confederate unit for a period of at least three months. To be eligible he had to show that he was indigent and incapacitated for manual labor because of wounds received during duty or because of his age, accident, or disease. Indigent widows of such veterans were also eligible for a pension if they were still married to their veteran husband when he died. Unfortunately, because of the lack of appropriated funds, all applications by widows younger than age sixty had to be rejected.

The Oklahoma Genealogical Society published an index of the applications and it has been microfilmed. It is available not only at the society's headquarters but also at the Oklahoma Historical Society. It gives the names of the applicants, the application number, and the microfilm roll number where the pension file may be found. The published version might be found in several genealogical libraries.

In 1910 at Ardmore, Oklahoma established a Confederate Home for the indigent or disabled Confederate soldiers or sailors, their wives and widows.

Since the Indians in the territory served in units from Texas, rather than in any unit having its own identity, the National Archives has no compiled service records relating to any Indian Territory military units.

KENTUCKY
DEPARTMENT OF ARCHIVES AND LIBRARIES
300 Coffee Tree Road, Frankfort 40602
(just off Route 676--the east-west connector)

HOURS: 8:00 a.m.-4:15 p.m., Monday-Saturday
closed: state holidays and the Saturday immediately preceding or following a
holiday

This facility houses the official state records. It also houses some material, in an assigned area of the search room, for the Kentucky Genealogical Society (not to be confused with the Kentucky Historical Society which is described below). As you register in the outer lobby, you must place your briefcase, purse, and such items in a locker outside the search room. Your belongings will be subject to search as you leave.

Inside the search room you will be shown a table where you will find several copies of the finding aids. These are notebooks which list all the archives' microfilm holdings. The listings are arranged first by subject and then by county. Opposite each item is a microfilm roll number. Using that number, you can find the roll you desire in one of the steel cabinets nearby. Help yourself to the film and drop it in a cart provided for that purpose when you are finished with it.

National Archives Microfilm

This archives has the following microfilm series which have been purchased from the National Archives. See chapter four for a complete description of these series.

Index to Compiled Service Records of Confederate Soldiers Who Served in Organizations From the State of Kentucky. M377 (14 rolls).

Compiled Service Records of Confederate Soldiers Who Served in Organizations From the State of Kentucky. M319 (136 rolls).

Register of Confederate Soldiers, Sailors, and Citizens Who Died in Federal Prisons and Military Hospitals in the North, 1861-1865. M918 (one roll).

Selected Records of the War Department Relating to Confederate Prisoners of War, 1861-1865. M598. (Only the records which related to the Louisville Military Prison's general register are available. These are rolls 88 and 89, located in drawer 335.)

Amnesty Rolls. M1003. (Only the records which relate to Kentucky citizens are available.) These are rolls 25 and 26 located in drawer 240-Row 2.

Pensions

Kentucky enacted pension laws for Confederate veterans or their widows in 1912. Because of the late date, it is obvious that only the more elderly could possibly have benefitted from it. The legislature created a pension board to administer the program and instructed the adjutant general to supply the board with military records and any other evidence needed to support an applicant's claim to military service with the Confederacy. Two years later, the board was replaced by a Confederate Pensions Department headed by a commissioner. He administered the program until 1936 when the department was abolished and the duties turned over to the newly created Division of Confederate Pensions under the sole authority of the adjutant general.

Applicants must have been residents of Kentucky since 1906, five years before the law became effective. Residence at the time of the war was not a factor in determining eligibility. Widows must have married the veteran before 1890. Military service for at least one year was required. As the years went by, amendments were made in the 1912 law. For instance, by 1942, a veteran could qualify if he had been a Kentucky resident since 1915. Widows who qualified received monetary awards based on a sliding scale according to when they had married the veteran. By 1952, all widows were eligible regardless of when they had married.

No pension was granted unless the applicant proved he or she was in financial need or was disabled. Initially, an applicant could own no property valued at more than $2,500 nor earn more than $300 per year. Also, a veteran with a wife who was able to support him or who lived in a confederate home was not eligible for a pension. The amount of the award at the time of the 1912 law was $10 per month, payable quarterly. All pensioners had to be recertified each year. By 1942, the monthly amount had been increased to $50 per month plus burial and funeral expenses. In 1958, the $300 ceiling on income was waived for all applicants.

The pension files were turned over to the Kentucky Historical Society in 1951. They were transferred to the Division of Archives and Records Management in 1976 and remain there. The files are not available to the public because of their fragile condition, but all have been microfilmed. A duplicate set of those microfilms may also be seen at the headquarters of the Kentucky Historical Society. Roll number one of the fifty-one roll series is the index to the other rolls. It is arranged in alphabetical order by name of either the veteran or a widow. If a widow is listed, her husband's name is also shown. Also, the index shows the county of residence at the time of application, the date, the maiden name of the widow (if given), and the application number.

Using the pension application number, you may find the roll on which your ancestor's file may be found. These are arranged in numerical order and located in drawer 188. The pension index found in this archives is also available in book form. It was compiled by Alicia Simpson in 1978 when she was the archivist of the Division of Archives and Records Management, then located on East Main Street, Frankfort.

Military Service Records

There is a two-volume work prepared by the state adjutant general which lists the names of persons who served in Confederate units raised in Kentucky. The names are arranged according to the name or number of the military unit. A brief history of each unit is given. The remarks column for each soldier often contains information concerning the soldier's place and date of enlistment and any information concerning promotions, wounds, or his death. This publication was reprinted in 1980 by Cook and McDowell Publications and includes an added index of names. This publication has also been placed on microfilm, and a staff member can direct you to that series.

Miscellaneous State Records

The Pewee Confederate Home served the Confederate veterans residing in Kentucky who required institutional care. In 1912, when the pension law was enacted, it specified that residents of the home were not eligible for a pension. A list of the residents at that time was prepared for easy reference by the pension board. That list has been microfilmed and is available at the archives. A staff member can direct you to it. A copy of this microfilm series, as well as the original handwritten list, is kept by the Kentucky Department of Military Affairs, located at the Boone National Guard Center. You may see this list and other state military records between the hours of 8:00 a.m. and 4:30 p.m., Monday through Friday. The center is located on Route 60 (the Louisville Road) southwest of Frankfort.

KENTUCKY HISTORICAL SOCIETY

A valuable adjunct to the state archives is the Kentucky Historical Society located at the corner of Broadway and Lewis Street next to the Old Capitol in downtown Frankfort. Many of the records on microfilm at the state archives are also available here. This society has several works that are valuable as references as you search for your Confederate ancestor. Some of the more important ones are listed below.

Report of the Adjutant General of the State of Kentucky, Confederate Kentucky Volunteers, War 1861-1865. 2 vols. See the description of this work above. The original card index, the muster rolls, and other related records which were used in the compilation of data in these two volumes may also be seen at the Kentucky Department of Military Affairs referred to above.

Index of Confederate Pension Applications, Commonwealth of Kentucky. This index as well as the pension files themselves are available on microfilm.

Registration of Veteran's Graves (Confederate and Union). This list, based on a 1939 field inspection of Kentucky cemeteries, is arranged by county and alphabetically thereunder by name. This list has also been indexed in alphabetical order without regard to county by the Department of Military Affairs referred to above. There, if you wish, you may also inspect the original field worker's reports.

Guide to the Manuscripts of the Kentucky Historical Society. This guide was prepared by G. Glenn Clift in 1955. It includes an index to the 4,840 Confederate pension files held by the society in that year. The catalog reference number for this index is "5730." There are other lists mentioned in the guide which may help you. They include:

1. Civil War--Adjutant General's Letters. Number 1142.
2. Civil War--Authorities Granted. Number 1143. These refer to recruitment, permits, passes, and such matters.
3. Pardons. Number 730. These are lists of persons granted a presidential pardon after the war.
4. Civil War--Kentucky Troops (Confederate). There are various citations and various manuscripts under this title.

KENTUCKY'S ROLE IN THE WAR

Kentucky made an effort to remain neutral between the seceding Southern states and the stubborn federal government. The attempt lasted only four months before it broke down. The counties chose up sides--thus causing their citizens to fight a truly civil war between themselves. Families were divided. The most classic example was Kentucky's Crittendens. Thomas L. Crittenden became a Union general; he had a brother, George G. Crittenden, who became a Confederate general. Generally, the blue grass section in the center of Kentucky and the western section favored the South. The mountainous eastern counties favored the North. There were sharp and bitter differences, though, within the counties and between neighbors. The predominant feeling throughout the state was that Kentucky should remain in the Union, but that the Southern states should be allowed to go in peace. Particularly abhorrent was the idea that the United States government would bring the force of arms against those sister states and even march through Kentucky to get to them. This was the dilemma facing the state legislature when it met in 1861. It could reach no clear conclusion and adjourned after taking only a weak action to arm both its home guards and its state guards purely for defensive purposes. Neither was to be used except in the event of an invasion from either the North or the South.

In April 1861, when Lincoln issued a call for four regiments from Kentucky, Governor Magoffin flatly refused. Lincoln, not wishing to risk pushing the state into the Confederacy, judiciously accepted the refusal. At another point, Lincoln also made an exception of Kentucky when a move was underway to declare all slaves freed. His main concern was to keep Kentucky in the Union, at all political costs, with or without slavery. In May, the legislature adopted a resolution of neutrality, and the governor issued the proclamation on 20 May. After the legislature adjourned, its members, various state officials, and many of the citizens, began to enlist their services on one side or another according to their own beliefs.

After four months, the federal government began to gather the members of the Kentucky Home Guards, secretly adding new recruits, at a place named Camp Dick Robinson. The purpose of this camp was to train for military action. The Confederate army interpreted this training camp, complete with arms, as a violation of neutrality and occupied Columbus, Kentucky, on the Mississippi River. Simon R. Buckner, commander of the Kentucky State Guards and a Southern sympathizer, organized his group into the second, third, fourth, and fifth regiments and became a Confederate general. Meanwhile, John H. Morgan was also raising several troops for the Confederacy at Lexington. Because of this Confederate action, General Grant occupied Paducah.

A new legislature sat in August 1861 and called for the Confederate troops to leave the state but failed to pass an offered resolution with regard to the Union troops. The governor vetoed the resolution, but the legislature approved it over his veto. This was the first move to bypass the governor, but it happened regularly from then on. On 18 September, the legislature declared formally in favor of remaining in the Union, and, not trusting the governor, placed Thomas I. Crittenden in charge of the state's military forces. In August 1862, the governor resigned his post and turned the leadership over to the Speaker of the House in accordance with state law.

To illustrate the deep schism within the state, the Southern sympathizers organized their own state convention with delegates from the counties not then under federal military control. They met at Russellville in November 1861 and adopted a constitution and elected a provisional governor and a ten man executive council. Negotiations with the Confederacy resulted in the unofficial state government being admitted as one of the Confederate States of America on 10 December 1861. A star was placed on the Confederate flag representing Kentucky.

As the political moves were taking place, General Buckner occupied Russellville and Bowling Green and set up a line of defense along the Green

River to prevent General Grant from operating in that area. Buckner raided and destroyed railroads near Louisville but was defeated by Union forces at Ivy Mills. He also lost five hundred men in a battle at Mill Springs and was forced to retreat. He abandoned Bowling Green and Columbus and set up camp in Tennessee--where he was later to surrender his army at Fort Donelson. A bit later, at Shiloh, Tennessee, an estimated 23,700 men were counted as casualties. Many of them were Kentucky men who had fought opposite each other.

In August 1862, Confederate General Kirby Smith advanced into Kentucky and joined Gen. Braxton Bragg who was driving toward Glasgow. They met each other on 29 August. After capturing approximately three thousand and occupying Lexington, Bragg forced the Union troops there back to Richmond. On 13 September, Bragg occupied Glasgow and attacked at Mumfordville where he captured four thousand more. He and Morgan then headed toward the state capital at Frankfort. The legislature fled toward Louisville and took the state archives with them. When Bragg moved into Frankfort, he "inaugurated" Richard Hawes as the new governor. Before the ceremonies were concluded, however, the noise of Union forces led by Gen. Don Carlos Buell was heard. Believing the invasion was underway, the celebrating group ran toward Lexington. They were unaware that Buell actually was heading for Bardstown--not Frankfort.

The Union army led by General Buell initially concentrated at Cumberland Gap and confronted Confederate troops wherever he found them. After Buckner's withdrawal to Tennessee, intent on taking Fort Donelson on the Kentucky-Tennessee border, he moved to the Green River. When he approached Bragg at Perryville on 2 October 1862, they engaged in the most destructive battle to take place inside Kentucky. Bragg then withdrew to Harrodsburg where he met General Smith and relocated with him to Tennessee.

There were no other major battles in the state, but the Confederates made several important and destructive raids into the state at various places. They were led by Gen. Nathan B. Forrest and by Gen. John H. Morgan and his cavalry. Morgan and his band made several lightning raids to destroy supply lines all throughout central Kentucky. He raided at such places as Mt. Sterling, Paris, and Cynthiana, becoming a legendary hero and a terrifying threat to the population wherever he chose to strike. When he first entered Kentucky he had nine hundred men; when he left he had twelve hundred, reflecting his recruitment successes along the way.[16] Eventually, the pressure to catch him became too intense and he was forced to retreat through the mountains into Virginia. He was killed at Greenville, Tennessee, on 4 September 1864.

When the war finally came to an end outside the state, Kentucky officially and wholeheartedly welcomed back all those who had fought and suffered regardless of whether they had thrown their lot with the South or the North. The new governor, a veteran of the Union army, publicly urged amnesty for all participants.

Military Units

The National Archives has the compiled service records for personnel who served in Confederate units from Kentucky as listed below. They may be found in Microcopy 319, consisting of 136 rolls. See chapter four for a complete description of this series.

First (Butler's) Cavalry
First (Helm's) Cavalry
First Battalion, Cavalry
First Mounted Rifles
Second Cavalry
Second (Duke's) Cavalry
Second (Woodward's) Cavalry
Second (Captain Dortch's) Battalion, Cavalry
Second Battalion, Mounted Rifles
Third Cavalry
Third and Seventh (Consolidated) Cavalry
Third Battalion, Mounted Rifles
Fourth through Tenth Cavalry
Tenth (Diamond's) Cavalry
Tenth (Johnson's) Cavalry
Eleventh Cavalry
Twelfth Cavalry
Eighth and Twelfth (Consolidated) Cavalry
Thirteenth Cavalry
Fourteenth Cavalry
Captain Corbin's Men

Jessee's Battalion, Mounted Riflemen
Kirkpatrick's Battalion
Morehead's Regiment, (Partisan Rangers)
Captain Bolen's Independent Company, Cavalry
Buckner Guards, Cavalry
Captain Dudley's Independent Cavalry
Captain Field's Company (Partisan Rangers)
Captain Jenkins' Company, Cavalry
Morgan's Men
Captain Rowan's Company (Partisan Rangers)
Captain Thompson's Company, Cavalry
Captain Byrne's Company, Horse Artillery
Captain Cobb's Company, Light Artillery
Captain Corbett's Company, Artillery
Green's Battery, Light Artillery
Lieutenant McEnnis' Detachment, Artillery
First Infantry
Second through Ninth Mounted Infantry
Ficklin's Battalion, Infantry
Miscellaneous, Kentucky

MARYLAND'S ROLE IN THE WAR

Maryland's eastern and southern areas were deeply into tobacco growing and had a flourishing slave economy. When a split between South and North appeared to be certain, those persons leaned toward supporting the South. Fewer in number were those living in the western part of the state who had little or no agriculture and had no use for slaves. They leaned toward the North. The federal government under Lincoln could not take a chance that this state, at the back door of the capital, would join the Confederacy and stationed many federal troops at crucial points inside the state. When a proposal was made to secede, regulations were adopted to permit furloughs by those who were already away in Union units so that they could vote in the election set for 27 April 1861. On the other hand, those who had rushed to join Confederate units were barred from voting. With federal soldiers standing outside the polls, the secession proposal was soundly rejected. The vote to remain in the Union was especially strong in the western parts and in Baltimore where there was a concentration of Germans.

Maryland was not enthusiastic, though, when it received a call for soldiers to fight for the Union. When troops from Massachusetts came through Baltimore enroute to Washington, D.C., mobs in Baltimore pelted them with rocks, and riots broke out. After that, Union troops passing through chose to take the longer way around the outskirts of the city. The young men in Southern and Eastern Maryland began to join Confederate units. They organized themselves and marched off to Virginia to join other units being amassed there. It has been estimated that approximately twenty thousand Marylanders fought for the Confederacy. Included in what was later called the Maryland Line were two regiments of infantry, the second replacing the first when it disbanded after the twelve month term ended. The first had been organized at Harper's Ferry, Point of Rocks, and Richmond. The second was organized at Winchester, Virginia. There were also four batteries of artillery, organized in 1861 and 1862, primarily created at Richmond. Small units became part of Virginia units but kept their identity. For instance, there was Company "B" (the Maryland Guard) of the Twenty-first Virginia; Company "K" of the First Virginia Cavalry and Company "B" of the Virginia Battalion (White's) Rangers.

Possibly even more important to the Confederacy than the soldiers Maryland provided was its strategic location near Washington and on the border between South and North. Since the people in the Eastern and Southern portions sympathized with the South, they were valuable in the carrying and transferring of messages through the state and for hiding Confederate prisoners who might have been fortunate enough to escape from a Northern prisoner of war camp. It is remembered that when John Wilkes Booth fled after assassinating the president, he headed directly for that part of Maryland where he knew he would receive assistance in his flight across the Potomac into Virginia where he assumed he would be safe. He did, in fact, receive such assistance and made it safely across the river only to be turned in by some Union soldiers whom he chanced to meet as he headed south through Virginia.

The "Eastern Shore" area of Maryland, east of the Chesapeake Bay, generally escaped the horrors of battle but was sometimes occupied by Union troops who ruled under martial law. Western Maryland was not so fortunate; it was the scene of Lee's invasions and the raids led by John S. Mosby. On 4

September 1862, Robert E. Lee crossed the Potomac into Maryland with the intention of encircling and capturing Harper's Ferry. His subordinate units did accomplish that objective on 15 September. Lee was fighting in the meantime at Sharpsburg, Maryland, with his own forces. He had been met there by General McClellan on 17 September. They fought there on the banks of the Antietam all day. The next day both armies stood fast, but on the second night Lee withdrew into Virginia. This was the bloodiest single day of battle of the war. Various estimates put the Confederate casualties at between ten thousand and fourteen thousand compared to 12,400 Union casualties.[17]

Lee invaded the North again in late June 1863. He marched his army across Maryland and to Gettysburg, Pennsylvania. Along the way, they fought off raids and harrassment-type skirmishes. After the disastrous battle at Gettysburg, Lee managed to get away again and took what was left of his army back to Virginia to fight another day. He never again left Virginia, though, and Maryland was relatively quiet after that, at least for several months.

In 1864 Confederate General Jubal Early headed into Maryland with the goal of taking over Fredericksburg. He raided federal stores at Harper's Ferry, marched to Sharpsburg where Lee had previously fought, and continued to Fredericksburg. He demanded $200,000 from the citizens under the threat that he would burn the town if the sum was not forthcoming. This was justified as an indemnity for the damage done by federal forces in Virginia's Shenandoah Valley some time earlier. He got the money but soon had to confront the Union General Lew Wallace who was coming to the scene. They met at the Monocacy River and Early triumphed although he lost eighteen hundred men. He then into Rockville the next day and then into Silver Spring, Maryland, at Fort Stevens on the Washington, D.C. line. While Early was encamped there, President Lincoln rode out to the scene to look at the enemy troops approaching. Early moved back to Rockville, rather than attempting to storm the capital. He had accomplished his primary mission of drawing strength from other Union armies while Lee was busy elsewhere.

While Early was busy in Maryland, a branch of his army led by General Johnston headed toward Point Lookout, Maryland, hoping to free Southern soldiers imprisoned there. Before reaching their objective, he was ordered to meet with Early at Silver Spring, where he learned of the impending withdrawal of all Confederate troops back to Virginia.

With the exceptions of frequent raids from Virginia, especially by Mosby's men, there were only skirmishes in Maryland for the remainder of the war.

After the war, two veterans organizations were formed in Maryland to perpetuate the memory of those who had contributed to the Confederacy. They were the Association of the Maryland Line and the Society of the Army and Navy of the Confederate States in Maryland. Those organizations jointly raised funds to assist impoverished Confederate veterans in their state, who, of course, were not eligible for a pension from the federal government. The Maryland legislature did not enact any Confederate pension laws but did turn over the old Pikeville Arsenal just outside Baltimore for use as a soldiers' home for Confederates. It was supported both by private donations and annual appropriations by the legislature. A report issued in 1898, ten years after the home opened, showed that it had admitted 235 persons and was still in operation. The official name of the home was The Maryland Line Confederate Soldier's Home.

The Hall of Records at Annapolis has no records of Confederate soldiers or sailors. The best source of names of the Confederate soldiers is the publication by William W. Goldsborough titled *The Maryland Line in the Confederate Army*. It contains some muster rolls and casualty lists of the units making up the Maryland Line. It also has a section describing the soldiers' home. A supplementary source is the publication by Louise Q. Lewis titled *Records of Marylanders in the Confederate Navy, 1861-1865.*

Military Units

The Hall of Records does not have any Confederate records purchased from the National Archives, but they may be seen at the National Archives itself which is about forty-five miles from Annapolis. There you may examine the following series of microfilm relating to Maryland Confederates. See chapter four for a complete description of this series.

First Cavalry
Second Battalion, Cavalry
First Battery, Artillery
Second Battery, Artillery
Third Battery, Artillery

Fourth Battery, Artillery
First Infantry
Second Battalion, Infantry
Weston's Battalion
Captain Walter's Company (Zarvona Zouaves)
Miscellaneous, Maryland

MISSOURI
OFFICE OF THE ADJUTANT GENERAL
1717 Industrial Drive, Jefferson City 65101

HOURS: 8:00 a.m.-4:30 p.m., Monday-Friday
closed: state holidays

The Missouri State Archives, located at 1001 Industrial Drive, Jefferson City, has no military records of any kind, so the only such resource in this city is the Office of the Adjutant General. The archives does have many other types of genealogical material, and you may wish to write or visit it for related information. It is in a very small building and is cramped for space. Perhaps it will someday move to larger quarters and take over the care and custody of the state's military records. Its mailing address is P.O. Box 778, Jefferson City, MO 65102. The State Library is located in the ultra-modern Harry S. Truman Building just west of the capitol. There you will find an excellent collection of publications relating to the Civil War. It is clear that the State of Missouri has supported its Department of Education, which is responsible for the library, far better than it has supported the Office of the Secretary of State, which is responsible for the archives. For now, at least, you must avail yourself of the friendly assistance offered at the Office of the Adjutant General where space and facilities are grossly inadequate.

NOTE: Just prior to publication, it was learned that the governor has ordered the adjutant general to turn over his military reocrds for storage at the State Archives. A final decision has also been made to begin immediate construction of a large, modern archives building. It is scheduled for completion in three years.

National Archives Microfilm

The Office of the Adjutant General was refused approval to buy any microfilm from the National Archives. Since the state archives also does not have such film, it is necessary for you to travel to Columbia, Missouri or to St. Louis, Missouri to use those sources. In Columbia, the State Historical Society, located in the east wing of the Ellis Library of the University of Missouri, is open from 8:00 a.m. to 4:30 p.m., Monday through Friday except on holidays. This facility is supported by state funds and is an excellent place to do Missouri genealogical research. It stores no Confederate military records but does have the following two microfilm series purchased from the National Archives. These are located in the newspaper library section where other microfilm is stored.

Index to Compiled Service Records of Confederate Soldiers Who Served in Organizations From the State of Missouri. M380 (16 rolls).
Compiled Service Records of Confederate Soldiers Who Served in Organizations from the State of Missouri. M322 (193 rolls).
The main St. Louis Library also has microfilm 322. In addition, it has the series titled *Consolidated Index to Compiled Service Records of Confederate Soldiers* (all states). M253 (535 rolls).
For a complete description of the above microfilm series, see chapter four.

Pensions

In the same manner that this state was ambivalent about throwing in its lot with either the Union or the Confederacy, it later was ambivalent about providing for pensions for Confederate veterans. It did not pass its first such law until 1913, and it remained in effect for only eleven years. The law provided for pensions amounting to a maximum of ten dollars per month to Confederate veterans who could qualify on the basis of their military service and their indigent status. No provision was ever made for their widows. The veteran was required to prove his service in a Confederate military unit, including what was called the Jackson State Militia, that he had been a Missouri resident for two years, was indigent because of wounds, disease, injury, or old age to the extent that he could not perform physical labor, and had no means of livelihood. If he was a resident of the state Confederate home, he was ineligible for a pension.

The actual amounts awarded as pensions depended upon the annual appropriations by the legislature, and these were usually not large enough to pay the full maximum allowable. For instance, during World War I in 1918, no funds were appropriated for Confederate pensions. In 1924, the opponents of Confederate pensions managed to have the entire law declared unconstitutional and payments ceased.

The state adjutant general was the administrator of the pension law. There was a board of review to handle complaints by persons who felt they had been unfairly dealt with. The Office of the Adjutant General created a card index of the 2,123 persons who applied for a pension during the period of the law's existence. Those cards as well as the original applications are filed in alphabetical order and will be shown to you upon request. They have not been microfilmed. The applications contain information about military service, a description of any wounds received, and evidence of inability to earn a living. Documents from the War Department collection of compiled service records were frequently used to support a claim of military service.

Military Service Records

There is an alphabetically arranged card index of approximately twenty thousand Confederate soldiers from Missouri, and these represent possibly one-half of the estimated forty thousand from this state who served somewhere in a Confederate unit. The cards refer to pension applications and also to those whose names appeared on a muster roll which might have survived.

Two large volumes of muster rolls are available for inspection in both the original or on microfilm. Because no adequate storage space has been made available, these valuable volumes are resting atop one of the file cabinets and are subject to dust and deterioration. The microfilm copies are on rolls J29, J30, and J31. These rolls cover the following Missouri units:

First through Sixth Regiments, Infantry
First through Third Regiments, Cavalry
Buibor's Battery, Artillery
King's Battery, Artillery
Landis' Battery, Artillery
McDonald's Battery, Artillery

Miscellaneous State Records

There is a card index of the names of those who were residents of the Confederate Home at Higginsville. The original applications for admission, approximately 300, are also available for inspection. They cover the years when the home was established in 1892 to 1951 when it was closed. Information on the application form includes the date and place of birth, county of residence, enlistment dates, and other miscellaneous facts relating to wives of veterans who also applied for admission.

MISSOURI'S ROLE IN THE WAR

Missouri was a Union state despite the fact that the governor and the legislature requested that it be admitted into the Confederate States of America. The request was granted and a star was added to the flag to represent Missouri. Citizens of the state, although split on the question of whether to permit the extension of slavery into the western territories, never waivered on the question of remaining in the Union. When the Democratic National Convention split into two parts in 1860, the states' rights faction of the South nominated John Breckenridge as its presidential candidate. Stephen A. Douglas, the candidate for the regular Democratic Party, was supported only in the North. In Missouri, for the sake of moderation, the voters elected Claiborne Jackson as governor. He was nominally a supporter of Douglas but actually was a believer in the Breckenridge philosophy. At his inaugural he swiftly let it be known where his true sympathies were when he said, ". . . Missouri will not shirk from its duty . . . to stand by the South." The legislature, not wishing to be rushed into action yet on a possible secession movement, called for a state convention to discuss what the state's relationship to the Union should be. When the citizens voted for delegates to the convention, not one district sent a delegate who favored secession. Of the total number of votes cast, approximately thirty thousand were for secessionist delegates while approximately 110,000 were for Unionist delegates. Despite the wishes of the governor and his captive legislature, the convention recommended overwhelmingly in favor of remaining in the Union. Even in the face of this, when Lincoln asked the governor to supply four regiments to the Union Army, he replied, "Your requisition, in my judgement, is illegal, unconstitutional, and revolutionary in its objects, inhuman and diabolical, and cannot be complied with."[18] In direct opposition, the governor sent two hundred men to the town of Liberty to seize the federal arsenal there and to remove the arms to another location. He instructed the state guards to assemble in west St. Louis at a place he named after himself--Camp Jackson. The legislature was called into special session for emergency purposes.

Opposing Jackson's actions was Francis "Frank" Blair, a Republican and Unionist from St. Louis. Supported by the Germans and the Irish of the city, he organized a Home Guards unit of volunteers. At his urging, the Union sent Gen. Nathaniel Lyon to St. Louis to defend against a threatened attack by the governor. Lyon arrived and took over the arsenal in south St. Louis. With his ten thousand troops, he overwhelmed Jackson and his force of eight hundred and sent them back to Jefferson City.

During this period, the legislature had passed an act requiring the state militia to take an oath of obedience to the governor and also authorized the governor to prepare for war. This was referred to as an "indirect secession ordinance." A more formal ordinance was passed when the legislature reconvened at Neosho on 28 October 1861. Representatives then traveled to Richmond to negotiate an alliance with the Confederacy. To fill the void, a state convention voted to declare the governor's office open and a Union governor, Hamilton Gamble, was elected. By that time, Jackson had retired to Arkansas where he presided over his officials who went with him. They claimed that they were the legal government of Missouri. Jackson died in Little Rock in December 1862. He was succeeded by Lieutenant Governor Thomas C. Reynolds who carried out his duties at Marshall, Texas until the war ended.

Before Jackson and his government left Missouri in the summer of 1861, they stoutly resisted the Northern invasions. On 11 June, Jackson and his colleagues!met with Lyon in St. Louis in an attempt at disarmament and a truce. Lyon, angered, accused Jackson of interfering with federal orders. Jackson and his friends hurried back to Jefferson City with Lyon in pursuit. En route, Jackson literally burned the bridges over the Gasconade and the Osage River bridges behind him to slow down Lyon. The next day, Jackson put out a call for fifty thousand volunteers and vowed to continue the fight in the field. He and the government moved out immediately to Boonville, permitting Lyon to take over Jefferson City. Lyon then routed Jackson and his military force near Boonville.

A few weeks later, on 5 July, Jackson met some Union troops at Charthage and fought them to a standstill thus preventing any further invasion by the Union for a time. Lyon continued to apply pressure, however, on pockets of Confederate resistance in many towns. He assigned Col. Franz Sigel, with his largely German troops from St. Louis, to take over the Pacific Railroad to its terminus at Rolla. Then they were to march to the southwest part of the state to head off a threatened attack by Jackson and his General Price and also the troops led by Arkansas' Gen. Benjamin McCulloch.

In August, Sigel and Lyon were together at Springfield, then a town of about two thousand persons. They met and fought the Confederate troops at Wilson's Creek just outside Springfield. In the two day battle there, Lyon was killed, and his troops pulled back to Springfield and then back to Rolla. Following this victory, General McCulloch went back to his home state of Arkansas, but Price moved in a northerly direction where he fought at Lexington for two days. He finally prevailed when his men were able to advance while hiding behind burning hemp bales which they pushed up the hills ahead of them.

Back in St. Louis, Gen. John C. Fremont, in overall command, had refused to reinforce his forces at Wilson's Creek and at Lexington on the proposition that he was saving his men for a big push down the Mississippi. When he imposed martial law over the city and ordered all Southern sympathizers shot and their slaves freed, President Lincoln became impatient and relieved him of his command and cancelled his orders at the same time. Before Fremont was informed, however, he had gone to Springfield himself, only to withdraw to Rolla. General Price and his men occupied Springfield for the winter of 1861-62.

Fremont was replaced by Gen. Samuel R. Curtis, who moved his ten thousand troops out of Rolla and back to Springfield. General Price rejoined McCulloch in Arkansas and they added thirty-five hundred Indians from the Indian Territory to their army. These combined forces totaling twenty-five thousand men were led by Gen. Earl Van Doren. They met Curtis at the Elk Horn Tavern at Pea Ridge, Arkansas, just below the Missouri border. The fighting, which took place on 7 and 8 March 1862, was the largest battle to take place west of Mississippi. When it was over, McCulloch had been killed, and Van Doren was forced to retreat. The Union armies were left in almost complete control of Missouri. There were many skirmishes and smaller attacks at many different places in the state below the Missouri River, but none of them were instrumental in taking over the state for the Confederacy.

The balance of the war in Missouri consisted primarily of guerrilla actions by such persons as William Quantrill and his henchmen who rode through the western part of the state terrorizing the people and wreaking havoc upon Union supply depots and railroads. Those depredations were directed not only toward the Union troops but also against the hated Kansas Jayhawkers who had previously raided western Missouri. The raiders killed and demolished property at such places as Osceola, Butler, and Parkville. On one occasion, Quantrill and his band rode into Lawrenceville, Kansas to murder and burn buildings in revenge for an earlier atrocity by the Kansas raiders.

At the command of his superior General Lane, Union General Ewing, in a move to try to lessen the impact of the local fighting in the western counties of Missouri, issued his famous Order Number Eleven. That edict required all residents of the counties of Jackson, Bates, Cass, and the northern portion of Vernon to deliver their crops to the nearest military post and destroy what they could not bring in. Then they were to vacate the area entirely. The only exceptions were those who lived within a mile of a Union military post or station. Those who would somehow prove their loyalty to the Union were also excepted, but such action would have been foolish since they would then automatically become the targets of the Confederate raiding parties. General Ewing authorized the Kansas troops to enforce his order. The result of this action was that soldiers on both sides moved in to plunder and burn any buildings left standing, and any citizen who had not left was murdered.

In 1864, General Price again decided to try to capture St. Louis. He met General Ewing at Pilot Knob. He later determined that St. Louis would be an unlikely prize and headed instead to Jefferson City. Upon finding that city quite well fortifed, he went around it to conduct raids at Glasgow and Lexington. He also fought at Westport on 21 October and at the Big Blue River where he was finally defeated and returned once more to Arkansas. He had fought forty-three skirmishes in different parts of Missouri.[19]

Except for continued guerilla warfare,which continued even after the war ended, there was no further fighting in Missouri. Outlaw gangs were formed and led by such men as the Younger brothers and a young Jesse James, all from northwest Missouri.

It has been estimated that during the war, Missouri had contributed 109,000 men to the Union forces and thirty to fourty thousand men to the

Confederate forces. The total comprised sixty-three precent of the state's eligible men.

Military Units

The National Archives has the compiled service records for personnel who served in Confederate units from Missouri as listed below. They may be found in Microcopy 322, consisting of 193 rolls. See chapter four for a complete description of this series.

First Cavalry
First Northeast Cavalry
First and Third (Consolidated) Cavalry
Second Cavalry
Second Northeast Cavalry (Franklin's Regiment)
Third Cavalry
Third Battalion, Cavalry
Fourth through Eighth Cavalry
Ninth (Elliott's) Cavalry
Tenth Cavalry
Twelfth Cavalry
Fifteenth Cavalry
Boone's Regiment, Mounted Infantry
Clardy's Battalion, Cavalry
Coffee's Regiment, Cavalry
Coleman's Regiment, Cavalry
Davies' Battalion, Cavalry
Ford's Battalion, Cavalry
Freeman's Regiment, Cavalry
Fristoe's Regiment, Cavalry
Hunter's Regiment, Cavalry
Jackman's Regiment, Cavalry
Lawther's Partisan Rangers
Lawther's Temporary Regiment, Dismounted Cavalry
Poindexter's Regiment, Cavalry
Preston's Battalion, Cavalry
Schnabel's Battalion, Cavalry

Shaw's Battalion, Cavalry
Slayback's Regiment, Cavalry
Snider's Battalion, Cavalry
Williams' Regiment, Cavalry
Wood's Regiment, Cavalry
Captain Beck's Company, Cavalry
Captain Hick's Company, Cavalry
Captain Hobbs' Company, Cavalry
Captain Stallard's Company, Cavalry
Captain Woodson's Company, Cavalry
First Battery, Light Artillery
Third Battery, Light Artillery
Thirteenth Battery, Light Artillery
First Field Battery, Light Artillery
Second Field Battery, Light Artillery
Third Field Battery, Light Artillery
Fourth (Harris') Field Battery, Light Artillery
Captain Barret's Company, Light Artillery
Capt. H. M. Bledsoe's Company, Light Artillery
Capt. Joseph Bledsoe's Company, Artillery
Captain Farris' Battery, Light Artillery (Clark Artillery)
Lieutenant Hamilton's (Prairie Gun) Battery, Light Artillery
Captain Landis' Company, Light Artillery
Captain Lowe's Company, Artillery (Jackson Battery)
Captain McDonald's Company, Light Artillery
Captain von Phul's Company, Light Artillery
Captain Walsh's Company, Light Artillery
First Infantry
First Battalion, Infantry
First and Fourth (Consolidated) Infantry
Second Infantry
Second and Sixth (Consolidated) Infantry
Third Infantry
Third Battalion, Infantry
Third and Fifth (Consolidated) Infantry
Fourth through Eighth Infantry
Eighth Battalion, Infantry

Ninth Infantry
Ninth Battalion, Sharp Shooters
Tenth through Twelfth Infantry
Sixteenth Infantry
Clark's Regiment, Infantry
Dorsey's Regiment
Douglas' Regiment
Parsons' Regiment
Perkins' Battalion, Infantry
Phelan's Regiment
Searcy's Battalion, Sharp Shooters
Thompson's Command
Winston's Regiment, Infantry
State Guard
Quantrill's Company
Miscellaneous, Missouri

WEST VIRGINIA
ARCHIVES AND HISTORY LIBRARY
Capitol Complex, Charleston 25305
(Washington Street, west of the Capitol)

HOURS: 9:00 a.m.-9:00 p.m., Monday-Thursday
       9:00 a.m.-5:00 p.m., Friday
       1:00 p.m.-5:00 p.m., Saturday
closed: most state holidays

This is a combination archives and library. You must register in the search room, but there are no specific security measures. Staff will assist you in your search if you so request. If you wish to use a microfilm reader, select any one and sign for it. In times of heavy usage, you may be restricted to a two hour period of use.

Since West Virginia was not a Confederate state, the military records to be found here are those of the parent state of Virginia. There is an emphasis here, however, on those who lived in the area which was to become the independent entity known as Kanawha and then the State of West Virginia.

National Archives Microfilm

There are no National Archives microfilm pertaining to West Virginia Confederate soldiers, but available here are two series pertaining to Virginia. See chapter four for a complete description of these series.

Index to Compiled Service Records of Confederate Soldiers Who Served from the State of Virginia. M382 (62 rolls).

Compiled Service Records of Confederate Soldiers Who Served in Organizations From the State of Virginia. M324 (1,075 rolls).

Pensions

West Virginia never enacted any legislation providing for its residents to collect a pension for service in the Confederate forces. If any veterans applied for pensions from Virginia, their files may be found at the Virginia archives at Richmond.

Military Service Records

There is a card index of Confederate soldiers that was evidently created by the Works Project Administration (WPA). This index is very incomplete and unreliable. It is divided into two parts:

CSA--Artillery, Cavalry, Infantry. In addition to the names of the soldiers, their rank and military unit are shown. This index is also available on microfilm titled "State of Virginia--Confederate Service Records of Virginia."

Soldiers' Graves--CSA. These cards contain data regarding next of kin, place of burial, and directions to the grave. Also given are the dates and places of birth and death and a brief summary of military service. This index is also available on microfilm titled "Virginia Adjutant General's Office--Burial and Cemetery Records."

Miscellaneous State Records

The manuscripts stored in this archives are listed in a black finding aids notebook titled "Alphabetical Main-Entry Listing of Manuscripts in the

Archives and History Division, June, 1980." Upon request, a staff person will lend you this notebook and will obtain any material listed in it that you may wish to examine. Among the many listings, the following are examples of some which may be pertinent to your search for a Confederate ancestor:

Civil War Collection (Artificial). MS 79-18. This collection consists of letters, diaries, lists of personnel in some military units, and other material.
Confederate Veterans From Charleston. MS 80-308.
Confederate States of America--Conscription Department, Tenth District--Exemptions and Substitution Records, 1862-1864. MS 79-239.

WEST VIRGINIA'S ROLE IN THE WAR

The story of the counties in the northwestern portion of Virginia, west of the Alleghenies, is a result of Virginia's decision to secede from the Union. The people in these mountainous counties never had much in common with their wealthier eastern neighbors. Some of them even voted for the Republican, Lincoln, for president. When the storm clouds of war began to form after Lincoln was elected, they were staunchly on the side of staying in the Union. During the many internal debates, those western counties began to hold mass meetings to protest the move by the other parts of the state to secede. The arguments became so intense that some of them even passed a resolution to the effect that they favored "striking West Virginia from East Virginia and forming a state independent of the South and firm to the Union."[20]

In Richmond, Governor Letcher called on the state to try to affect a compromise between the North and the South but added that if that failed they should side with the South. The legislature called for a secession convention but the delegates who were chosen to participate were primarily on the side of remaining in the Union. Only thirty of the 152 delegates voted for ouright secession. Most preferred to wait and see if the federal goverment would enforce the runaway slave laws and protect the property rights of slave owners. After the rash actions by John Brown at the federal arsenal at Harper's Ferry at the junction of Virginia and Maryland, and after Lincoln's announcement that he would occupy federal posts wherever they were located, the mood in Virginia began to change. A second try at secession failed, also, by a vote of eighty-five to forty-five. A third attempt, however, garnered a vote of eighty-eight to fifty-five to secede, subject to a popular vote on 23 May 1861. The people voted in favor of secession, and the wheels were set in motion for Virginia's entrance into the Confederate States of America, and it officially became a Confederate state. Early the next month, the Confederate capital was moved from Montgomery, Alabama to Richmond.

Opposed to the state's action at the last convention, only fifteen of the forty-seven delegates from the north-western counties voted for secession.[21] The others, feeling very unpopular in Richmond and possibly in danger, sneaked back to their home counties. There they were met by enthusiastic crowds all eager for separation from the mother state. The question was debated at length at a series of conventions held by this section at Wheeling. One sticking point was whether the new state should be a slave or a non-slave state. On 1 July 1861, the so-called "Reorganized Government" elected replacements to the United States House of Representatives and the United States Senate to replace the Virginians who had resigned when the state seceded. On 20 August, they approved "an ordinance to provide for the formation of a new state out of a portion of the territory of this state." It was to be composed of thirty-nine counties and to be named Kanawha. In 1862 when the United States Senate drafted a bill for admission of the new state, it provided for an additional fifteen counties but that provision did not hold up. The bill stipulated that slavery in the new state would gradually be abolished--the Emancipation Proclamation had not yet been issued. A compromise bill was sent to the president who was not sure the action conformed to the constitution which stated that both the new state and the old state had to consent to a separation before the Union could accept the new state. Virginia, prior to its secession, obviously had not so consented. Nevertheless, he signed the bill on 1 January 1863. After the new state adopted a new constitution by public vote on 20 June 1863, Lincoln proclaimed that West Virginia was the nation's thirty-fifth state--effective sixty days later. Two counties, Jefferson and Berkeley, were annexed later.

While the wheels of government were turning, the young men in the area voted with their feet--some of them heading south and some heading north. It has been estimated that seven to nine thousand from those counties served in Confederate units compared to twenty-eight to thirty-six thousand who served in Union units. Virginia's Twenty-second Infantry was composed almost entirely of soldiers from that portion of Virginia, and the Thirty-first and the Forty-sixth Infantry also have large numbers from that area.

Fighting was comparatively light--the most spectacular being John Brown's raid before the war had started and later actions between the Confederates and the Union troops also at Harper's Ferry. Union forces raided the area several times but fought no large battles such as took place in Tennessee, Virginia, and other states. The raids were upon towns such as Grafton, Clarksburg, Philippi, and also Charleston. Most of these were attempts to gain control of the Baltimore and Ohio Railroad which ran through the mountains. Usually, the Confederate forces were able to slip away from their Union tormentors and generally retained control over the Kanawha Valley. The opposite was true, through, in the Monongahela Valley where the Union forces prevailed. In addition to the raids, the citizens were able to observe the many marching units which passed through enroute to bigger and more devastating battles in Maryland, Pennsylvania, and eastern Virginia.

CHAPTER 4

Searching in the National Archives

After you have searched the records in the archives of the appropriate Southern or border states, there is still the important collection of records at the National Archives in Washington, D.C. As noted in previous chapters, some of the microfilmed service records and their indexes filmed by the National Archives have been purchased by some of the state and local archives and libraries; you may have seen them there before you use the facilities of the National Archives. There are thousands of other rolls of microfilmed Confederate records in Washington which have not been purchased by the states. No matter what success you might or might not have had in the states, it is important that this vast treasurehouse of material in Washington D.C. be explored. Access to these records may be gained by written request, by use of an experienced genealogical researcher who lives in the area (including Maryland and Virginia), or by making a personal visit yourself. Each of these methods is discussed below.

Written Request

You may write the National Archives and request a supply of Form 80. The address is Reference Services Branch (NNIR), National Archives and Records Service, 8th and Pennsylvania Avenue, NW, Washington, D.C. 20408. Complete the form when you receive it, and mail it back. Send no money with the form. After the Archives staff completes its search, you will be notifed and told how much the copies will cost. Upon receipt of your payment, the copies will be mailed to you. Extensive searches will not be made, and you must fairly well identify the record you want or it cannot be located. If there are fewer than five records of veterans with the same or nearly the same name, all will be searched for you in an attempt to identify the one you want. Expect to wait a minimum of eight to ten weeks for a reply.

Professional Researcher

For quicker service and a more individualized and innovative search, you may engage a professional genealogical researcher. You should determine in advance what his or her rates are, and, unless your request is a simple one, obtain some estimate of the total cost. Upon receipt of the first report, you can decide whether to continue with that researcher or try another one. There are two good sources of names and addresses of professional genealogical researchers in the Washington, D.C. area. These are the advertisements in *The Genealogical Helper,* published by The Everton Publishers, Inc., and the Board for Certification of Genealogists, P.O. Box 19165, Washington, D.C. 20036. The majority of the researchers have not applied for or obtained certification from this board, however, but are generally fully experienced, honest, and helpful nevertheless.

Personal Visit

Location: Pennsylvania Avenue NW--at 8th Street
HOURS: 8:30 a.m.-9:45 p.m., Monday-Friday
        8:30 a.m.-5:00 p.m., Saturday
closed: Sundays and national holidays

Upon arrival you must sign a register maintained by a security guard in the lobby and show some personal identification. No pass is needed to use the services and records in the microfilm room (room 400). If it appears, however, that you will need to research in any of the other rooms you will need a pass. The guard will direct you to the appropriate desk for this purpose, and the pass will be issued without delay and at no cost. There is no charge for the use of any facilities at this archives except for photocopying. Upon leaving the building, it is necessary to sign the register again. Briefcases and purses are subject to inspection by the guard to prevent theft or unintentional taking of valuable historical documents from the building.

When you enter room 400 you must sign another in-out register before beginning your search in the microfilm. You will notice a row of steel file cabinets on the left wall as you enter. Each of these has a small number on the upper left hand corner; these are used to locate a particular microfilm series explained below. To the right of the aisle are many microfilm readers and staff will instruct as to their use should you need such assistance. Select any reader--it need not be signed for. At the end of the room and to the left is a door leading to another room full of steel file cabinets. We shall call this room 400-A, although it is not especially marked as such. Staff is seated at a desk at the entrance of room 400 to answer your questions or to assist you in finding the microfilm reels you need. For difficult problems or for special help, you may be referred to one of the consultants on duty in room 205, except during the evenings or on Saturday.

MICROFILMED RECORDS OF MILITARY PERSONNEL

The National Archives stores the collection of Confederate papers which were gathered and classified by the War Department several years after the close of the Civil War. The Confederate records, for the most part, have all been microfilmed.

The gathering of the Confederate records began immediately upon General Lee's surrender and the evacuation of Richmond, Virginia in April 1865. The records were taken by the Confederate adjutant and inspector general to Charlotte, North Carolina, where they were voluntarily turned over to the Union officials for posterity. They were then transferred to Washington, D.C. They were held and preserved there by the War Department along with other papers captured at various places during and just after the war. In 1903 the War Department began to organize the mountain of papers to construct a service record for as many Confederate soldiers and sailors as was possible. For that purpose, the department asked the Southern governors to also lend their Civil War documents for copying and return. The response was not unanimous or complete, but generally the states cooperated. Many federal records from other sources contained references to both Union and Confederate personnel. Primarily, these came from the Provost Marshal and the Department of the Treasury.

Once in possession of the above documents, the War Department hired a legion of clerks and set them to work inspecting each piece of paper and placing it in one of the several specialized series of documents. They were classified according to subject or the office which handled them during the war. As each document was examined, the name of each soldier or sailor mentioned was placed at the top of an "abstract card." His rank and military unit were also recorded. A few words were written on the card to identify the basis for the creation of the card. Often this was a statement merely that the individual was present at a certain place at a certain time or was paid some amount of money at a certain place at a certain time. Such information was entered when the name appeared on a muster roll, a payroll, or a similar list. Names on a list of jail or hospital inmates also triggered the preparation of a card. In many instances, a paper appeared with only one name on it rather than being one of a list of names. In those instances, the paper itself was placed in a file along with any abstract card created for the individual name.

In modern times there is a central folder maintained for each soldier; all of his records are placed in this. No such folder existed in the Confederate army. Rather, the War Department had to compile such folders, called "jackets," after the fact with whatever records survived. A separate jacket was made for each soldier for whom an abstract card or a solitary piece of paper was prepared or located. When this project was completed in 1927, the jackets were divided into three main groups: those in units identified with a particular state; those in units raised directly by the Confederate government; and those in units above the regimental level or performing some unique specialied function. The jackets were then placed in order according to the name or number of the unit and then in alphabetical order according to the name of the person. At that point, the task of creating "compiled service records" for Civil War personnel was complete.

During the early 1940s, the recently established National Archives acquired these War Department collections of both Confederate and Union records and their indexes. A program to microfilm them was begun. However, after the Confederate phase was completed, the project was abandoned. For that reason, one who is searching for a Confederate ancestor may be able to confine most or all of his search to the National Archives for reading the microfilm. One who is searching for a Union ancestor must use both a microfilmed index and the actual paper documents.

A search for a Confederate ancestor definitely should not end with the service records. There are many papers relating to soldiers and sailors which did not find their way into the compiled service records. Further, the service records may only have a few words in them. A reference on an abstract card, through, may lead to the original document where further information may be uncovered. In some instances, material found in one of the many series of documents was made a part of the service record, but in other instances it was not. Also, there are collections of data concerning civilians associated with the Confederate army or government which are not included in the military records. A study of the titles and descriptions of both the microfilmed and unmicrofilmed series set forth on the following pages may lead to extensive searching.

For each microfilm series described below there is an identifying "M" number and a location symbol. Since the Archives operates on a self-serve system, reference to these location symbols will enable you to go directly to the proper file cabinet to get the microfilm roll you desire without needing to ask for staff assistance. As an example, a location symbol, "FC 30-5," signifies that the microfilm roll is in file cabinet number 30, the fifth drawer from the top. If a "10" precedes the location symbol, the file cabinet will be found in room 400-A. Thus, "FC10-32-2," signifies that the microfilm roll is in file cabinet nubmer 32, located in room 400-A, the second drawer from the top. When you locate the proper drawer, you will see the "M" number you are looking for written on the box of film.

Indexes to Service Records

Consolidated Index to Compiled Service Records of Confederate Soldiers. M253 (535 rolls) FC 29-3.

Before going to the compiled service records directly, it is necessary to find your ancestor's name in an index and then refer to a special pamphlet to ascertain the microfilm roll number for the correct service record. There are two sets of indexes to the compiled service records, both a consolidated index for all Confederate units and a set of separate indexes for each of the Southern and border states. The consolidated index covers the groups of service records not only for state volunteer units but also for those in units raised directly by the Confederate government including general officers and others in high-level command units.

After you have found a name in the consolidated index, make a note of the unit or units in which your ancestor served. Units were often merged with other units, so a soldier may have been listed in several units during his service. It will be necessary to check each of them to be sure you do not miss him. Go next to a black, bound notebook marked "Confederate" to be found atop one of the file cabinets. Therein you will find a pamphlet for each of the Southern and border states, a pamphlet for units raised directly by the Confederate government, and a pamphlet for the command type units not associated with a particular state. Each pamphlet lists the units by name or number and the alphabetical grouping of the names of the soldiers in those units. Opposite each listing is a microfilm roll number, and that number will lead you to the service records.

State Indexes to Compiled Service Records of Confederate Army Volunteers.

There is a separate index for each state which provided volunteer units to the Confederate army. If you already know that your ancestor served in one of those units, you may choose to ignore the consolidated index and go directly to the appropriate state index. It may pay, however, to check both indexes to make sure that he did not serve in some organization other than a state volunteer unit. As when using the consolidated index, it will be necessary to refer to the black notebook marked "Confederate" to obtain the microfilm roll number for the appropriate name or number of the unit and the alphabetical grouping of the soldiers' names. The list of state indexes follows:

State	"M" Number	Number of Rolls	Location
Alabama	374	49	FC 29-7
Arizona Territory	375	1	FC 29-7
Arkansas	376	26	FC 29-7
Florida	225	9	FC 29-7
Georgia	226	67	FC 29-7
Kentucky	377	14	FC 29-8
Louisiana	378	31	FC 29-8
Maryland	379	2	FC 29-8
Mississippi	232	45	FC 29-8
Missouri	380	16	FC 29-9
North Carolina	230	43	FC 29-9
South Carolina	381	35	FC 29-9

Tennessee	231	48	FC 29-9
Texas	227	41	FC 29-10
Virginia	382	62	FC 29-10

Index to Compiled Service Records of Confederate Soldiers Who Served in Organizations Raised Directly by the Confederate Government and of Confederate General and Staff Officers and Non-regimental Enlisted Men. M818 (26 rolls) FC 30-1.

This separate index is a guide to the two groups of compiled service records described later (M258) (M331). It may be used as an alternative to the consolidated index of compiled service records (M253). It might pay you to check both these indexes, however, to be sure that your ancestor was not missed in one of them. In either case, it will be necessary to refer to the black notebook marked "Confederate" to obtain the microfilm roll number for the alphabet grouping for the name you seek.

Compiled Service Records

After checking the appropriate indexes and obtaining the microfilm roll number for the service record you desire, you are ready to inspect the record itself. A description of those records, by type, are described below.

Compiled Service Records of Confederate Army Volunteers

If you have found your ancestor's name listed as a member of one of the state volunteer units, you will find his compiled service record in one of the series listed below by state. The record will consist of abstract cards made on the basis of a muster roll, payroll, hospital or prison list, roster, or other such list. It may also contain a copy of an individual document which pertains specifically to him rather than a list of persons.

State	"M" Number	Number of Rolls	Location
Alabama	311	508	FC 30-5
Arizona Territory	318	1	FC 30-8
Arkansas	317	256	FC 30-8
Florida	251	104	FC 30-1

Georgia	319	607	FC 31-1
Kentucky	319	136	FC 31-5
Louisiana	320	414	FC 31-6
Maryland	321	22	FC 31-1
Mississippi	269	427	FC 31-1
Missouri	322	193	FC 32-3
North Carolina	270	580	FC 32-4
South Carolina	267	392	FC 32-9
Tennessee	268	359	FC 33-2
Texas	323	445	FC 33-5
Virginia	324	1,075	FC 33-8

Compiled Service Records of Confederate Soldiers Who Served in Organizations Raised Directly by the Confederate Government. M258 (123 rolls) FC 30-3.

After you have found your ancestor's name in the consolidated index or in the separate index (M818) and have found his unit and alphabetical grouping in the black notebook marked "Confederate," you may obtain the microfilm roll for the name you are seeking.

Personnel in these units cannot be identified with any one state. They are comprised of units either raised by the Confederate government, and therefore part of the regular Confederate army, or they were formed into cavalry, artillery, or infantry units by additions and consolidations of smaller units originally created by a state. Some units were raised in the Indian Territory, some from foreigners, and some from prisoners of war serving in Confederate prisons. Specialized units were created, and these included the signal corps, corps of engineers, nitre and mining bureau, and the musical bands.

Compiled Service Records of Confederate General and Staff Officers and Nonregimental Enlisted Men. M331 (275 rolls) FC 30-1.

Persons in this category served in some command type unit such as a division, brigade, corps, or some other unit above the regimental level. They included the generals, other officers and enlisted men assigned to the offices of the Adjutant and Inspector General, the Quartermaster General, the Commissary General, the Medical Department, and the Ordnance Department.

Persons with specialized skills such as chaplains, drillmasters, agents, military judges, and aides-de-camp are also included in this series. Many officers and enlisted men served part of their time in one of these units as well as in a state volunteer unit, and there could be two sets of documents and index cards for such a person although the intent was to put all the records pertaining to one person in the same file.

Unfiled Papers and Slips Belonging to Confederate Compiled Service Records. M347 (442 rolls) FC 34-6.

This series is usually overlooked by the researcher simply because he or she does not know of its existence and no one suggests he look at it. The papers in this series are not identified in any of the indexes. For one or more reasons, they never made their way into a service record. When the War Department clerks went through the warehouse of papers to prepare abstract cards and create service records, they often came across a document which was impossible to identify as relevant to a certain person. In other cases there was no matching documentation of the person's name to prove that he had been in a particular military unit. In still other cases it appeared that he was merely a member of a home guard or some similar local unit. Sometimes it was unclear whether he was a military person, a civilian employee of the Confederate government, or a private citizen. Often a separate file was not created because there was only one paper which contained meager information.

Because of the large number of these "problem papers," they were arranged in alphabetical order according to the name and placed in a separate category. When those papers were microfilmed separately, 442 reels of film were required for the job. Because you may have more family information than did the clerks, you may have better luck identifying these papers. It might pay to find any such papers which contain the name of your ancestor and try to decide whether to include or exclude them for your family history. At the front of each roll in this series is a list of the rolls, by number, for the various alphabet groups.

Navy and Marine Corps Records

Theoretically, the Consolidated Index to the Compiled Service Records (M253) contains the names of sailors and marines as well as soldiers. The records of the navy and marine corps which survived are notoriously incomplete, however, and it may very well be that your ancestor was missed unless he was a land soldier. Nevertheless, you may find a reference to him in one of the compiled service records or in the records of a particular naval vessel. Your chances of finding your ancestor in one of the series described below will be greatly enhanced if you are fortunate enough to already know the name of the vessel on which he served.

Records Relating to Confederate Naval and Marine Personnel. M260 (7 rolls) FC 29-7.

The records in this series are similar to the service records pertaining to land soldiers in that they include abstract cards created on the basis of original documents as well as copies of original documents themselves. For each person, the record will show his name, rank, and the name of his ship or the naval station to which he was attached. Other data, such as date of capture, hospital admissions, and similar events are also included if relevant.

This series of papers is divided into two groups, one for the navy and the other one for the marine corps. Each group is arranged in alphabetical order according to the name of the sailor or marine. There is no separate index.

Papers Relating to Vessels of or Involved with the Confederate State of America "Vessel Papers." M909 (32 rolls) FC 10-32-4.

During the war there was a great amount of naval activity involving not only bona fide naval ships but also privately owned or operated vessels mustered into use or which furnished cargo to the Confederate government-- the so-called "blockade runners," which eluded the Union ships and shore batteries intent on closing the Southern ports to outside commerce. Other vessels were confiscated by the Confederate government either for occasional or sustained use. The legal owner or operator of the vessel could have been either a willing or an unwilling participant.

For several years following the hostilities, many vessel owners or their heirs filed claims against the federal government for alleged damage or loss of their vessels by the Union navy or as a result of their forces losses to the Confederate government. To enable the claims commission to determine whether a claim was to be allowed or disallowed, it was first necessary to ascertain whether or not the claimant had been a citizen loyal to the Union rather than a rebel sympathizer. For that purpose, papers relating to these many vessels were gathered together and organized for speedy retrieval of information concerning any particular individual should they be needed by the commission.

The papers were classified by name of the vessel or the steamship company which owned the vessels; each was given its own file and file number which serves as an index to the papers in this series. Roll number one carries this index and gives the specific roll numbers where the papers may be found. The "subject" (vessels or companies) are arranged alphabetically throughout the series. In each case, names of persons may be found among the related papers although many papers merely describe types and amounts of cargo, financial transactions, and similar commercial matters. It is evident that most of the persons named in this series were civilians, but, because of their waterbased occupations or activities, were classed in some records as naval personnel.

Subject File of the Confederate States Navy, 1861-1865. M1091 (63 rolls) FC 10-27-3.

Many naval records were lost or destroyed, but some were saved and became part of a much larger set of files maintained by the United States Navy titled "Subject File of the United States Navy, 1775-1910." This file was made up of documents from many sources. For instance, former Confederate naval officers who had retained their logs and related papers were asked to turn them in. Also, in 1904 and 1906, Congress required all executive departments to turn their naval records over to the Navy Department. In 1963, the National Archives extracted from the above "Subject File," all the Confederate States Navy material and consolidated it into this new series. The records in this series are all copies of the original papers rather than being abstract cards based on such papers. Incidentally, many of these papers were also reproduced in the publication *Official Records of the Confederate Navies in the War of the Rebellion* (see chapter five).

There is no index to this series and it is difficult to use unless a considerable amount of time is set aside for leisurely searching or browsing through it in hopes of finding something pertinent. There is a definite classification system, but it is necessary to inspect papers classified under one or more file headings to find what you are looking for. Each category of subjects is given an alphabetical order code. Within each category are subcategories, each with its own alphabetical code. To really understand this sytem and to use it, you must refer to the explanations in front of each roll, where the complete system is set forth. You may then pick out the categories and subcategories which appear to be promising and then go to the proper microfilm roll to see what you can find.

Unit Events, Casualties, Prisoners, Hospitalizations

The first goal in locating your Confederate ancestor, of course, is to learn his name and identify him as a member of a specific military unit or as a civilian. The next goal is to find some material that will enable you to fill in the personal history with regard to the places where he was stationed or resided and what events he might have been involved in during the time he served. The following are some of the questions to be answered. Did he serve all the time with the same unit? If not, in what other units did he serve? Was he injured in battle or did he suffer from some disease or ailment? Where was he hospitalized or treated? Was he taken prisoner by the Union forces and where was he confined? Was he ever paroled from confinement? The microfilm series described on the following pages provide you with opportunities to learn the answers to these questions about your ancestor. The abstract cards in your ancestor's compiled service record will give you the clues. To follow up on the clues, check one or more of the following series to see if you can find a copy of the original document where his name was listed. There may well be more information there than was stated briefly on the abstract card.

Compiled Records Showing Service of Military Units in Confederate Organizations. M861 (74 rolls) FC 10-31-5.

From the same mass of papers which the War Department sifted through to create the compiled records of individual soldiers and sailors of the Confederate army and navy, there were created a number of compiled records of the military units themselves. For each mention, an abtract card labeled "Captions and Record of Events" was prepared. These cards were grouped together according to unit and they form the content of this microfilm series. Unfortunately, the records are incomplete and this source is only partially helpful. They are worth a look, though, and if your ancestor's unit is present, the cards will give you a summary of the locations and dates of the campaigns and stations relative to the unit. One must be careful, though, to trace the ancestor's company, as well as his regiment, since one or more companies were frequently slipped off from the regiment and dispatched to some other location. Your ancestor's company may have been fighting a major battle while the other companies of the regiment were in some distant location doing routine camp duties--or vice versa.

Chances are that your ancestor will not be mentioned by name in this series unless he was an officer, but the story of the unit provides the framework upon which your ancestor's story can be told and may well explain an injury or capture. This series should be used to augment or confirm historical data in any published regimental history which you may also find listed in chapter five.

These records are arranged alphabetically, first by state and then by type of military unit such as artillery, cavalry, and infantry. In addition to state volunteer units, there are also records of units raised directly by the Confederate government and of units of a specialized or command type. Reserve and militia units are also included in some instances where their record survived and became a part of the War Department collection. Because of the alphabetical arrangement, there is no index to this series.

Confederate States Army Casualties. Lists and Narrative Reports, 1861-1865. M836 (7 rolls) FC 10-31-6.

During the course of the war, each unit of the Confederate army filed official reports to the Confederate adjutant and inspector general pertaining to each battle in which it played a part. Those reports listed numbers and names of those killed, wounded, or missing. A narrative description of the battle was also part of the report. After the war, reports came into possession of the United States adjutant general.

The majority of the reports were reproduced in the multi-volume work, *Official Records of the Union and Confederate Armies in the War of the Rebellion* (see chapter five). This microfilm series contains these reports which were either not included in that publication or were duplicated for the publication with the original remaining in this series. It would be advantageous to first check the publication and then inspect this mirofilm only if necessary to find material which was rejected for the publication. It is easier to find and read the material in the publication than it is in this microfilm. Some of the reports were the basis of an abtract card which was placed in a compiled service record. When that took place, the word "carded" and the date were written in the report.

The reports are arranged alphabetically by state in which the battle took place, then by name of the battle or engagement, and lastly by the names of the units that participated. In roll number seven, the battles which occurred in more than one state and the battles in which only one unit participated are listed chronologically. Also in roll number seven, the reports for the Indian Territory are listed alphabetically by name of the battle. A word of caution is necessary in that a particular soldier may actually have fought in one of these battles although his unit is not listed here. This may be so because he might have been especially detailed to the location at the time of the battle and thus was out of his normal area and unit. Also, there were errors and missing documents causing gaps in the complete histories of these engagements.

To use this series it is very important that you already have some idea that your ancestor fought in a particular battle. If you have that information, you should first inspect roll number one to see the listing of the battles and the number of the roll where the reports for that battle may be found.

Selected Records of the War Department Relating to Confederate Prisoners of War. M598 (145 rolls) FC 10-31-8.

When the War Department was preparing the compiled service records on individuals and military units, it kept separate a group of bound volumes containing records of military prisoners of war and the prisons in which they were confined. Those volumes were numbered in various fashions at different times,but when the National Archives microfilmed them they were renumbered--from one to 427. Those numbers are stamped on the front cover or first available page of each volume. Some of the records in these volumes were from the Office of the Commissary General of Prisoners who was responsible for Confederate military prisoners of war, political prisoners confined in Union prisons, and related matters. A smaller number of other records were in volumes kept by the Surgeon General's Office and by individual army commands. The majority of the reports were submitted by the individual prisons and are reproduced in this series. Records from these sources were kept by various federal agencies after the war, but they became part of the War Department collection and were microfilmed by the National Archives as a separate series.

Some of the reports were selected for inclusion in *Official Records--War of the Rebellion* (see chapter five). They are distinguishable by a circular stamp placed on them which reads, "COPIED, WAR RECORDS, 1861-1865." The first twelve microfilm rolls in this series reproduce the records of the commissary general of prisons and the surgeon general and relate to all prisoners regardless of the prison in which they were confined. Rolls thirteen through 142 reproduce the records of individual prisons, and rolls 144 and 145 reproduce the records relating to more than one prison. To use this resource, it is important that you already know, at least tentatively, in which prison your ancestor was confined, assuming he was captured by the Union or was considered a political prisoner by the United States government. Once you know that, it is possible to select certain rolls to examine in the hope of finding his name on one of the registers. Roll number one lists the contents of each roll in this series. For convenience, however, that listing is set forth below to enable you to decide whether to use this series or not and to help speed your search if you do.

Rolls 1-6	Registers compiled by the commissary general of Prisoners. (Roll number four lists deaths of prisoners).
Rolls 7-8	Registers compiled by the commissary general of prisoners. (Roll number eight lists applications for release, approvals for release).
Roll 9	Registers of unclaimed money, effects of deceased soldiers, permits for furnishing of clothing to prisoners, deaths.
Roll 10-12	Registers of deaths compiled by the surgeon general, arranged by state.

Rolls 13-139	Registers of Federal Prisons:
	Alton, Illinois
	Bowling Green, Kentucky
	Camp Butler, Illinois
	Camp Chase, Ohio
	Cincinnati, Ohio
	Fort Columbus, New York
	Fort Delaware, Delaware
	Camp Douglas, Illinois
	Elmira, New York
	Gratiot and Myrtle Streets Prison, St. Louis, Missouri
	Department of the Gulf (lists parolees)
	Hart Island, New York
	Hilton Head, South Carolina
	Johnson's Island, Ohio
	Knoxville, Tennessee
	Fort Lafayette, New York
	Little Rock, Arkansas
	Fort McHenry, Maryland
	McLean Barracks, Cinncinnati, Ohio
	Memphis, Tennessee
	Camp Norton, Indiana
	Newport News, Virginia
	Old Capitol Prison, Washington, D.C.
	Point Lookout, Maryland
	Richmond, Virginia
	Rock Island Barracks, Illinois
	Ship Island, Mississippi
	Fort Warren, Massachusetts
Rolls 140-142	Division of West Mississippi
Roll 143	District of West Tennessee, Provost Marshal's Office
Rolls 144-145	Records relating to various military prisons

Register of Confederate Soldiers, Sailors, and Citizens Who Died in Federal Prisons and Military Hospitals in the North. M918 (1 roll) FC 32-4.

Because a system of prisoner exchange between the Confederate and Union forces did not work out well, many Confederate prisoners remained in custody even though their deaths were imminent. When they died, in most cases, they were buried at the prison. A small wooden slab was usually erected at the gravesite, but sometimes there was no marker at all. A series of national cemeteries was established for deceased Union soldiers, and a few Confederate soldiers were buried in those cemeteries. Three Confederate burial grounds were established just after the turn of the present century. These included a section of the National Cemetery at Arlington, Virginia, just outside Washington, D.C.; Confederate Mound, Oak Woods Cemetery, Chicago, Illinois; and Camp Chase, Columbus, Ohio.

In 1906, Congress enacted legislation instituting a program of locating and marking the graves of soldiers and sailors of the Confederate army and navy who died in Northern prisons and who were buried there. A register of those graves consisting of 665 pages was completed in 1912. It is arranged first by location of the grave and then by name of the deceased. In each case, the person's rank, his unit, the date of his death, and the specific spot where he is buried is given. There is no master index of names, so if one's ancestor is thought or known to have been buried in a Northern prison, it would help considerably if the location of the prison were known. There are sixty or more prisons with burial grounds listed in this microfilm series, and it would take considerable time to go through each of those lists looking for one name. It is possible, though, because each list is alphabetized. The names of the prisons may be found at the front of roll number one.

Original Letters and Telegrams--Confederate Offices

In modern times it has been said that an army cannot fight a war without a typewriter. During the Civil War there were no typewriters, but a mountain of paperwork was accumulated, nevertheless, all written by hand with pen and ink. Three departments of the Confederate army received and replied to most of the correspondence. From the large volume of letters on hand at the close of hostilities, it would appear that most of the letters received by those departments were saved for posterity. This windfall of data has been indexed and microfilmed. Many of the letters were taken out of this series for use in publishing *Official Records--War of the Rebellion,* and others were taken out to be placed in some compiled service record. The remainder are available for inspection in one of the microfilm series described below. Since the indexes were based on the registers in which entries were made upon receipt of a letter (or telegram), a name may appear in the index even though the correspondence itself was later removed or transferred to some other office.

The three departments that provided the collections of letters and telegrams were the Office of the Secretary of War, the Office of the Adjutant and Inspector General, and the Office of the Quartermaster. Before searching the correspondence itself, it is necessary that you use the indexes. They are described below.

Index to Letters Received by the Confederate Secretary of War. M409 (34 rolls) FC 10-31-3.

This is a microcopy of index cards prepared in 1892 by the War Department. They refer to the letters which found their way to the Confederate Secretary of War and which were turned over to the Union officers after the Confederate surrender. Many of them were initially sent to some other office or person, such as the president, and forwarded to the Secretary of War for handling.

During the first year of the war, the letters were assigned a file number as they were received and were logged into a register. The number was followed by the year, "1861," or "1862." The system was modified by February 1862. From that time on, the letters were arranged by alphabet groups according to the name of the writer or the principal person referred to in the letter. Then a serial number, plus the year, was assigned to each letter. A file number which reads "234-W-1864" indicates that it was the 234th letter by or referring to a person whose name begins with the letter "W" in the year of 1864.

Letters Received by the Confederate Secretary of War. M437 (151 rolls) FC 10-31-1.

Each letter received by the Office of the Secretary of War was endorsed on the back or on a cover sheet giving the name of the sender, or the person to which it referred, and the dates it was sent and received. The general content of the letter was also summarized before it was logged into the register. Primarily, the letters which came to this office were from high level military officers or government officials. Their content dealt largely with such things as deployment of troops or equipment, the acquisition and use of military supplies, the organization and transfer or consolidation of military units, and other important business relating to the conduct of the war. It was seldom that an enlisted man, a junior officer, or a civilian holding a minor post was mentioned in this type of correspondence. There were exceptions, though, and a close check of the index is worthwhile and may bring unexpected results. If the commanding officer of a soldier's unit is known, it would pay to check his name in the index to see if there might be some information relating to the unit in which your ancestor served, and this would add flavor to your family history.

Index and Register for Telegrams Received by the Confederate Secretary of War, 1861-1865. M618 (19 rolls) FC 10-31-3.

The telegrams sent to the Confederate secretary of war were entered into a register and kept separate from the letters. As with the letters, the telegrams were endorsed on the back, giving the name of the sender, the dates they were sent and received, and the general content of the message. They were then given a file number and logged. Some of the telegrams were later taken out for use in the publication *Official Records--War of the Rebellion,* and some were taken out to become part of a compiled service record. No adjustments to the registers were made, however, when such transfers were made. Some of the telegrams in this series were initially received by other Confederate offices or persons but forwarded to the secretary of war for handling.

This microfilm series contains both the registers and the telegrams themselves arranged in chronological order. Each register has its own index of names, so you will have to search more than one index to see if your ancestor might be mentioned among these telegrams. The earliest time period, February 1861 to June 1862 is on roll number one, and this pattern continues throughout the nineteen rolls.

Index to Letters Received by the Confederate Adjutant and Inspector General and the Confederate Quartermaster General. M410 (41 rolls) FC 10-31-1.

The letters sent to the two offices mentioned in the above title were grouped separately and later microfilmed in separate series as described below. The two collections were lumped together, however, for the purpose of indexing. Not only the names of the senders but also the names of those who attached enclosures or endorsements are included in the index. The rank and unit of any military personnel were also listed. Each index card contains either the symbol "A & IGO" (Adjutant and Inspector General) or "QMC" (Quartermaster General).

The letters to the Adjutant and Inspector General were grouped first by year the letter was sent and then arranged alphabetically by the person's first initial only. Each letter in each category was then given a serial number as it was entered into a register. Thus, a file number "2345-B-1863" indicates that it was letter number 2345 sent by or relating to a person whose name began with the letter "B" in 1863.

When you use this index, be careful about those letters dated after July 1862, because the initial "I" and "J" are indexed together. It is very difficult in most cases to distinguish between those two letters in the script of the day. Some cards were made solely for cross-reference purposes and they may be helpful to you.

Letters Received by the Confederate Adjutant and Inspector General. M474 (164 rolls) FC 10-31-1.

The Office of the Adjutant and Inspector General was reponsible for the administration of the Confederate army. His office exercised jurisdiction over such things as issuing and enforcing orders and regulations, and this required actual inspection of the units in the field. It kept registers of officer nominations and confirmations, issued commissions, and acted as an arbiter in cases involving succession rights and the ranking of officers. It also kept detailed records of each unit including its origination, any consolidations, and its disbandment. This office kept records relating to military personnel. Lastly, it acted on court-martial documents.

The letters received by this office were endorsed on the back or on a separate cover sheet with the name of the writer, or primary person to which it referred, the dates it was sent and received, and the general content of the letter. It was then given a file number and entered into a register established for that purpose. When the War Department began assembling and categorizing these letters, it first arranged them by year, then alphabetically by the initial only of the writer or the office he represented, or the person to whom the letter referred. Several letters were taken out for use in the publication *Official Records--War of the Rebellion,* and the others were taken out to become part of a compiled service record. The register, however, lists all the letters regardless of their ultimate destination, and since the index is based on the register, some entries may not have a corresonding letter in this series.

Letters Received by the Confederate Quartermaster General. M469 (14 rolls) FC 10-31-3.

The quartermaster general was responsible for provision of quarters, supplies, clothing, fuel, food, horses, and related material necessary to the functioning of the Confederate army. His office also collected "taxes in kind" as a means of obtaining material for use by army personnel or for transfer to the Treasury Department.

As with letters described in other microfilm series letters to the Quartermaster General were endorsed, given a file number, and entered into a register established for that purpose. Each register or book was numbered successively and used until it was full usually after three to six months. When the War Department began to arrange these letters, it first arranged them by the number of the book into which it had been entered. This series consists of the entries of twelve of those books plus the entries of a thirteenth book which was subsequently lost. The letters are arranged by alphabetical order according to the first initial only of the writer, or the person to whom the letter referred, and then by serial number assigned when it was received and entered into the book.

Several letters in this series were taken out for use in the publication *Official Records--War of the Rebellion,* and some were taken out to become part of a compiled service record. The registers, however, list all the letters regardless of their ultimate destination. Since the index is based on the registers, some entries may not have a corresponding letter in this series.

Official Records of the Union and Confederate Armies in the War of the Rebellion. M262 (128 rolls) FC 10-32-1.

These records were published after extracting letters, reports, and other documents from various sources in order to create this huge collection of papers arranged according to campaigns and battles. For a complete description of this set of 128 volumes, see chapter five. This microfilm series duplicates the printed volumes. The last volume contains the general index, and there is a separate supplementary index in each volume which lists the actual page on which an indexed name appears. Both indexes must be used in conjunction with each other.

Union Volunteers from Southern and Border States

Despite the fact that a Southern state officially seceded from the Union and formed a Confederate army, there were many citizens who did not agree with the Southern philosophy toward the war. Some of those persons chose to volunteer to serve in the Union army rather than consider themselves "rebels." This was especially predominate in the border states whose loyalties were often sharply divided between the North and the South. Those states sent organized units in both directions. Compiled service records are available at the National Archives for those soldiers who volunteered to serve the Union despite their state of residence. Those records may be found in the following microfilm series. If you have not been able to locate your ancestor in the Confederate forces as you had expected, perhaps you should examine these records to see if he might have joined the Union instead. Incidentally, there were many instances where a man served on both sides during the course of the war.

Compiled Service Records of Volunteer Soldiers Who Served in Organizations From the State of:

Alabama M276 (10 rolls)	Index-M263
Arkansas M399 (60 rolls)	Index-M399
Florida M400 (11 rolls)	Index-M264
Georgia M403 (1 roll)	Index-M388
Kentucky M397 (515 rolls)	Index-M386

Louisiana M396 (50 rolls)	Index-M387
Maryland M384 (238 rolls)	Index-M388
Mississippi M404 (4 rolls)	Index-M389
Missouri M405 (854 rolls)	Index-M390
Territory of New Mexico (Arizona)	
M427 (46 rolls)	Index-M242
North Carolina M401 (25 rolls)	Index-M391
Tennessee M395 (220 rolls)	Index-M392
Texas M402 (13 rolls)	Index-M393
Territory of Utah M392 (1 roll)	Index-M556
Virginia M398 (7 rolls)	Index-M394
West Virginia M508 (261 rolls)	Index-M507

MICROFILMED RECORDS OF CIVILIANS

In addition to the records about the one million or so Confederate soldiers and sailors, there are records which survived for possibly hundreds of thousands of civilians who either were actively affiliated with the Confederate government or the Confederate army or simply were Southern citizens with varying degrees of loyalty to the Confederate cause. If you have exhausted all the possible resources for locating your military ancestor, it is time to attempt to locate something about his family members. If you have no military ancestor who served the Confederate armed forces, perhaps you can locate a civilian who was associated with it. The National Archives has a store of records relating to those persons, and the records are described below.

There are many references to civilians in the collections of letters to Confederate army officers, as previously described. In addition, the following sources contain records of civilians with some mentions of military personnel. These records are primarily of three types: (a) papers relating to business dealings with the Confederacy, (b) lists and reports kept by the Union Provost Marshal pertaining to civilians in the Southern and border states or pertaining to military personnel in Northern prisons and hospitals, and (c) papers relating to Southerners who filed for a pardon or amnesty after the war in order to regain their citizenship in the United States. With the exception of a person who might also have been a veteran of the fighting forces, none of the persons listed in these civilian sources were included in the indexes of compiled service records. Therefore, it will be necessary to check the separate indexes, where they exist, for each of the following series.

Records of the Commissioners of Claims (Southern Claims Commission), 1871-1880. M87 (14 rolls) FC 10-51-1.

Despite popular impressions, not all Southerners were in sympathy with the secessionist movement, and many remained steadfast in their belief that the Southern states should remain in the Union and attempt to solve their differences by peaceful means. Some families had members who threw their lot in with both the Northern and Southern sides, and some worked as spies or double agents for the Union. The majority, however, simply went about their own businesses or tended their own farms without getting too involved with their secessionist neighbors. Often those individuals, through no fault of their own, suffered financial losses or damages growing out of the hostilities. After the war, a commission was established to consider the claims of those loyal Southerners who wished to be compensated for their reverses.

The papers dealing with the claims have been microfilmed and may be examined at the National Archives. They deal with the monetary amounts of loss or damage, the merits of the claim, and the evidence to show that the claimant actually remained loyal to the Union. The papers are arranged first by state, then by county, and then by name of the claimant--with the amount of each claim listed. Many papers relating to the 22,298 claims processed by the commission are indexed in roll number thirteen of this series. Since the words "allowed" or "disallowed" were written next to some of the entries, it is apparent that this index was used for record keeping purposes for a short time. Roll number fourteen is a consolidated index of the claims arranged by the name of the claimant. The nature and amount of the claims as well as the state and county of the claimant are given. This is a copy of the index prepared by the commission and submitted to the House of Representatives. It has also been published in book form by the Government Printing Office. A copy may be found in the West Reading Room of the National Archives. See also the publication *Civil War Claims in the South* by Gary Mills (see chapter five).

Confederate Papers Relating to Citizens or Business Firms. M436 (1,158 rolls) FC 10-90-1.

As mentioned above in relation to claims filed by Southerners for loss or damage, it was necessary to determine if the claimant had remained loyal to the Union. To facilitate the task of answering that question, it was necessary to comb through a half million papers for any record that the claimant might have done business with the Confederacy and thus be disqualified from any compensation rights. The papers were gathered from those turned over to the War Department, from the Treasury Department, from various quartermaster officers and commissaries. Also, some papers originally placed by the War Department in other series were transferred to this collection with a cross reference to keep track of them. They were all classified and placed in jacket type files which were in turn stored in 1,349 file boxes. These were referred to as the "Citizen File."

The most common type of document found in this collection is a voucher form usually signed by a government official and the citizen or the business that provided goods or services to the Confederate government or the Confederate army. In the case of a large business there might be a large number of such vouchers as well as other kinds of business papers relating to many transactions. In many instances, a file was made up under the name of the president or other officer of the business and in other instances it showed up under the name of the firm instead. In addition to files for firms and individuals who conducted business, there were some files for military officers, government employees, and other specialized agents or employees of the Confederate government.

Since the files are arranged in alphabetical order throughout all the rolls in this series, there is no index. As a guide, there is a listing by alphabet groups with the corresponding microfilm roll number. There is also a separate and lengthy select list of files for persons or businesses that have an unusually large number of papers in their files.

Union Provost Marshal's File of Papers Relating to Individual Citizens. M345 (300 rolls) FC 10-26-6.

The provost marshals, in the role of military police, served in territorial commands and in the armies. As such, they were concerned with both

Confederate and Union army deserters, spies, and persons suspected of being disloyal to the Union. They investigated theft of government property, arrested and detained military and civilian prisoners, and maintained records of paroles and oaths of allegiance. They also approved transportation and travel between and within the states. They even established courts in some areas and tried civilians charged with violation of military laws and military personnel charged with violation of civil laws.

After the war their records were classified by the War Department and separated according to which ones referred to only one person and which ones referred to more than one person. The first group comprises this microfilm series, and the names are in alphabetical order. On occasion, a paper is cross referenced to the other group which is primarily arranged according to geographical area or by subject matter. There is a list of the alphabet groups and the corresponding roll numbers in this series. There is no index. A caution is in order here--all papers bearing the same name are filed in the same jacket without regard to whether they all refer to the same person.

Union Provost Marshal's File of Papers Relating to Two or More Civilians. M416 (94 rolls) FC 10-26-8.

The papers in this series are similar to those that refer to only one person, and cross references in that series are helpful in finding a name in this series. This group of papers was a bit more difficult to arrange and finding a certain name takes more time. The series consists of five parts: (a) a geographical and subject index (incomplete), (b) numbered documents arranged chronologically, (c) unnumbered documents arranged chronologically, (d) names of prisoners (both civilian and military) arranged by name of the prison, and (e) names in papers relating to property which was confiscated or destroyed.

The geographical listings are particularly interesting in that sometimes a person is named among a group of citizens of a town or county. Noted is his supposed loyalty or disloyalty to the Union with information about members of his family and their politicial leanings and whether they had enlisted in either the Confederate or the Union forces. Those residing in border states were more subject to this type of personal checking because of the larger numbers of people with divided loyalties.

Case Files of Investigation by Levi C. Turner and Lafayette C. Baker, 1861-1866. M797 (137 rolls). FC 10-19-5.

Levi C. Turner was the United States Army judge advocate between 1862 and 1866. Lafayette C. Baker was a provost marshal and special agent between 1861 and 1865. This series is comprised of the papers relating to the cases those two either investigated or tried during those years. They were involved in cases of subversion by both Southerners and Northerners. There are thousands of names in these papers and there is a general index.

Most of the 7,748 cases mentioned in this series were handled by Turner. His jurisdiction included the District of Columbia and the adjacent Virginia counties. It included both civilian and military persons accused of disloyalty, giving aid to the Confederates, defrauding the government, resisting the draft, trading in contraband with the enemy, and prisoners convicted in a state court but confined in a federal prison. They dealt also with Confederate army deserters and with those who tried to evade the blockade of Southern ports.

The cases handled by Baker, fewer in number, included cases of subversion, confiscation of abandoned rebel property in the areas in and around the District of Columbia, secessionists, contraband, and fraud against the government. The papers also include documents relating to prospective employment of detectives in the provost marshals' forces.

Both Turner's and Baker's files were merged with the records of the adjutant general in 1894 but were arranged and indexed as a separate collection because of their uniqueness. A file number was assigned to each document with a "B" following it if it was from Baker's collection. Some files consist of only one paper, but others consist of dozens of papers. The index provides the general content of the papers in each file. Roll number one identifies the other rolls in this series according to groups of file numbers.

Confiscated Property--Case Papers of the United States District Court for the Eastern District of Virginia, 1863-1865. M435 (1 roll) FC 10-9-5.

This series contains only a few papers and there is no index. The cases are related to legal procedures regarding the seizure of Confederate property in the Virginia counties of Alexandria, Fairfax, and Loudon.

Confederate Papers of the United States District Court for the Eastern District of North Carolina, 1861-1865. M436 (1 roll) FC 10-9-6.

This series contains papers filed in the above cited courts relating to "sequestration of estates, property and effects of alien enemies." There are also papers relating to persons accused of harboring deserters, of treason, and of robbery of the mails. They also include jury lists, court orders, and subpoenas. The cases related to a portion of North Carolina primarily in and around Salisbury, Wilmington and Cape Fear. The papers are arranged by subject, and there is no index.

Case Files of Applications from Former Confederates for Presidential Pardons (Amnesty Papers), 1865-1867. M1,003 (73 rolls) FC 10-33-9.

In 1863, while the war was still going strong, President Lincoln issued a proclamation of amnesty to Southern "rebels." There were few who took advantage of the opportunity, however, since there remained considerable doubt as to which side would be victorious. This proclamation specifically excluded six types of persons (a seventh would be added later) who were barred from amnesty unless a personal application was made to the president and unless such application was approved. Near the war's end on 29 March 1865, President Johnson who had succeeded Lincoln reissued the proclamation and added his seventh exception. Generally, Lincoln's exceptions included persons who held high level military or government positions and those who had left the North to fight for the South. Johnson's exception added those who owned property valued at more than $20,000, and this eliminated a considerable group of persons who could otherwise have been automatically pardoned. Subsequent proclamations tended to erase some of the exceptions until a final proclamation dated 25 December 1869, provided amnesty for all--"unconditionally and without reservation."

During the period 1865-67, a flood of applications was received by President Johnson. Half of them were in response to his restriction on owning property valued at more than $20,000. Those property owners feared confiscation of their lands and also feared being tried for treason. They were, therefore, anxious for a pardon as a means to obviate such ill fortune. They frequently sought recommendations and affidavits from persons in high places to support their pleas. There were approximately 14,000 applications, and, by the fall of 1867, the president had granted pardons to 13,500.

The records in this series are divided according to where the applications were filed--Southern states, states in the North or West, and where no state was identified. The papers are arranged under the name of the state, and thereunder by alphabet according to name. Also, under each state there is a group of files which contain two or more names as well as a group of miscellaneous files.

This microfilm series contains the papers of those who filed for amnesty without regard to whether or not their requests were approved. To determine the names of those who were actually pardoned, it is possible to read the published *Congressional Reports* which listed such persons. While at the National Archives, you might visit the West Reading Room and ask the librarian for assistance in locating these reports:

Thirty-ninth Congress, First Session, H. Document 99, Serial 1263. *Message of the President*. May 14, 1866. (Contains a list of those persons who owned property valued at more than $20,000.)

Thirty-ninth Congress, Second Session, H. Document 31, Serial 1289. *Message of the President. January 8, 1867.*

Thirty-ninth Congress, Second Session, H. Document 116, Serial 1293. *Message of the President. March 2, 1867.*

Fortieth Congress, First Session, H. Executive Document 32, Serial 1311. *Message of the President. July 8, 1867.*

Fortieth Congress, Second Session, H. Executive Document 16, Serial 1330. *Final Report of the Names of Persons Engaged in Rebellion Who Have Been Pardoned by the President. December 4, 1867.*

RECORDS NOT ON MICROFILM

Because most of the Confederate records at the National Archives have been microfilmed, it is unlikely that you will ever need to search those which are stored away in their original form. You may have some evidence, however, of the existence of your Confederate ancestor, either military or civilian, being employed or stationed at a certain place during the war years but have not been able to locate a reference to him in the microfilmed material. In those instances, you may want to make one last attempt at finding him in the unmicrofilmed material. Also, you may have found a reference to your ancestor on microfilm but feel you might uncover additional material in the original papers. In these instances, you might discuss your problem or desire with one of the Archives' consultants in room 205.

The consultant will advise you concerning the material available to you and probably will refer you directly to one of the specialized branches. These probably would be either the Military Service Branch or the Navy and Old Army Branch. They might also be the Legislative and Diplomatic Branch or the Cartographic and Architectural Branch. If so, the consultant will direct you to the branch where you can get the most expert service and assistance. An Archives search card is required to use one of these branches or to gain entry into the reading rooms just off room 203. If the branch locates material for you, it will send it to room 203 where you may pick it up and examine it at your leisure.

When you confer with the consultant or one of the staff in the branches, it may help them and speed things up for you if you will refer to the descriptions of the records set forth below.

Index of Appointment of Confederate Officers. Location: Military Services Branch (Section 8-E). Entry 21, Record Group 109.

A card index of Confederate officer appointments was prepared by the United States Adjutant General from the entries placed in the registers of the Confederate Secretary of War and the Confederate Adjutant and Inspector General. That index was never microfilmed but is available for inspection upon request. If the person was confirmed as an officer you probably can find his record in the microfilmed records and need not bother with this card index. However, he may have been nominated but not confirmed or had never entered duty. In those instances, you may find a card bearing his name in this index and nowhere else. The card shows the name, rank, state, and sometimes other data. To facilitate the search, provide the name of your ancestor so that only the one box which contains the cards of the alphabet group for the name you seek will be brought to you.

Registers of Officers, Confederate States Navy, 1861-1865. Location: Military Services Branch (section 8-E).

Rather than being a collection of papers, this is a bound volume prepared by the Office of Naval Records and Library. It consists of an alphabetical list of officers with brief biographical statements for each. It includes the place of birth, if known, the place from which appointed, rates and ranks, ships and stations to which assigned, and whether captured or released on parole.

Shipping Articles for Enlisted Men in the Confederate Navy. Location: Navy and Old Army Branch (Section 8-W). Entry 420, Record Group 45.

This is a huge, bound volume containing data relative to persons who agreed to enlist in the Confederate Navy. The entries are listed in chronological order, dated between 18 September 1861 and 29 April 1864. The entries include the name, date of enlistment, rate, monthly wages and bounty paid (in a few rare instances), and the signature of the recruit. There is a typewritten index arranged alphabetically by name, attached to this volume. The data in this volume may well be found in the compiled service records which are on microfilm, but there may be supplemental data here which was not included on the abstract card used in compiling those records. Also, the signature may be of particular interest.

Muster Rolls and Payrolls of Ship and Shore Establishments of the Confederate Navy. Location: Navy and Old Army Branch (Section 8-W). Entry 419, Record Group 45.

These records are filed according to the name of the ship or the location of the shore establishment. To use them you must know where your ancestor was stationed. There is no index. The records consist of flat ledger sheets listing the names, rank, date, amounts of money paid and deducted from the pay, and the signature of the payee.

Civilian Personnel at Confederate Shore Establishment. Location: Navy and Old Army Branch (Section 8-W). Entry 422, Record Group 45.

These records consist of six drawers of ledger sheets used to record the pay of those persons employed at the shore establishments at the following locations: Albany, Georgia; Atlanta, Georgia; Charleston, South Carolina; Jackson, Mississippi; Little Rock, Arkansas; Memphis, Tennessee; Mobile, Alabama; New Orleans, Louisiana; and Petersburg, Virginia. There is no index.

Payrolls of Civilian Workers of the Confederate Government, 1861-1865.
Location: Navy and Old Army Branch (Section 8-W). Entry 56, Record
Group 45. The index is Entry 58.

These are standard payroll forms used to record payments to both
civilian and military personnel employed at various establishments of the
Confederate government. The index consists of slips of paper each containing the name of a payee. The source of the payroll is given in the index, in
many instances, but others merely list a name with no additional information
or reference.

Slave Payrolls, Confederate Government. Location: Navy and Old Army
Branch (Section 8-W). Entry 57, Record Group 109.

These are standard payroll forms used to record payments to civilians
who furnished slave labor for use in construction of Confederate buildings
and fortifications and for other work. The entries show for whom the slave
was hired, the slave's name (usually only a given name) and occupation followed by the slave, the time worked and wages earned, and the signature of
the slaveowner who received the payment. The names are indexed in Entry
58.

Register of Slaves, Charleston, South Carolina Harbor, 1862-1863.
Location: Navy and Old Army Branch (Section 8-W). Entry 436, Record
Group 45.

This is a bound volume containing lists of slaves who worked on military fortifications. Given are the dates, name of the slaveowner, and name of
the slave (usually only a given name).

Oaths of Allegiance to the Federal Government. Location: Legislative and
Diplomatic Branch (Section 5-E). Record Group 59.

Persons granted amnesty by President Johnson before 1868 were
required to take an oath of allegiance. There are several boxes of these oaths
made on thin, fragile paper forms. They contain the name, date and place the
oath was signed, and the signature. The signer agreed to obey the

Constitution of the United States as well as the official proclamations made during the war with regard to the emancipation of slaves. The papers are arranged first by state and then alphabetically by the first two letters of the name of the oath taker.

Maps Relating to Captured and Abandoned Property. Location: Cartographic and Architectural Branch, 841 S. Pickett Street, Alexandria, Virginia.

Staff at the National Archives will provide directions to this storehouse located outside Washington, D.C. A free shuttle bus may be used if desired. Hours are 8:00 a.m. to 4:00 p.m., Monday through Friday, except on national holidays.

This branch has manuscripts and maps pertaining to Civil War era plantations of a few selected counties or parishes, as follows: Arkansas, the counties of Chicot and Desha; Louisiana, the parishes of Caroll, Madison, and Tensas; Mississippi, the counties of Adams, Bolivar, Claiborne, Issaquena, Jefferson, Warren, Washington, and Wilkinson.

CHAPTER 5

Searching in Publications

In addition to searching the records of the Civil War for information about your Confederate ancestor, you will want to peruse some of the hundreds of publications pertaining to specific Confederate military units. There are two categories of such publications. One category consists of those which give the history of a company, regiment, or brigade, mentioning only the names of the generals and other high level commanding officers; the other consists of those which also contain lists of the soldiers who served in the unit. These may include muster rolls, casualty lists, prisoner lists, and names provided by correspondents who contributed to the publication. An exhaustive search was made to locate as many publications of the latter category as possible. The results of that search are the titles listed in this chapter. They are arranged by "general works" which involve units from more than one state and by name of the individual states.

Shown below are various sources and places you might explore to locate unit histories which may or may not contain names of the unit's personnel. Before you start, it probably would pay to examine the two bibliographies described so you will have some idea of what is available in the printed word. Then decide on which libraries you will visit first. Somewhere, in that vast treasurehouse, your ancestor's name will be listed.

Civil War Books, a Critical Bibliography by Allen Nevins, James I. Robertson, and Bell I. Wiley. This is a two volume work containing a lengthy list of regimental histories, diaries, narratives, and other books about the Civil War. In each case, there is a comment relative to the book's usefulness and its accuracy so you will be able to determine whether a search for a particular book is worth your time. The entries are arranged alphabetically by name of the author and include both Union and Confederate works.

Military Bibliography of the Civil War by Charles E. Dornbusch. This is a three volume work containing a very complete list of Union and Confederate regimental histories as well as articles relating to military units to be found in journals and history magazines. Included also are memoirs, diaries, and similar narratives. Volume one covers the Southern, border, and Western states; volume two covers the Northern states; and volume three covers specific units which fought at certain selected battle sites. Each entry is coded according to the name of one or more libraries where the work might be located. If needed, your librarian will be able to help you interpret those code symbols and assist you in the use of the *National Union Catalog,* a series of volumes which list books and where they are located anywhere in the United States. The military units in this bibliography are arranged according to the name of the state and thereunder by name or number of the unit. The books and publications which refer to each unit are listed under the name or number of the unit.

Southern Historical Society Papers. Dozens and dozens of regimental histories as well as registers and lists have been published by the Southern Historical Society. These have been bound into fifty-two volumes covering the years 1876 to 1959. A two volume "Index Guide" to the volumes was published in 1980 by James I. Robertson and is an indispensible aid in locating articles about Confederate units. None of the publications listed in this chapter include articles either from these papers or from other journals or magazines, so be sure to check the indexes of such publications for additional sources.

Library of Congress

A high proportion, but not all, of the publications listed in this chapter may be found at the Library of Congress located just east of the Capitol in Washington, D.C. Visit the local History and Genealogy Room in the Thomas Jefferson Building (the main building) and ask for assistance from the staff. The publications you wish to see must first be located either in the card catalog or on a computer terminal. Once the catalog data is found, the publication may be ordered by submitting a call slip. In most cases, the Library of Congress catalog number you need will be found in this chapter, thus obviating the need for you to look it up in the card catalog or to use the computer terminal. If you cannot arrange a personal visit to this library, an alternative is to use the services of a professional genealogical researcher. He or she can find the book you want and can make copies from it at the rate of ten cents per sheet.

Military History Institute, Carlisle Barracks, Pennsylvania

This library and museum is lcoated in Upton Hall of the military post. It is open to the public between 8:00 a.m. and 4:30 p.m., Monday through Friday, except on holidays. As you enter the building, you will register and be given an identification tag. Upon request, the library staff will provide you with a long list of their Confederate holdings. You will then be shown where to find the publications on that list. They are in open stacks and you are invited to browse among them at your leisure. You will find that there have been many additions to their list of holdings since it was printed. Many of the works listed in this chapter may be found at this library.

State, University, and Local Libraries

Many of the publications listed in this chapter, as well as those publications which give only background historical information, may be found in the state libraries. You will also find some of them in the historical or genealogical sections of libraries of colleges and universities and the public libraries of the larger towns and cities. Especially helpful in state or regional type libraries are county and city histories. In many of those you will find lists of persons who served in the Civil War. None of those local histories are included in the publications listed in this chapter, so be sure not to overlook this additional valuable source.

Bookshops

There are specialized bookshops which carry Civil War regimental histories, many of which are out of print. If the shop you contact does not have the volume you are seeking, it may be able to locate it for you from one of the other shops with which it cooperates. One of the large shops is the Broadfoot's Bookmark, Route 4, Box 508C, Wilmington, NC 28405. It recently announced that it has a set of forty volumes of Civil War material selling for $1,000, plus shipping and handling charges. A two volume index to that series is also available at $40 plus shipping and handling charges. Also, see its 1978 priced booklist available in some libraries. You may write to this shop to inquire if it has any material relating to the specific military unit in which you are interested or to inquire about their current price list.

Another leading Civil War bookshop is the Morningside Bookshop, a combination reprint publishing house and bookstore. You may obtain an up-to-date catalog by writing to them at P.O. Box 1087, Dayton, OH 45401. Their store is at 258 Oak Street in Dayton.

Virginia Historical Society Library

This society, located at the corner of Boulevard and Kensington Avenues in Richmond, Virginia (off exit 14 of I-95), has a large collection of Civil War publications including many regimental histories of Confederate units. You may wish to write to see if it has a particular book which you may be seeking. The mailing address is P.O. Box 7311, Richmond, VA 23221. You may visit in person between 9:00 a.m. and 4:45 p.m., Monday through Saturday, except on national holidays and national holiday weekends. The books are on closed stacks, and you must inspect the card catalog and use a request slip for each book you wish to see. This library is only one example of similar libraries maintained by other state historical or genealogical societies in other Southern or border states or even counties. It may pay you to check out the holdings in such a society in your own state or county. Many of them publish their own journals which sometimes contain Confederate names. An example is the *Alabama Historical Quarterly.*

Libraries at Civil War Sites Operated by the National Park Service

When you visit a battleground maintained by the National Park Service, ask to speak with the historian for that site. He can provide you with a copy of the catalog entitled *Sunshine and Shadows.* This is a list of both Union and Confederate histories and personal narratives housed in the libraries of the various parks associated with Civil War battle sites. Each entry is coded to show which of the parks has the books in this collection. An extensive library of this type is the one at Fredericksburg, Virginia (at the Chatham section).

The staff there will make available to you their large collection of microfilm purchased from the National Archives. It has the series of film listing the personnel of the military units from each of the Confederate states as listed in each state section of chapters two and three of this book and as listed in chapter one.

This library is creating a collection of papers, documents, letters, diaries, and anything written during the Civil War, and urges you to donate a copy (not the original) of any such material you might possess.

Other large libraries of the above type are maintained at the Civil War sites at Petersburg, Virginia, Wilson's Creek, Missouri, and Gettysburg, Pennsylvania, among others.

In addition to the use of these park service libraries, a personal visit to the site where your ancestor fought will provide you with detailed and authenticated information about the battle fought there--usually accompanied by a movie, slide show, or a battle map complete with lights, and a short lecture or tour. The following battle sites associated with the Civil War are operated by the National Park Service.

Andersonville (Georgia)
Antietam (Maryland)
Appomattox (Virginia)
Brice's Cross Roads (Mississippi)
Chancellorsville (Virginia)
Chickamauga and Chattanooga (Tennessee)
Cumberland Gap (Tennessee, Virginia, Kentucky)
Fort Donelson (Tennessee)
Fort Pulaski (Georgia)
Fort Sumter (South Carolina)
Fredericksburg (Virginia)
Gettysburg (Pennsylvania)
Harpers Ferry (West Virginia)
Kennesaw Mountain (Georgia)
Manassas (Virginia)
Pea Ridge (Arkansas)
Petersburg (Virginia)
Richmond (Virginia)
Shiloh (Tennessee)

Spotsylvania (Virginia)
Stones River (Tennessee)
Tupelo (Mississippi)
Vicksburg (Mississippi)
Wilson's Creek (Missouri)

PUBLICATIONS WITH LISTS OF NAMES

The following are publications personally inspected by the author and found
to have some type of list of names of Confederate soldiers or sailors.

General Works

Barbiere, Joseph. *Scraps from the Prison Table at Camp Chase and
Johnson's Island.* Doylestown, Pa.: W. W. H. Davis, 1868.

Beitzell, Edwin W. *Point Lookout Prison Camp for Confederates.* Abell,
Md.: By the Author, 1972 (E616 118 .B4)

Brice, Marshall M. *The Stonewall Brigade Band.* Verona, Va.: McClure Co.,
1967. (E581 .5 4th .B4)

Brock, R. A. *The Appomattox Roster.* Richmond: The Society. Reprint. The
Antiquarian Press, 1962. (E548 .C66)

Brown, Dee A. *The Galvanized Yankees.* Urbana, Ill.: Urbana Press, 1863.
(E83 .863 .B7)

Buzzett, Isabelle S. *Men Signing the "Confederate Hall" Register at the Cotton States Exposition, Atlanta, Georgia, 1895.* Atlanta: United
Daughters of the Confederacy, 1895.

Carroll, J. M. & Co. *The Confederate Roll of Honor.* Mattituck, N.Y.: J. M.
Carroll & Co., 1985.

Confederate Medical and Surgical Journal. 14 vols., Jan, 1864-Feb. 1865.
Reprint. Metuchen, N.J.: Scarecrow Press, 1976. (R11 .C62)

*Confederate Soldiers, Sailors, and Civilians who Died as Prisoner's of War
at Camp Douglas, Chicago, Illinois, 1862-1865.* Kalamazoo, Mich.:
Edgar Gary, 1968. (E616 .D6C6)

Confederate Veteran. 40 vols. Nashville: N.p. 1893-1932. (E482 .C74) (LOC micro #10929)

Confederate Veteran Index. Dayton: The Morningside Bookshop, 1982.

Crute, Joseph H., Jr. *Confederate Staff Officers, 1861-1865*. Powhatan, Va.: Derwent Books, 1892. (E548 .C83)

Dickinson, Sally B. *Confederate Leaders*. Staunton, Va.: McClure Co., 1935. (E467 .D54)

Donnelly, Ralph W. *Biographical Sketches of the Commissioned Officers of the Confederate States Marine Corps*. Alexandria, Va.: By the Author, 1973. (E467 .D66)

_____. *Service Records of Confederate Enlisted Marines*. New Bern, N.C.: By the Author, 1973. (E596 .D663)

Dotson, Susan M. *Who's Who in the Confederacy*. San Antonio: The Naylor Co., 1966. (E467 .D68)

Elliott, William, comp. *Lists of Confederate Soldiers Who, While Prisoner's of War, Died at Columbus and Camp Denison, Ohio, and Buried at Camp Chase Confederate Cemetery*. Washington, D.C.: Government Printing Office, 1907.

Estes, Claude, comp. *List of Field Officers, Regiments, and Battalions in the Confederate States Army, 1861-1865*. Macon, Ga.: J. W. Burke Co., 1912. Reprint. Mattituck, N.J.: Carroll Co., 1983. Originally printed: Government Printing Office. N.d. (E548. E79) (E548 .U785)

Evans, Clement E. *Confederate Military History*. 12 vols. Atlanta: Confederate Publishing Co., 1899. (E484 .E9)

Fuzzlebug, Fritz [pseud]. *Prison Life During the Rebellion, Being a Brief Narrative of the Miseries and Sufferings of Six Hundred Confederate Prisoners Sent from Fort Delaware to Morris' Island to be Punished*. Singer's Glen, Va.: Joseph Funk's Sons; Printers, 1869. (615 .D92) (Dunkle, John J.)

Glover, Ruth. *Confederate Service Records of all Southern States and a few Federal Veterans: From Biographical Souvenirs of the States of Georgia and Florida*. N.p., n.d.

Handy, Isaac W. K. *United States Bonds; or Duress by Federal Authority; a Journal of Current Events During Fifteen Months at Fort Delaware*. Baltimore: Turnbull Brothers, 1887.

Helsely, Mrs. Wilford and West, Mrs. Warren R. *Undertaker's List of Confederate Dead in the Bethel Cemetery, Knoxville, Tennessee*. Knoxville:

United Daughters of the Confederacy, Knoxville Chapter #89, 1973. (E548 .H44)

Hewitt, Lawrence L. and Bergeron, Arthur W., Jr. *Post Hospital Ledgers, Port Hudson, Louisiana, 1862-1863.* Baton Rouge: Les Comte des Archives de la Louisiane, 1981. (E548 .H48)

Hodge, Robert A. *A Death Roster of the Confederate General Hospital at Culpeper, Virginia.* Fredericksburg, Va.: By the Author, 1977. (E548 .H68)

Hollywood Memorial Association, Richmond. *Register of the Confederate Dead, Interred in Hollywood Cemetery, Richmond, Virginia.* Richmond: Gary, Clemmit and Jones, 1869. (E548 .H72)

Holmes, Clay W. *The Elmira Prison Camp: A History of the Military Prison at Elmira, New York, July 6, 1864 to July 10, 1865.* New York: G. P. Putnam's Sons, 1912. (E616 .E4H7)

Ingmire, Frances T. *Confederate Prisoners of War: Soldiers and Sailors Who Died in Federal Prisons and Military Hospitals in the North.* St. Louis: Ericson Books, 1984. (E548 .I55)

Johnson, David E. *The Story of a Confederate Boy in the Civil War.* Portland: N.p. 1914. (E605 .J72)

Knaus, William H. *The Story of Camp Chase.* Nashville and Dallas: Publishing House of the Methodist Episcopal Church, South, 1906. (E616 C4K67)

Krick, Robert K. *Lee's Colonels, a Biographical Roster of the Field Officers of the Army of Northern Virginia.* Dayton, Oh.: Morningside Bookshop, 1979.

_____. *The Gettysburg Death Roster--The Confederate Dead at Gettysburg.* Dayton, Oh.: Morningside Bookshop, 1981. (E494 .K74)

Kurtz, Lucy. *A Roster of Confederate Soldiers Buried in Stonewall Cemetery, Winchester, Virginia.* N.p., n.d.

Mills, Gary B. *Civil War Claims in the South, an Index of Claims Filed Before the Southern Claims Commission, 1871-1880.* Laguna Hills, Calif.: Aegean Park Press, 1980. (E480.5 .M54)

Murray, J. Ogden. *The Immortal Six Hundred, A Story of Cruelty to Confederate Prisoners of War.* Roanoke, Va.: The Stone Printing and Manufacturing Co., 1911. (E615 .M90)

Norton, Herman W. *Rebel Religion: The Story of Confederate Chaplains.* St. Louis: Bethany Press, 1961. (E547 .7 .N6)

Office of Naval Records and Library. *Register of Officers of the Confederate States Navy, 1861-1865.* Washington, D.C.: Government Printing Office, 1898. Reprint. 1931. (E597 .N585)

Peterson, Clarence S. *Last Civil War Veteran in Fifty States.* Washington, D.C.: By the Author, 1971. Typescript.

Piton, Mrs. Phillip. *Register of Confederate Dead Interred in Camp Chase Confederate Cemetery, Columbus, Ohio, and in Johnson's Island Confederate Cemetery, near Sandusky, Ohio.* Columbus: Ohio Genealogical Society, Franklin County Chapter, 1960.

Poe, J. E., ed. *The Raving Foe: The Civil War Diary of Major James T. Poe, C.S.A. and the Eleventh Arkansas Volunteers, and a Complete List of Prisoners.* Eastland, Tex.: Longhorn Press, 1967. (E605 .P65)

Pompey, Sherman L. *Members of the First Alabama, Mississippi, and Tennessee Infantry, C.S.A. Buried at Oakwood Cemetery, Chicago, Illinois.* Fresno, Calif.: By the Author, 1968. (E548 .P62)

_____. *Burial List of the 2,436 Confederate Soldiers Mostly Taken Prisoner of War at the Battle of Gettysburg . . . Interred at Finn's Point National Cemetery, near Salem, New Jersey.* Harrisburg, Ore.: Pacific Specialties, 1875. (E548 .P56) Note: Sherman L. Pompey has written several such works, and you will want to examine these when searching bibliographies.

Powell, William H., ed. *Officers of the Army and Navy, Regular and Volunteer, Who Served in the Civil War.* Philadelphia: L. R. Hamersley & Co., 1894. (E467 .P88)

Robertson, James I., Jr., ed. *An Index Guide to the Southern Historical Society Papers, 1876-1959.* 2 vols. Millwood, N.J.: Kraus International Publications, 1980. (E483 .7 .762R62)

Southern Claims Commission. *Consolidated Index of Claims Reported by the Commissioners of Claims to the House of Representatives, 1871-1886.* Washington, D.C.: Government Printing Office, 1892.

Southern Historical Society. *Southern Historical Society Papers.* 52 vols. Richmond: 1876-1959. (E483.7 .S76)

Spencer, Thomas. *Wayside Home Register, Union Point, Georgia.* Atlanta: By the Author, 1956. Typescript.

Taylor, Elizabeth C. *Confederate Soldiers Buried at Vicksburg, February 15, 1862-July 4, 1862.* N.p., n.d.

United States Congress. *Cotton Sold to the Confederate States.* Sixty-third Congress, Third Session, S. Document 987. Serial 6348.

United States War Department. *General Officers Appointed . . . Confederate States, 1861-1865.* Washington, D.C.: Government Printing Office, 1908. Reprint. Mattituck, N.J.: Carroll Co., 1983. (E548 .U617)

_____. *List of Staff Officers of the Confederate Army.* Washington, D.C.: Government Printing Office, 1891. Reprint. Mattituck, N.J.: Carroll Co., 1983. (E548 .U76)

_____. *Medical and Surgical History of the War of the Rebellion.* Vol. 2, Part 3. Washington, D.C.: Government Printing Office, 1883.

_____. *Memorandum of Field Officers in the Confederate States Service.* Washington, D.C.: Government Printing Office. N.d. (E548 .U785)

_____. *Official Records of the Union and Confederate Armies in the War of the Rebellion.* 128 vols. Washington, D.C.: Government Printing Office, 1901. Reissue. Gettysburg, Pa.: National Historical Society, 1971. (E464 .U6) See also: Irvine, Dallas. "A Guide-Index to the Official Records of the Union and Confederate Armies, 1861-1865." (National Archives: Ref. Box 337, VII F5).

_____. *Official Records of the Union and Confederate Navies in the War of the Rebellion.* 31 vols. Washington, D.C.: Government Printing Office, 1894-1927. (E591 .U58)

Wakelyn, Jon L. *Biographical Dictionary of the Confederacy.* Westport, Conn.: Greenwood Press, 1977. (E467 .W20)

Warner, Donald C., ed. *From an Autograph Album of Civil War Days.* Cleveland: N.p., ca 1933.

Wilson, Beverly E. *General Officers of the Confederacy, 1861-1865.* Baytown, Tex.: By the Author. Typescript. (E548 .W54)

Alabama

Alabama. Infantry. *Roll and History of Company C, Nineteenth Alabama Regiment.* (Report from annual unit reunion, 12 August 1904). (E551 .5 19th A3)

Barnard, Harry V. *Tattered Volunteers; The Twenty-seventh Alabama Infantry Regiment, C.S.A.* Northport, Ala.: Hermitage Press, 1965. (E551 .5 40th W54)

Botsford, T. F. *A Sketch of the Forty-seventh Alabama Regiment, Volunteers, C.S.A.* Montgomery: Paragon Press, 1909 (?). (E551 .5 47th B6)

Brewer, Willie. "Brief Historical Sketches of Military Organizations Raised in Alabama During the Civil War." *Alabama, Her History . . . From 1540 to 1872.* Alabama Civil War Centennial Commission, 1962. (F326 .B84)

Hoole, William S. *Alabama Tories: The First Alabama Cavalry, U.S.A., 1862-1865.* Tuscaloosa: Confederate Publishing Co., Inc., 1960. (E495 .6 1st H6)

Hurst, M. B. *History of the Fourteenth Regiment, Alabama Volunteers.* Tuscaloosa: Confederate Publishing Co. Reprint. University, Ala.: University of Alabama Press, 1982. (E551 .5 14th)

Little, George. *A History of Lumsden's Battery, C.S.A.* Tuscaloosa, Ala.: R. E. Rhodes Chapter, United Daughters of the Confederacy, 1965. (E551 .8 .L9L7)

McMorries, Edward Y. *History of the First Regiment, Alabama Volunteer Infantry, C.S.A.* Montgomery: The Brown Co., 1904. (E551 .4 1st M35)

Mims, Captain Wilbur F. *War History of the Prattville Dragoons* (Company H, Third Alabama Cavalry). Autauga County, Ala.: N.p., n.d. (E551 .5 3re M4)

Montgomery Greys Retired Corps (Roster of the Sixth Infantry Regiment, Alabama Volunteers). Montgomery: The Brown Co., 1907.

Oates, William C. *The War Between the Union and the Confederacy and Its Lost Opportunities, With a History of the Fifteenth Alabama Regiment and the Forty-Eight Battles in Which It Was Engaged . . .* New York: Neale Publishing Co., 1905. Reprint. Dayton, Oh.: Morningside Bookshop, 1974. (E551 .5 15th 38)

Smith, Daniel P. *Company K, First Alabama Regiment, Or Three Years in the Confederate Service.* Prattville, Ala.: By the Survivors, 1885. (E551 .5 1st S45)

Willett, Elbert D. *History of Company B (Originally Pickens Planters), Fortieth Alabama Regiment, Confederate States Army, 1862 to 1865.* Anniston, Ala.: Norwood, 1902. (E551 .5 40th W54)

Arizona

Pompey, Sherman L. *Colonel P. T. Herbert's Battalion, Arizona Cavalry, C.S.A.* Independence, Calif.: Historical and Genealogical Publishing Co., 1865. (E552 .6 H47P65)

Arkansas

Arkansas. Adjutant General's Office. *Report of the Adjutant General of Arkansas, for the Period of the Late Rebellion and to November 1, 1866.* Washington, D.C.: Government Printing Office, 1867. (UA43 .A8)

Collier, Calvin L. *First In--Last Out: The Capitol Guards, Arkansas Brigade.* Little Rock: Pioneer Press, 1961. (E553 .5 6th C64)

_____. *They'll Do To Tie To; The Story of the Third Regiment, Arkansas Infantry, C.S.A.* Little Rock: J. D. Warren, 1959. (E553 .5 3rd C6)

_____. *The War Child's Children: The Story of the Third Regiment, Arkansas Cavalry, Confederate States Army.* Little Rock: Pioneer Press, 1965. (E553 .6 3rd C6)

Dacus, Robert H. *Reminiscences of Company "H", First Arkansas Mounted Rifles.* Dardenelle, Ark.: Post-Dispatch Print, 1971. (E553 .6 1st MR D33)

Gammage, Washington L. *The Camp, the Bivouac, and the Battlefield, Being a History of the Fourth Arkansas Regiment . . . .* Little Rock: Arkansas Southern Press, 1958. (E553 .5 4th G3)

Hammock, John C. *With Honor Untarnished--First Arkansas Infantry Regiment, C.S.A.* Little Rock: Pioneer Press, 1961. (E553 .5)

Lavender, Captain John W. *They Never Came Back (Company "F", Fourth Arkansas Cavalry).* Pine Bluff: The Perdue Co., 1956. (E558 .5 4th .L3)

Leeper, Wesley T. *Rebels Valiant; Second Arkansas Mounted Rifles (Dismounted).* Little Rock: Pioneer Press, 1964. (E553 .6 2nd MR L4)

Pompey, Sherman L. *Civil War Veteran Burials from Arkansas Regiments, C.S.A.* 1972. (#553 .4 .P65)

Woodruff, William E. *With the Light Guns in '61-'65.* (Eleventh Arkansas, Missouri, and Texas Light Batteries) Little Rock: Central Printing Co., 1903. (E553 .5 SW89)

Wright, Marcus J. *Arkansas in the War, 1861-1865.* Batesville, Ark.: The Independence Historical Society, 1963. (E553 .W7)

Florida

Bittle, George C. "In the Defense of Florida: The Organized Florida Militia From 1821 to 1920." Ann Arbor: M.A. thesis, Florida State University, 1965.

Dickison, John. *Military History of Florida.* Atlanta: Confederate Publishing Co., 1899. (E484 .D9 v.11)

Dickison, Mary E. *Dickison and His Men, Reminiscences of the War in Florida*. Louisville, Ky.: Courier-Journal Printing Co., 1890. (E448 .6 2d D52)

Florida. Board of State Institutions. *Soldiers of Florida in the Seminole Indian, Civil, and Spanish-American Wars*. Live Oak, Fl.: Democrat Book and Job Print, 1903. (E558 .3 .568)

Glover, Ruth. *Confederate Service Records of all Southern States and a Few Federal Veterans*. From Biographical Souvenirs of the States of Georgia and Florida.

Pompey, Sherman L. *Civil War Veteran Burials From Florida*. Fresno, Calif.: By the Author, 1968. (E558 .3 .P65)

United Daughters of the Confederacy, Florida. Annie H. Darracott Chapter, Lakeland. *Records of Confederate Veterans*.

Georgia

Austin, Aurelia. *Georgia Boys With "Stonewall" Jackson, Jones Thomas Thompson and the Walton Infantry*. Athens, Geo.: University of Georgia Press, 1967. (E559 .4 11th A87)

Calhoun, W. L. *History of the Forty-second Regiment, Georgia Volunteers, Confederate States Infantry*. 1900. Reprint. University, Ala.: Confederate Publishing Co., 1977. (E559 .5 42d C34)

Croom, Wendell D. *The War History of Company "C", (Beauregard Volunteers), Sixth Georgia Regiment*. Fort Valley: "Advertisers" Office, 1879. (E559 .5 6th C76)

Georgia. State Division of Confederate Pensions and Records, Henderson, Lillian, ed. *Roster of the Confederate Soldiers of Georgia, 1861-1856*. Hapeville, Ga.: Longino and Porter, 1959. (E559 .4 J76)

Glover, Ruth. *Service Records of the Georgia Confederate Soldiers Registered by Florida United Daughters of the Confederacy, and Others Buried in Florida*.

_____. *Confederate Service Records of all Southern States and a Few Federal Veterans*. From Biographical Souvenirs of the States of Georgia and Florida.

Hart, Sally L. *Old Records*. (Thomas County, Georgia Confederate Pensioners). Thomasville, Ga.: Pascal Burke, 1981.

Henderson, Lindsey P., Jr. *The Oglethorpe Light Infantry*. Savannah: The Civil War Centennial Commission of Savannah and Chatham County, 1961. (E547 .4H4)

Herbert, Sidney. *A Complete Roster of the Volunteer Military Organizations of the State of Georgia.* Atlanta: J. P. Harrison, 1878. (E5559 .4 H3)

Huxford, Folks. *Pioneers of the Wiregrass Georgia.* 7 vols. Adel, Ga.: The Patten Publishers, 1951. (F285 .H8)

Jones, Charles C. *Historical Sketch of the Chatham Artillery During the Confederate Struggle for Independence.* Albany, Ga.: Joel Munsell, 1867. (E559 .7 .CHA J65)

Lake Blackshear Regional Library. *Index to Roster of the Confederate Soldiers of Georgia, 1861-1865.* Spartansburg, S.C.: The Reprint Co., 1982. (E559 .A5)

Murray, Alton J. *South Georgia Rebels--Twenty-sixth Regiment, Georgia Volunteer Infantry (CSA),* St. Mary's, Ga.: By the Author, 1976. (E559 .5)

Nichols, G. W. *A Soldier's Story of His Regiment (Sixty-first Georgia).* N.p., 1898. (E559 .6 61st N53)

Powers, J. Tracy. *Index to Confederate Soldiers in Gwinnett County, Georgia Units During the War Between the States, 1861-1865.* Lawrenceville, Ga.: Gwinnett Historical Society, 1975.

Rockwell, Captain W. S. *The Oglethorpe Light Infantry of Savannah In Peace and In War.* Savannah: J. H. Estil, 1894. (E559 .5 .04 R7)

Sams, Anita B., ed. *With Unabated Trust* (the muster rolls of Company "H", Eleventh Regiment, Georgia Volunteer Infantry, C.S.A. Walton, N.C.: The Historical Society of Walton County, North Carolina, 1911. (E577 .M33)

Stegman, John F. *These Men She Gave.* Athens: University of Georgia Press, 1964. (F294 .A758)

Thomas, Henry W. *History of the Doles-Cook Brigade, Army of Northern Virginia C.S.A.* (muster rolls of the Fourth, Twelfth, Twenty-first, and Forty-fourth Georgia Regiments) Atlanta: The Franklin Printing and Publishing Co., 1903. (E559 .4 D6745)

United Daughters of the Confederacy, Oglethorpe Chapter. *This They Remembered, 1861-1865.* Washington, Ga.: Washington Publishing Co., 1969.

Kentucky

George, Henry. *History of the Third, Seventh, Eighth, and Twelfth Kentucky, C.S.A.* Louisville: C. T. Deering Printing Co., 1911. (E564 .4 .K4G46)

Johnson, Adam R. *The Partisan Rangers of the Confederate States Army*. Louisville: G. G. Fetter, 1904. (E564 .6 .Par J64)

Kentucky. Adjutant General's Office. *Report of the Adjutant General of the State of Kentucky--Confederate Kentucky Volunteers, War of 1861-1865*. 2 vols. Frankfort: The State Journal Co., 1915. (E564 .3 .K37)

Mosgrove, George D. *Kentucky Cavaliers in Dixie*. Jackson, Tenn.: McCowat-Mercer Press, Inc., 1987. (E605 .M882)

Simpson, Alicia. *Kentucky Confederate Veteran and Widows Pension Index*. Hartford, Ky.: Cook and McDonald Publications, 1979. (E514 .3 .C61)

_____, comp. *Index of Confederate Pension Applications, Commonwealth of Kentucky*. Frankfort: Division of Archives and Records Management, Department of Archives and Library, 1981. (E564 .3 .K38)

Thompson, Edwin P., ed. *History of the First Kentucky Brigade*. Cincinnati: Gaxton Publishing House, 1868. (E564 .4 .06T56)

_____. *History of the Orphan Brigade*. Louisville: L. N. Thompson, 1897. (E564 .4 .06T56)

Louisiana

A Soldier's Story of the War, Including the Marches and Battles of the Washington Artillery . . . . New Orleans: Clark and Hoffline, 1874. (E565 .8 .Was S6)

Bartlett, Napier. *Military Records of Louisiana, Including Biographical and Historical Papers Relating to the Military Organizations of the State*. Baton Rouge: Louisiana State University Press, 1964. (E565 .4 .B293)

Carter, Howell. *A Cavalryman's Reminiscences of the Civil War*. New Orleans: American Printing Co., N.d. (E565 .6 1st C37)

Hall, Winchester. *The Story of the Twenty-sixth Louisiana Regiment, in the Service of the Confederate States*. N.p., 1890. (E565 .6 26th H34)

Louisiana. Commission of Military Records. Booth, Andrew B., comp. *Records of Louisiana Confederate Soldiers and Louisiana Commands*. New Orleans: N.p., 1920. (E565 .3 .L87)

Marchand, Sidney A. *Forgotten Fighters, 1861-1865*. Donaldsonville, La.: By the Author, 1966. (E565 .95 A7M3)

Owen, William M. *In Camp and Battle With the Washington Artillery of New Orleans*. Boston: Ticknor and Co., 1885. (E565 .8 .Was 084)

Tunnard, William H. *A Southern Record: The History of the Third Regiment, Louisiana Infantry*. Baton Rouge: By the Author, 1866. Reprint.

Dayton, Oh.: Morningside Bookshop, 1970. (contains an index by Maggie R. Bearss and rosters by Edwin C. Bearss). (E565 .5 3d T8)

Maryland

Booth, George W., comp. *Maryland Line Confederate Soldier's Home. Pikesville, Md.: N.p., 1894. (E566 .4 .B72)*

Goldsborough, William W. *The Maryland Line in the Confederate Army, 1861-1865.* Port Washington, N.Y.: Kennikat Press, 1972. (E566 .4 .G6)

Michel, Robert E. *Colonel Harry Gilmore's Raid Around Baltimore.* Baltimore: Erbe Publishers, 1976. (E566 .G54 .M52)

Pompey, Sherman L. *Muster Lists of the American Rifles of Maryland, Baltimore Artillery, Dias, Maryland Artillery, Maryland Guelle Zouaves, Walter's Company, Maryland Zarvons Zouaves of the Confederacy.* By the Author, 1965. Typescript. (E565 .3 .P65)

Mississippi

Bearss, Edwin C. *Decision in Mississippi.* Jackson: Mississippi Commission on the War Between the States, 1962. (E568 .B4)

Brown, Maud M. *The University Grays: Company "A", Eleventh Mississippi Regiment, Army of Northern Virginia, 1861-1865.* Richmond: Garrett and Massie, 1940. (E568 .5 11th B8)

Howell, H. Grady, Jr. *Going to Meet the Yankees--A History of the "Bloody Sixth," Mississippi Infantry (C.S.A.).* Jackson: Chicksaw Bayou Press, 1981. (E568 .5 6th .H68)

Liveritte, Rudy H. *Ole Rosinheels . . . . Major Amox McLemore, Twenty-seventh Mississippi Infantry Regiment, Provisional Army of the Confederate States of America.* Boise, Id.: By the Author, 1979. (E569 .5 .32L58)

Pompey, Sherman L. *Register of the Civil War Dead, Confederate and Federal Troops, Missisippi.* Clovis, Calif.: N.p., 1970.

Missouri

Anderson, Ephraim M. *Memoirs: Historical and Personal; Including the Campaigns of the First Missouri Confederate Brigade.* Dayton, Oh.: Morningside Bookshop, 1972. (E569.4 1st A54)

Bailey, Elizabeth, comp. *Missouri Ex-confederate Soldiers--Pension Lists and Deaths at the Confederate Soldier's Home, Higginsville, Missouri.* Columbia, Mo.: State Historical Society of Missouri, 1984.

Bevier, R. S. *History of the First and Second Missouri Confederate Brigades, 1861-1865.* St. Louis: Bryan, Brand, and Co., 1879. (E569 .4 B57)

Lanham, Mrs. B. M. *Records From the Confederate Cemetery at Higgins-ville, Missouri.* N.p., n.d.

Miles, Kathleen W. *Bitter Ground* (Benton, Henry, and St. Clair Counties). Warswa and Clinton, Mo.: The Printery, 1971. (E569 .M5)

Personal Experiences of C. B. Lotspeich, 1861-1865 (contains roster of Company "A", Sixteenth Missouri Infantry).

Pompey, Sherman L. *Muster Lists of the Missouri Confederates.* 9 vols. Independence, Calif.: Historical and Genealogical Publishing Co., 1965. (MF2 .M0118)

Shelton, Alonzo. *Memoirs of a Confederate Veteran* (some who fought at Wilson's Creek). Liberty, Mo.: William Jewell College, N.d. Mimeo.

Woodruff, William E. *With the Light Guns in '61-'65.* (Eleventh Arkansas, Missouri, and Texas Light Batteries). Little Rock: Central Printing Co., 1903. (E553 .5 W89)

New Mexico

Hall, Martin H. *The Confederate Army of New Mexico.* Austin: Presidial Press, 1978. (E547 .N4H3)

North Carolina

Birdsong, James C. *Brief Sketches of the North Carolina State Troops.* Raleigh: Josephus Daniels, State Printer and Binder, 1894. (E573 .4 .B61)

Clark, Walter. *Histories of the Several Regiments and Battalions From North Carolina in the Great War, 1861-1865.* 5 vols. Raleigh: State of North Carolina, E. M. Uzzell, Printer and Binder, 1901. (E573 .4 .C59)

Crow, Vernon H. *Storm in the Mountains; Thomas' Confederate Legion of Cherokee Indians and Mountaineers.* Cherokee, N.C.: Press of the Museum of the Cherokee Indian. N.d.

Hall, Harry H. *A Johnny Reb Band From Salem; The Pride of Tarheelia.* Raleigh: North Carolina Confederate Centennial Commission, 1963. (E573 .5 26th H3)

Harris, James S. *Historical Sketches, Seventh Regiment North Carolina Troops.* 1893. Reprint. Ann Arbor: University Microfilms, 1972. (E573 .5 7th H3)

Iobst, Richard W. *The Bloody Sixth--The Sixth North Carolina Regiment (C.S.A.)* Raleigh: North Carolina Confederate Centennial Commission, 1965. (E573 .5 6th I6)

Leinbach, Julius. *Regiment Band of the Twenty-sixth North Carolina.* Winston-Salem: Moravian Music Foundation, 1958. (E573 .3 26th L3)

Leon, Louis. *Diary of a Tarheel Confederate Soldier.* (The Charlotte Grays, Company "C", Fifty-Third North Carolina Regiment). Charlotte: Stone Publishing Co., 1913. (E573 .5 .L46)

Manarin, Louis H., comp. *North Carolina Troops, 1861-1865, A Roster.* 6 vols. Raleigh: State Department of Archives and History, 1966. (E573 .3 .M3)

_____, ed. *Report on Cavalry Units From North Carolina, 1962.* Misc. Civil War Pamphlet.

Manarin, Louis H. and Jordan, Weymouth. *North Carolina Troops, 1861-1865, A Roster.* 9 vols. Raleigh: State Department of Archives and History, 1981-1983. (E573 .3 .M3)

McCallum, James H., Martin County Historical Society. *Martin County During the Civil War.* Williamston, N.C.: Enterprise Publishing Co., 1971.

North Carolina. Moore, John W., ed. *Roster of North Carolina Troops in the War Between the States.* 4 vols. Raleigh: Ashe and Gatling, State Printers, 1882. (E573 .3 .N87)

_____. Infantry. *Twentieth Regiment. History of Company "E", Twentieth North Carolina Regiment: 1861-1865.* Ann Arbor: University Microfilms, 1974. (E573 .5 20th N6)

_____. Infantry. *Forty-third Regiment. Sketch of the Duplin Rifles . . . .* Raleigh?, 1895? (E573 .Pl8)

_____. *Sketch of the Forty-third Regiment, North Carolina Troops, 1861-1865.* Raleigh: N.p., 1895. (E573 .P18)

Pamlico Chapter of the Daughters of the Confederacy. *The Confederate Reveille, Memorial Edition.* Raleigh: Edwards and Broughton, Printers and Binders, n.d. (E573 .U58)

Stedman, Charles H. *Memorial Address . . . , A Sketch of the Life and Character of General William MacRae.* Wilmington: William L. DeRosset, 1890. (E573 .P18)

Sloan, John A. *Reminiscences of the Guilford Grays. Company "B", Twenty-seventh North Carolina Regiment.* Washington, D.C.: R. I. Polkinhorn, 1883. (E573 .5 275h S56)

Smith, William W. *The Anson Guards* (Company "C", Fourteenth Regiment, North Carolina Volunteers). Charlotte: Stone Publishing Co., 1914.

Underwood, George C. *History of the Twenty-sixth Regiment, North Carolina Troops.* Goldsboro: Nash Brothers, 1928. (E573 .5 26th)

Wall, H. D. *Historical Sketch of the Pee Dee Guards* (Company "D", Twenty-third North Carolina Regiment). Raleigh: Edwards and Broughton, 1876.

Williams, Julie C. *War Diary of Kinchan Jahu Carpenter* (Company "K", Fiftieth North Carolina Regiment). Rutherford, N.C.: By the Author, 1955. (E573 .5 50th C3)

Oklahoma

Cunningham, Frank. *General Stand Watie's Confederate Indians.* San Antonio, Tex.: Naylor Co., 1959. (467 .1 .W33C8)

Oklahoma Genealogical Society. *Index to Applications for Pensions From the State of Oklahoma Submitted by Confederate Soldiers, Sailors and Their Widows.* Oklahoma City: N.p., 1969. (UB 374 .5 .I53)

South Carolina

Andrews, W. J. *Sketch of Company "K", Twenty-third South Carolina Volunteers.* Richmond: Whillet and Shepperson, 1974. (E577 .5 23rd A5)

Brunson, Joseph W. *Pee Dee Light Artillery.* University, Ala.: Confederate Publishing Co., 1983.

Caldwell, J. F. J. *The History of a Brigade of South Carolinians Known First as "Gregg's" and Subsequently as "McGowan's Brigade".* Philadelphia: King and Baird, 1866. Reprint. Dayton, Oh.: Morningside Bookshop, 1951. (E577 .4 .M3C34)

Coker, James L. *History of Company "G", Ninth South Carolina Regiment Infantry, and Company "E", Sixth South Carolina Regiment Infantry.* Greenwood, S.C.: The Attic Pres, Inc., 1979. (E577 .5 9th C64)

Cote, Richard N., ed. *Dictionary of South Carolina Biography, Vol. 1.* Easley, S.C.: Southern Historical Press, 1985.

Dickert, D. Augustus. *History of Kershaw's Brigade, with A Complete Roll of Companies, Biographical Sketches,* . . . Newberry, S.C.: Elbert H. Aull, 1899. Reprint. Dayton, Oh.: Morningside Bookshop, 1976. (E577 .4 D54)

Dunlop, William W. . . . *Lee's Sharpshooters; or the Fore-Front of Battle* (McGowan's Brigade). Little Rock: Tunnah and Pittard, Printers, 1899. (E605 .D72)

Hagood, Johnson.*Memoirs of the War of Secession, From the Original Manuscripts of . . . .* Columbia: The State Company, 1910. (E577 .4 .H14)

Izlar, William V. *A Sketch of the War Record of the Edisto Rifles, 1861-1865* (Company "A", First Regiment, and Company "G", Twenty-fifth Regiment). Columbia: August Korn, 1914. (E577 .5 25th I94)

Salley, Alexander S., Jr. *South Carolina Troops in Confederate Service.* 3 vols. Columbia: South Carolina Historical Commission, 1913. (E577 .3 .S72)

_____. *Tentative Roster of the Third Regiment, South Carolina Volunteers, Confederate States Provisional Army.* Columbia: South Carolina Historical Commission, 1908. (E577 .5)

South Carolina. Commissioner of Confederate Rolls. *Report of M. P. Tribble, South Carolina Commissioner of Confederate Rolls to the General Assembly, 1903.* Columbia: The State Company, 1904. (E577 .S82)

_____. *The Washington Light Infantry of Charleston, South Carolina.* Charleston: Walker, Evans and Cogswell, 1873. (UA448 .W2)

_____. Infantry. *Washington Light Infantry . . . An Historical Sketch of the . . .* New York: D. Appleton, 1875. (E173 .P18 Number 287)

_____. Infantry. *Washington Light Infantry. Annual Observance of Washington's Birthday of the . . .* Charleston: News and Courier Presses, 1878. (E312 .6 .S68)

Taylor, John S. *Sixteenth South Carolina Regiment, C.S.A. From Greenville County, South Carolina.* Privately printed, 1964. (E577 .5 16th T39)

Tompkins, D. A. and Tompkins, S. A. *Company "K", Fourteenth South Carolina Volunteers.* Charlotte: Observer, 1897. Reprint. Ann Arbor: University Microfilms, 1972. (E577 .5 14th T6)

United Daughters of the Confederacy, South Carolina Division. *South Carolina Women in the Confederacy.* Columbia: The State Company, 1903. (E628 .U58)

Walker, Cornelius I. *Rolls and Historical Sketch of the Tenth Regiment, South Carolina Volunteers in the Army of the Confederate States.* Charleston: Walker, Evans, and Cogswell, Printers, 1881. (E577 .5 10th W34)

War Memorials of the Washington Light Infantry (Twenty-fifth Regiment). Charleston: Edward Perry & Co., 1894. (E577 .5)

Wells, Edward L. *A Sketch of the Charleston Light Dragoons*. Charleston:
Lucas Richardson & Co., 1888. (E577 .6 .W4)

Tennessee

Dyer, Gustavus W. and Moore, John T., comps. *The Tennessee Civil War
Veterans Questionnaires*. 5 vols. Easley, S.C.: Southern Historical
Press, 1985. (E494 .T46)

Elliott, Colleen M. and Armstrong, Louise, eds. *Tennessee Civil War
Questionnaires*. 5 vols. Nashville: Tennessee State Library, 1985. (See
Tennessee State Library for Index--below)

Hancock, Richard R. *Hancock's Diary; Or, A History of the Second Tennes-
see Confederate Cavalry, With Sketches of First and Seventh Battalions;
Also, Portraits and Biographical Sketches*. Nashville: Brandon Printing
Co., n.d. (E579 .6 2nd H35)

Head, Thomas A. *Campaigns and Battles of the Sixteenth Regiment, Tennessee Volunteers . . . .* Nashville: Cumberland Presbyterian Publishing
House, 1885. (E579 .5 16th H43)

Lindsley, John B. *Military Annals of Tennessee Confederates*. Nashville: J.
M. Lindsley & Co., 1886. (E579 .4 .L75)

McBrien, Joe B. *The Tennessee Brigade*. Chattanooga: Hudson Printing &
Lithographing Co., n.d. (E579 .4 .M32)

McMurray, W. J. *History of the Twentieth Tennessee Regiment, Volunteer
Infantry, C.S.A.* Nashville: Tennessee Regimental Association Publishing Committee, 1904. (E579 .5 20th M33)

Rennolds, Edwin H. *A History of the Henry County Commands Who Served
in the Confederate Army . . . .* Jacksonville, Fl.: Sun Publishing Co.,
1904. (E579. 95 .HRr)

Tennessee. Civil War Centennial Commission. *Tennesseeans in the Civil
War: A Military History of Confederate and Union Units With Available
Rosters of Persons*. 2 vols. Nashville: Tennessee Historical Commis-
sion, 1904. (E579 .4 .A53)

_____. State Library and Archives. Manuscript Division. *Index to Question-
naires of Civil War Veterans*. Nashville: Tennessee State Library and
Archives, 1962. (E494 ..T45)

United Confederate Veterans, N. B. Forrest Camp, Chattanooga, Tennessee.
*roster of Our Dead Buried in the Confederate Cemetery at Chat-
tanooga, Tennessee*. Chattanooga: N.p., 1894. (E475 .81 .U53)

United Daughters of the Confederacy, Tennessee Division. *Confederate Patriot Index, 1924-1978, Vol. 2.* Columbia, Tenn.: P-Vine Press, 1978.

Vaughan, Alfred J. *Personal Record of the Thirteenth Regiment, Tennessee Infantry.* Memphis: S. C. Toof, 1897. (E579 .5 13th V38)

Vaughan, Jack C. *Vaughan's Brigade, Army of Tennessee (C.S.A.)* Vols. 11-17. Arlington, Tex.: By the Author, 1959-1974. (#579 .5 .V3)

Worsham, William J. *Old Nineteenth Tennessee Regiment, C.S.A.* Knoxville: Paragon Printing Co., 1902. (E579 .5 19th W67)

Young, John P. *The Seventh Tennessee Cavalry (Confederate).* Dayton, Oh.: Morningside Bookshop, 1976. (E579 .5 Y68)

Texas

Boethel, Paul C. *The Big Guns of Fayette, Texas.* Austin: Jones, 1965. (E580 .6 5th B6)

Chance, Joseph E. *The Second Texas Infantry.* Austin: Eakin Press, 1984. (E580 .5 2nd C47)

Davis, Nicholas A. *Chaplain Davis and Hood's Texas Brigade.* San Antonio: Principia Press for Trinity University, 1962. (E580 .6 24th F67)

_____. *The Campaign From Texas to Maryland.* Austin: The Steck Co., 1961. (E580 .4 H6 D32)

Duanne, Carl L. *The Dead Men Wore Boots; An Account of The Thirty-second Texas Volunteer Cavalry, C.S.A., 1861-1865.* Austin: San Felipe Press, 1966. (E580 .6 32nd D8)

Femley, Bradford K. and Grady, John C. *Suffering To Silence; Twenty-ninth Texas Cavalry, C.S.A., Regimental History.* Quanch, Tex.: Nortex, 1975. (E580 .7 29th F44)

Fitzhugh, Lester N., ed. *Cannon Smoke.* Hillsboro, Tex.: Hill Junior College, 1971. (E580 .6 G3 G66)

_____. *Texas Batteries, Battaliona, Regiments, Commanders, and Field Officers, Confederate States Army, 1861-1865.* Midlothian, Tex.: Mirror Press, 1959. (E580 .3 .F5)

Griscom, George L. *Fighting With Ross' Texas Cavalry Brigade, C.S.A. . . .* Hillsboro: Hill Junior College Press, 1976. (E580 .4 R6 G75)

Hamilton, D. H. *History of Company "M", First Texas Volunteer Infantry . . .* Waco: W. M. Morrison, 1962. (E580 .4 1st H34)

Johnson, Sidney S. *Texans Who Wore the Gray.* Tyler, Tex.: N.p., 1907. (E580 .J69)

Kinney, John M., comp. *Index to Applications for Texas Confederate Pensions*. Austin: Archives Division, Texas State Library, 1977. (E548 .KS6)

Ledbetter, Barbara N. *Civil War Days in Young County, Texas, 1861-1865*. Newcastle, Tex.: By the Author, 1965. (E580 .95 Y7L4)

Nunn, W. E., ed. *Ten Texans in Gray*. Hillsboro: Hill Junior College Press, 1968. (E580 .N8)

Polk, J. M. *The North and South American Review*. Ann Arbor: University Microfilms, 1974. (E580 .5 4th P65)

Polley, Joseph B. *Hood's Texas Brigade, Its Marches, Its Battles, Its Achievements*. Dayton, Oh.: Morningside Bookshop, 1976. (E580 .4 T4 P64)

Simpson, Harold B. *Gaines' Mill to Appomattox; Waco and McLennan County in Hood's Texas Brigade*. Waco: Texian Press, 1963. (E580 .4 H652)

_____. *Hood's Texas Brigade: A Compendium*. Hillsboro, Tex.: Hill Junior College Press, 1974. (E580 .4 H6 S525)

_____. *Hood's Texas Brigade in Reunion and Memory*. Hillsboro, Tex.: Hill Junior College Press, 1974. (E580 .4 T4 S53)

_____. *History of the Old Settlers and Confederate Reunion Grounds*. Hillsboro, Tex.: Hill Junior College Press, 1986. Note: Write to Hill Junior College, P.O. Box 619, Hillsboro, TX 76645, for a catalog of Civil War books sold there.

Spencer, John W. *Terrell's Texas Cavalry*. Burnet, Tex.: Eakin Press, 1982. (E580 .6 34th S64)

Spurlin, Charles, comp. *West of the Mississippi With Waller's Thirteenth Texas Cavalry Battalion, C.S.A.* Hillsboro, Tex.: Hill Junior College Press, 1971. (E580 .5 1st T63)

Todd, George T. *First Texas Regiment*. Waco: Texian Press, 1911. (580 .5 1st T63)

Wood, Captain W. D. *Officers and Men Raised in Leon County, Texas for Confederate Service*. Waco: W. M. Morrison Bookseller, 1962. (E580 .95 L46)

Woodruff, William E. *With the Light Guns in '61-'65*. (Eleventh Arkansas, Missouri, and Texas Light Batteries). Little Rock: Central Printing Co., 1903. (#553 .S W89)

Wright Marcus J., comp. *Texas in the War, 1861-1865*. Hillsboro, Tex.: Hill Junior College Press, 1965. (E580 .W7)

Yeary, Mamie. *Reminiscences of the Boys in Gray, 1861-1865.* Dallas: Smith & Lamar, 1912. (E580 .3 Y39)

Virginia

Bean, William G. *The Liberty Hall Volunteers; Stonewall's College Boys.* Charlottesville: University Press of Virginia, 1964. (E581 .5 4th B4)

Beatley, Lt. R. W. *History of the Seventeenth Virginia Infantry, C.S.A.* Baltimore: Kelly, Piet & Co., 1870.

Casada, James A. *History of the Forty-sixth Virginia Infantry, Series 11.* Abingdon, Va.: Historical Society of Washington County, Virginia, n.d.

Chamberlaine, William W. *Memoirs of the Civil War Between the Northern and Southern Sections of the United States of America, 1861-1865.* Washington, D.C.: Press of B.S. Adams, 1912. (E605 .C44)

Chamberlayne, Edwin H. *War History and Roll of the Richmond Fayette Artillery, Thirty-eighth Virginia Battalion, Artillery, C.S.A.* Richmond: E. Waddey, Printer, 1883. (E581 .8 .R53)

Chapla, John D. *Forty-eighth Virginia Infantry Regiment, C.S.A.* (Smyth, Russell, Scott, Washington, Lee Counties)

Couper, William. *The V.M.I. New Market Cadets; Biographical Sketches . . .* Charlottesville: Michie, 1933. (E476 .64 .C76)

Cutchins, John A. *A Famous Command--The Richmond Light Infantry Blue.* Richmond: Garrett and Massie, Publishers, 1934. (UA508 .R5C2)

Delaney, Wayne R. *The Seventeenth Virginia Volunteer Infantry Regiment, C.S.A.* Washington, D.C.: American Printing Co., 1961. (E581 5 17th D4)

Eliot, Ellsworth, Jr. *West Point in the Confederacy.* New York: G. A. Baker & Co., Inc., 1941. (E586 .U535)

Fauguier County Civil War Centennial Committee. *The Years of Anguish, Fauquier County, Virginia, 1861-1865.* Warrenton, Va.: The Fauguier Democrat, 1965. (E581 .95 F3R3)

Fonerden, Clarence A. *A Brief History of the Military Career of Carpenter's Battery.* Ann Arbor: University Microfilms, 1971. (E581 .8 Car F65)

Graves, Joseph A. *The History of the Bedford Light Artillery, 1861-1865.* Bedford City, Va.: Press of the Bedford Democrat, 1903. (E581 .8 Bed G73)

Hale, Louis V. and Phillips, Stanley S. *History of the Forty-ninth Virginia Infantry, C.S.A.* Lanham, Md.: S. S. Phillips & Associates, 1981. (E581 .3 49th H34)

Headquarters, Department of Southwestern Virginia, August 20, 1862. *A List of Men Absent From the Eighth Cavalry.* Wytheville, Va.: D.S. St. Clair Press, n.d.

Irby, Richard. *Historical Sketch of the Nottoway Grays; Afterward Company "G", Eighteenth Virginia Regiment, Army of Northern Virginia.* Richmond: J. W. Ferguson and Son, 1878. (E581 .5 18th I72)

Krick, Robert K. *Ninth Virginia Cavalry.* Lynchburg, Va.: H. E. Howard, Inc. 1982. (E581 .6 9th K74)

_____. *Parker's Virginia Battery, C.S.A.* Berryville, Va.: Virginia Book Company, 1975. (E581 .8 Par K74)

Loehr, Charles T. *War History of the Old First Virginia Infantry Regiment, Army of Northern Virginia.* Richmond: W. Ellis Jones, 1884. Reprint. Dayton, Oh.: Morningside Bookshop, 1970. (E581 .4 1st L64)

Macon, Thomas J. *Reminiscences of the First Company of Richmond Volunteers.* Ann Arbor: University Microfilms, 1972. (E581 .8 Ric M3)

Manarin, Louis H., and Wallace, Lee A. *Richmond Volunteers: The Volunteer Companies of the City of Richmond and Henrico County, Virginia, 1861-1865.* Richmond: Westover Press, 1969. (E581 .4 M35)

McDonald, Captain William N. *A History of the Laurel Brigade (Ashby's Cavalry and Chew's Battery).* Baltimore: Sun Job Printing Office, 1907. (#581 .4 .L3M3) Also available as *Laurel Brigade, Originally Ashby's Cavalry.* Arlington, Va.: Beatty, 1969. (E581 .4 .L3M3)

Moore, Edward E. *The Story of a Cannoneer Under Stonewall Jackson.* New York and Washington, D.C.: The Neale Publishing Co., 1907. (E581 .8 Rock M65)

Neal, Lois A., comp. *A Personal Name Index to Expanded Version of Jedediah Hotchkiss' "Virginia."* Vol. 3 of *"Confederate Military History"* by Clement A. Evans. Raleigh: N.p., 1976. (E581. H682 N4)

Page, Richard C. M. *Sketch of Page's Battery, or Morris' Artillery, Second Corps, Army of Northern Virginia, by One of the Company.* New York: T. Smeltzer, 1885. (E581 .8 Page P34)

Shoemaker, John J. *Shoemaker's Battery, Stuart Horse Artillery, Pelham's Battalion.* Memphis: S. C. Toof & Co., 1880. (E581 .8 Shoe S56)

Tubbs, Edward F. *History of the Ninth Virginia Cavalry.* Richmond: B. F. Johnston Publishing Co., 1899. (E581 .6 9th B4)

Turner, Edward R. *The New Market Campaign, May, 1864.* Richmond: Whillet & Shepperson, 1912. (E476 .64 .T95)

Under the Stars and Bars; A History of the Surry Light Artillery . . . .
Richmond: E. Waddey, 1909. (E581 .8 Surry J65)

Williamson, James J. *Mosby's Rangers; A Record of the Operations of the
Forty-third Battalion, Virginia Cavalry* . . . . New York: R. B. Kenyon,
1896. (E581 .6 43d W54)

Wise, George. *History of the Seventeenth Virginia Infantry, C.S.A.*
Baltimore: Kelly, Piet and Co., 1870. Reprint. Arlington, Va.: Beatty,
1960. (E581 .5 17th W52)

Wood, William N. *Reminiscences of Big "I". Company "A", Nineteenth Virginia Regiment.* Jackson, Tenn.: McCowat-Mercer Press, Inc., 1956.
(E605 .W89)

Worsham, John H. *One of Jackson's Foot Cavalry.* Jackson, Tenn.:
McCowat-Mercer Press, Inc., 1964. (E581 .5 21st W62)

Virginia Regimental Histories Series

The publishing company of H. E. Howard, Inc., P.O. Box 4161, Lynchburg,
Virginia 24502, is making available a one hundred volume set of regimental
histories dealing with Virginia units in the Confederate States army. To date
it has published twenty-two volumes and uses the research and writing
talents of several authors. Each volume contains a unit history, an annotated
muster roll of every man who served in that unit, and relevant photographs
and maps. The authors and titles of the volumes published so far are listed
below.

Chapla, John D. *Forty-second Virginia Infantry.*
Davis, James A. *Fifty-first Virginia Infantry.*
Delauter, Roger U., Jr. *Eighteenth Virginia Cavalry.*
Divine, John E. *Eighth Virginia Cavalry.*
_____. *Thirty-fifth Battalion, Virginia Cavalry.*
Driver, Robert J. *Fifty-second Virginia Infantry.*
Fields, Robert K. *Twenty-eighth Virginia Infantry.*
Frye, Dennis E. *Second Virginia Infantry.*
Henderson, William D. *Twelfth Virginia Infantry.*
Krick, Robert K. *Thirtieth Virginia Infantry.*
_____. *Fortieth Virginia Infantry.*
_____. *Ninth Virginia Cavalry.*

Rankin, Thomas M. *Twenty-third Virginia Infantry.*

Riggs, David F. *Seventh Virginia Infantry.*

Robertson, James I. *Fourth Virginia Infantry.*

_____. *Eighteenth Virginia Infantry.*

Scott, J. L. *Thirty-sixth and Thirty-seventh Battalion, Virginia Cavalry.*

Stiles, Kenneth L. *Fourth Virginia Cavalry.*

Trask, Benjamin H. *Ninth Virginia Infantry.*

Wallace, Lee A., Jr. *First Virginia Infantry.*

_____. *Third Virginia Infantry.*

Wiatt, Alex L. *Twenty-sxith Virginia Infantry.*

West Virginia

Calhoun, Harrison M. *Twixt North and South.* Franklin, W.V.: McCoy Publishing Co., 1974. (E581 .95 .P3C3)

Hornbeck, Betty D. *Upshur Brothers of the Blue and Gray.* Parsons, W.V.: McClain Printing Co., 1967. (E582 .95 .U6H6)

Reader, Frank W. *History of the Fifty West Virginia Cavalry and Battery "G", First West Virginia, Light Artillery, 1861-1864.* N.p., 1870. (E536 .6 5th R5)

United Daughters of the Confederacy, West Virginia Division, Randolph Chapter 267. *Confederate Soldiers Who Enlisted From Randolph County, 1861-1865.* N.p., 1920? (F247 .R2U6)

Appendix

UNITED DAUGHTERS OF THE CONFEDERACY

Immediately following the Civil War several memorial, monument, and Confederate home associations were created to honor and assist Confederate veterans. The United Confederate Veterans once boasted sixty-five thousand members and published the magazine *Confederate Veteran* (see chapter five). There also was the United Sons of Confederate Veterans. The one organization which has survived and is still active, however, is the United Daughters of the Confederacy.

Two state-wide women's organizations came into being in 1890 and late in 1894. They and various other similar local groups merged to become the United Daughters of the Confederacy. This organization is active in providing scholarships for descendants of Confederate servicemen or servicewomen at many colleges, and it may pay you to look into this opportunity if you know of a possibly deserving and qualified young student. It also furnished financial support for many needy or hospitalized descendants of Confederate veterans or their families. They emphasize that their present day mission is service rather than simply "marching and waving the flag."

A woman may become a member of this organization if she is invited by a local chapter and qualifies as a descendant of a man or woman who served honorably in the army, navy, or the civil services of the Confederate States of America, and is "personally acceptable to the organization." A pamphlet which gives more details entitled *How to Become a Member* may be obtained by writing the headquarters at 328 North Boulevard, Richmond, VA 23220.

The headquarters building maintains some records of Confederate service, but they are not available for public inspection. The building is closed to all non-members. When requested, a chapter registrar, using the material stored at that building, will attempt to verify Confederate service for a prospective member. Any other research is not possible because of limited funds for the employment of staff.

Footnotes

1. Clement Eaton, *A History of the Southern Confederacy* (New York: The MacMillan Co., 1959), 16.

2. John S. Bowman, ed., *The Civil War Almanac* (New York: Bison Books, 1982), 42.

3. Michael B. Dougan, *Confederate Arkansas* (University, Ala.: The University of Alabama Press, 1976), 45.

4. William W. Davis, *The Civil War and Reconstructionin Florida* (New York and London: Columbia University, 1913), 52.

5. Ibid, 148.

6. Ibid, 323.

7. Thomas C. Bryan, *Confederate Georgia* (Athens, Geo.: The University of Georgia Press, 1953), 158.

8. *Governor's Message,* Documents of the Second Session of the Fifth Legislature of Louisiana, 1861 (Baton Rouge, 1861).

9. John K. Bettersworth, *Confederate Mississippi* (Baton Rouge: Louisiana State University, 1943), 3.

10. Daniel H. Hill, *A History of North Carolina in the War Between the States* (Raleigh: Edwards and Broughton Co., 1926), 35.

11. W. Buck Yearns and John G. Barrett, *North Carolina Civil War Documentary* (Chapel Hill: The University of North Carolina Press, 1980), 125.

12. Charles E. Cauthen, *The James Sprint Studies in History and Political Sciences,* Vol. 32, *South Carolina Goes to War, 1861-1865* (Chapel Hill: The University of North Carolina Press, 1950), 70.

13. David D. Wallace, *The History of South Carolina,* Vol. 3 (New York: The American Historical Society, Inc., 1934), 171.

14. Cartter Patten, *A Tennessee Chronicle* (N.p. 1953), 219.

15. James Farber, *Texas, C.S.A.* (New York: The Jackson Co., 1965), 25.

16. Joseph O. Van Hook, *The Kentucky Story* (Chattanooga: Harlow Publishing Corp., 1959), 294.

17. Craig L. Symonds, *A Battlefield Atlas of the Civil War* (Annapolis, Md.: The Nautical and Aviation Publishing Company of America, 1983), 43.

18. Meyer, Duane, *The Heritage of Missouri: A History* (Hazlewood, Mo.: State Publishing Co., Inc., 1963), 351.

19. Ibid, 398.

20. Charles H. Ambler, *West Virginia--the Mountain State* (New York: Prentice Hall, Inc., 1940), 308.

21. Ibid, 321.

Bibliography

Ambler, Charles H. *West Virginia--the Mountain State.* New York: Prentice-Hall, Inc., 1940. (F241 .A523)

Amman, William F. *Personnel of the Civil War.* 2 vols. New York: Thomas Yoseloff, 1961. (E494 .A4)

Battles and Leaders of the Civil War. 4 vols. Syracuse, New Jersey: Castle, a Division of Book Sales, Inc., Reprint. Century Co., 1887.

Beers, Henry P. *Guide to the Archives of the Confederate States of America.* National Archives Publication Number 631. Washington, D.C.: Government Printing Office, 1968. (CD3047 .B4)

Bettersworth, John K. *Confederate Mississippi.* Baton Rouge: Louisiana State University Press, 1953. Reprint. Philadelphia: Porcupine Press, 1978. (E568 .B47)

Blay, John W. *The Civil War--A Pictorial Profile.* New York: Thomas Y. Crowell Co., 1958.

Bowman, John S., ed. *The Civil War Almanac.* New York: Bison Books, 1982.

Bragg, Jefferson Davis. *Louisiana in the Confederacy.* Baton Rouge: Louisiana State University Press, 1941. (E565 .B7)

Broadfoot, Tom, ed. *Civil War Books, a Priced Checklist.* Wendell, N.C.: Avera Press, 1978. (Z1242 .B86)

Brownlee, Richard S. *Gray Ghosts of the Confederacy.* Baton Rouge: Louisiana State University Press, 1958. (E470 .45 .B76)

Bryan, Thomas C. *Confederate Georgia.* Athens, Georgia: The University of Georgia Press, 1953. (E559 .B89)

Cauthen, Charles E. *The James Sprint Studies in History and Political Sciences.* Vol. 32. *South Carolina Goes to War, 1861-1865.* Chapel Hill: The University of North Carolina Press, 1950. (E577 .C347)

Collins, Lewis. *History of Kentucky.* 2 vols. Covington, Kentucky: Collins & Co., 1878. Reprint. Easley, S.C.: Southern Historical Press, 1979. (F451 .C73)

Colton, Ray C. *The Civil War in the Western Territories.* Norman, Ok.: University of Oklahoma Press, 1959. (C470 .9 C7)

Cowles, Calvin D. *The Official Military Atlas of the Civil War.* New York: Thomas Yoseloff, 1891-1895. Reprint. 1978. (G1201 .S506)

Davis, William W. *The Civil War and Reconstruction in Florida.* New York: Columbia University, 1913. (E559 .D3)

Denman, Clarence P. *The Secession Movement in Alabama.* Montgomery, Alabama: Alabama State Department of Archives and History, 1933. (F326 .D36)

Dornbusch, Charles E. *Military Bibliography of the Civil War.* 3 vols. New York: New York Public Library. Arno Press, Inc., 1961-62. Reprint. 1971. (Z1242 .D612)

Dougan, Michael B. *Confederate Arkansas.* University, Alabama: The University of Alabama Press, 1976. (E553 .D68)

Dubay, Robert W. *John J. Pettus.* Jackson, Miss.: University Press of Mississippi, 1975. (F341 .P47 .D82)

Dupuy, R. Earnest and Dupuy, Trevor N. *The Compact History of the Civil War.* New York: Hawthorn Books, Inc., 1960. (E468 .D96)

Eaton, Clement. *A History of the Southern Confederacy.* New York: The MacMillan Co., 1959. (E487 .E15)

Farber, James. *Texas, C.S.A.* New York: The Jackson Co., 1947. (E580 .F3)

Faulk, Odie B. *Arizona--A Short History.* Norman, Ok.: University of Oklahoma Press, 1970. (E811 .E2)

Fischer, LeRoy E., ed. *The Western Territories in the Civil War.* Manhattan, Kansas: Journal of the West, Inc., 1977. (E470 .9 .W47)

Folmsbee, Stanley J., et al. *History of Tennessee.* Vol. 2. New York: Lewis Historical Publishing Co., Inc., 1960. (F436 .F64)

Gragg, Rod. *Civil War Quiz and Fact Book.* New York: Harper and Row, 1985. (E468 .9 .G73)

Groene, Bertram H. *Tracing Your Civil War Ancestor.* Winston-Salem, N.C.: John F. Blair, Publishers, 1973. (CD3047 .G76)

Goldsborough, William W. *The Maryland Line in the Confederate Army, 1861-1865*. Reprint. Port Washington, N.Y.: Kennikat Press, 1972. (E566 .G61)

Hill, Daniel H. *A History of North Carolina in the War Between the States-- Bethel to Sharpsburg*. 2 vols. Raleigh, N.C.: Edwards and Broughton Co., 1926. (E573 .H64)

Irvine, Dallas, comp. National Archives and Records Service. *Military Operations of the Civil War: A Guide Index to the Official Records of the Union and Confederate Armies, 1861-1865*. Washington, D.C.: Government Printing Office, 1967.

Kerby, Robert L. *The Confederate Invasion of New Mexico and Arizona, 1861-1865*. Los Angeles: Western Lore Press, 1958. (E470 .9 .K4)

Lewis, Louise Q. *Records of Marylanders in the Confederate Navy, 1861-1865*. October 1944, Typescript.

Long, Everette B. *The Civil War Day by Day--an Almanac, 1861-1865*. Garden City, N.Y.: Doubleday & Co., 1971. (E468 .3 .16)

Mankee, Harold R. *Maryland in the Civil War*. Baltimore: Maryland Historical Society, 1961. (#512 .M33)

McPherson, James M. *Ordeal by Fire. Vol. 2. The Civil War*. New York: Alfred A. Knopf, 1982.

Meyer, Duane. *The Heritage of Missouri--A History*. Hazlewood, Mo.: State Publishing Co., Inc. (F466 .M578)

Moore, Albert B. *Conscription and Conflict in the Confederacy*. New York: The MacMillan Co., 1924. (E545 .M82)

_____. *History of Alabama*. University, Ala.: University Supply Store, 1934. (F326 .M82)

Nevins, Allen, et al. *Civil War Books, a Critical Bibliography*. 2 vols. Baton Rouge: State Press, 1967. (Z1242 .N35)

Newman, Harry W. *Maryland in the Confederacy*. Annapolis, Md.: the author, 1976. (E66 .N48)

Patten, Cartter. *A Tennessee Chronicle*. N.p., 1953. (E436 .P3)

Poppenheim, Mary B., et al. *The History of the United Daughters of the Confederacy, 1894-1929*.Raleigh, N.C.: Edwards and Broughton Co., 1925. (E483 .5 A27)

Porter, David D. *Naval History of the Civil War*. Castle, a Division of Book Sales, Inc., 1984. (E581 .P84)

Rampp, Lary C., and Rampp, Donald L. *The Civil War in the Indian Territory*. Austin, Tex.: Presidial Press, 1975. (R540 .13 .R3)

Rice, Otis K. *West Virginia History*. Lexington, Ky.: The University Press of Kentucky, 1985. (F421 .R515)

Roland, Charles P. *The Confederacy*. Chicago: The University of Chicago Press, 1960. (#487 .R7)

Scharf, John T. *History of the Confederate States Navy From Its Origin to the Surrender of Its Last Vessel*. New York: Rogers and Sherwood, 1887. (E596 .S31)

Schweitzer, George K. *Civil War Genealogy*. Knoxville, Tenn.: the author, 1984. (Z1242 .S35)

Smith, Page. *A People's History of the Civil War and Reconstruction. Vol. 5. Trial by Fire*. New York: McGraw Hill Book Co., 1982. (E468 .S64)

Steen, Ralph W. *The Texas Story*. Austin, Tex.: The Steck Co., 1960. (E568 .S855)

Stephenson, Richard W., comp. *Civil War Maps in the Library of Congress, an Annotated List*. Library of Congress. (Z6027 .U5) 1961. Reprint. Falls Church, Va.: Sterling Press, 1977.

Smith, Myron J., Jr. *American Civil War Navies*. Metuchen, N.J.: Scarecrow Press, 1972. (Z1242 .S63)

Symonds, Craig L. *A Battlefield Atlas of the Civil War*. Annapolis, Md.: The Nautical and Aviation Publishing Company of America, 1983.

Tancig, William J., comp. *Confederate Military Land Units*. New York: Thomas Yoseloff, 1967. (E546 .T3)

Thomas, David Y. *Arkansas in War and Reconstruction*. Little Rock: Arkansas Division, United Daughters of the Confederacy, 1926. (F411 .T45)

Van Hook, Joseph O. *The Kentucky Story*. Chattanooga: Harlow Publishing Corp., 1959. (F451 .3 .V3)

Wagoner, Jay J. *Arizona Territory, 1863-1912*. Tucson: The University of Arizona Press, 1970. (F811 .3 .W38)

Wallace, David D. *The History of South Carolina*, Vol. 3. New York: The American Historical Society, Inc., 1934. (F269 .225)

Wallace, Lee A. *A Guide to Virginia Military Organizations, 1861-1865*. Richmond: Virginia Civil War Commission, 1964. (E581 .4 .W4)

Wright, Marcus J. *Texas in the War, 1861-1865*. Waco, Tex.: Hill Junior College Press, 1865. (E580 .W7)

United States Record and Pension Office. *Organization of State of Missouri Troops (Union and Confederate) in Service During the Civil War*. Washington, D.C.: Government Printing Office, 1902.

Yearns, W. Buck and Barrett, John G. *North Carolina Civil War Documentary.* Chapel Hill: The University of North Carolina Press, 1980. (E573 .9 .N67)

Index

J

Jackson, Claiborne, 200-01
Jackson, Gen. Thomas J. "Stonewall,"
    5, 168
Johnson, Andrew, 142
Johnson, Capt. J. R., 174
Johnston, Capt. C. F., 174
Johnston, Gen. Joseph E., 68, 114, 126,
    139-40, 174, 195
Jones, Capt. A. J., 174
Jones, Capt. L. F., 174

K

Kanapaux, Capt. J. T., 128
Kentucky
    military service records, 187
    military units, 192-93
    miscellaneous state records, 188
    pension records, 186-87
    printed sources, 259
    role in the war, 189-92
Kentucky Historical Society, 188-89
Kentucky, Department of Archives and
    Libraries, 185
Knights of the Golden Circle, 153-54
Ku Klux Klan, 142

L

Lee, Gen. Robert E., 14, 16-17, 20, 124,
    153, 167-70, 195
letters and telegrams, Confederate
    offices, 227-32
Lewis, Louise Q., 196
Library of Congress, 245-46
Lincoln, Abraham, 2-4, 168, 190, 195,
    202, 209
Longstreet, Gen. James, 140
Louisiana
    military service records, 79
    military units, 84-89
    miscellaneous state records, 80
    pension records, 77-79
    printed sources, 259-60
    role in the war, 80-84
Louisiana, secession of, 5
Louisiana, State Archives and Records
    Service, 76
Lyon, Gen. Nathaniel, 19, 51, 201-02

M

Manassas, battle of, 15
Maryland
    military units, 196-97
    printed sources, 260
    role in the war, 193-96
McClellan, Gen. George B., 15, 195
McCulloch, Gen. Ben, 50, 155, 202
McDowell, Gen. Irvin, 15
McLane, Bobbie J., 49
Meade, George C., 16
Merrimack, 21, 168
Military History Institute, 246
military records, Texas, 157-62
Military Rosters, 39 39
Military service records
    Alabama, 39
    Arkansas, 49
    Georgia, 64-65
    Kentucky, 187
    Louisiana, 79
    Mississippi, 92-94
    Missouri, 199
    North Carolina, 108
    South Carolina, 121
    Tennessee, 133-34
    Texas, 150-51
    Virginia, 165
    West Virginia, 207
Military units
    Alabama, 42-46
    Arkansas, 52-55
    Florida, 61
    Georgia, 69-76
    Kentucky, 192-93
    Louisiana, 84-89
    Maryland, 196-97
    Mississippi, 95
    Missouri, 204-06
    North Carolina, 114-17
    South Carolina, 126-30
    Tennessee, 142-47
    Virginia, 171-81
Miscellaneous state records
    Alabama, 40
    Arkansas, 50
    Florida, 57-58
    Georgia, 65
    Kentucky, 188
    Louisiana, 80
    Mississippi, 94
    Missouri, 200-04